MW01630138
This Word Sauce! belongs to:

Mrs Wordsmith®

Word Sauce!™

Made with ♥ by free-range
teams in London and Los Angeles.

Words hand-picked by our brilliantly
clever data science engine.

Word Sauce was formulated by
Mrs Sally J. Wordsmith in 2018.

Only she knows the exact recipe.

mrswordsmith.com

 USNJ4D01B

For **FREE** downloads and teaching materials, visit:

mrswordsmith.com

Mind-blowing
inspiration ahead!
You're a writer now, with a pen in one hand and Word Sauce! in the other. It's time to spice things up, to create stories that will make mouths water and heads spin. Add a few drops, or lay it on thick.
Think you can handle this sauce?
Then start pouring!

Table of Contents

Seriously sweet words ahead.

Use the next six pages to find the themes, categories, and words you need to get writing.

PAGE 17

Action

184 astonishing action nouns

PAGE 103

Character

164 clever character words

PAGE 187

Emotion

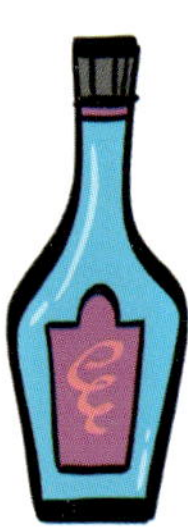

PAGE 259

Setting

373 serene setting nouns

PAGE 357

Taste & Smell

167 decadent taste & smell nouns

PAGE 435

Weather

97 whistling weather nouns

Get to know your illustrated dictionary

Go on, take a bite.

WORD TIP

Some words are longer than others, but that doesn't always make them better. Sometimes short, simple words work best.

WORD TIP

Some words have more than one meaning. For example, a **sleepy** baby is tired, while a **sleepy** lagoon is quiet and peaceful. Definitions in Word Sauce! focus on the meaning of the word that's most helpful for storytelling.

Category tabs

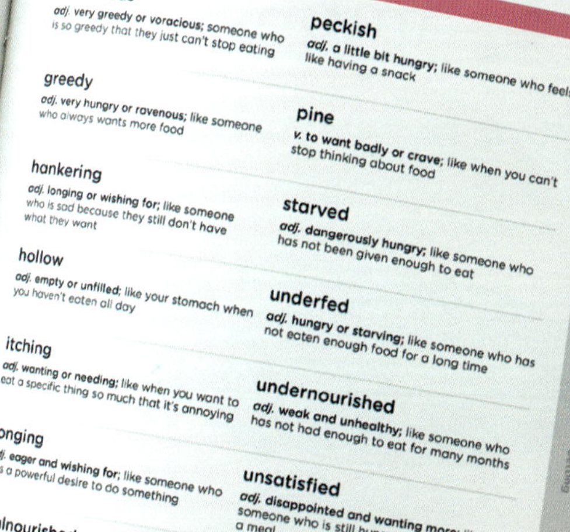

WHAT TYPE OF WORD?

A *noun* or naming word

An *adjective* or describing word

A *verb* or doing word

Express your originality

Shake up your stories and inject some originality to create your own spicy little number. Find the noun you need here, and use the word pairs around the edge to kick your creativity into overdrive.

sports car

Oz parked her **expensive sports car** next to her diamond-encrusted swimming pool.

Oz's **imported sports car** gave her a real air of Italian chic.

Oz raced away from the police in the **stolen sports car**.

URE > THE CHASE

noisy • turbocharged
n. otorcycle

torn • built-in • billowing
n. parachute

sinking • derelict
n. ship

powerful • elegant • military
n. speedboat

eching • punctured
n. tire

large • burned-out • clanking
n. trailer

ed • bulletproof
n. shield

private • cruising • palatial
n. yacht

ACTION AND ADVENTURE > THE CRIME

skilled • dim-witted • suspected
n. accomplice

masked • desperate • bumbling
n. burglar

photographic • solid • forensic
n.
evidence
an object that proves what really happened; like a doughnut forgotten by a criminal during a robbery

single • important • hidden
n. clue

gruesome • contaminated
n. crime scene

private • bumbling • cynical
n. detective

clever • ridiculous • ingenious
n. disguise

powerful • dim • rechargeable
n. flashlight

covert • botched • clandestine
n. operation

deadly • corrosive • radioactive
n. poison

retired • undercover • corrupt
n. police officer

locked • fireproof • impenetrable
n. safe

hidden • digital • hacked
n. security camera

91

Action | Character | Emotion | Setting | Taste & Smell | Weather

An explosion just over the ridge shook the ground and flung stones and clods of earth high into the air. Lyra cried out, and Will had to clutch his chest. "Hold on," Iorek growled, and began to **charge**.

His Dark Materials: The Amber Spyglass
by Philip Pullman

Action

chaos and confusion words

n.

commotion

DEFINITION

chaos or uproar;
like animals set loose in a kitchen causing a crazy mess

SAMPLE SENTENCE

Oz caused a loud **commotion** at the party when she arrived by helicopter.

chaos and confusion words

adj.

devastating

DEFINITION

terrible or destructive; like flinging a bowling ball along the dinner table

SAMPLE SENTENCE

The powerful hose had a **devastating** effect on Grit's tulips, which were ripped to shreds.

n.

chaos and confusion words

havoc

DEFINITION

great damage or chaos;
like the mess caused by a giant bear smashing through a city

SAMPLE SENTENCE

The supervillain spread **havoc** by releasing thousands of bees into the children's hospital.

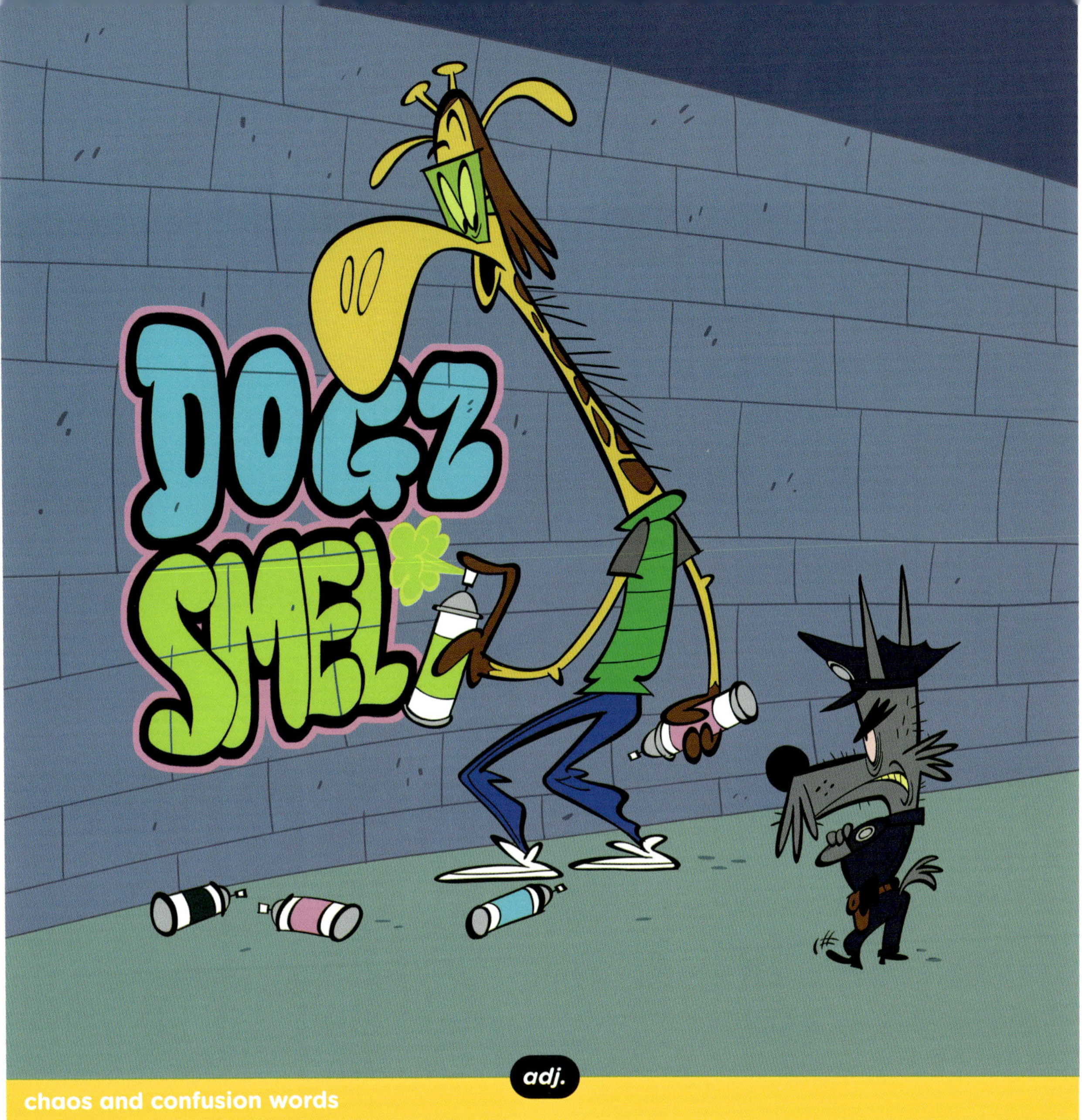

chaos and confusion words

adj.

rebellious

DEFINITION

naughty or disobedient;
like a giraffe who breaks the rules and draws on the walls

SAMPLE SENTENCE

The **rebellious** teenager stayed out way past her bedtime.

chaos and confusion words

adj.

turbulent

DEFINITION

violent and unstable;
like a plane that gets knocked around by heavy clouds

SAMPLE SENTENCE

The **turbulent** journey was so bumpy that everyone felt sick.

unruly

DEFINITION

wild, rowdy, and rebellious;
like long, frizzy hair at the beach

SAMPLE SENTENCE

The **unruly** students never gave their teacher a moment of peace.

or you can try...

Topsy-turvy chaos and confusion words!

anarchy
n. **a state of disorder;** like a country with no laws and no leaders

blackout
n. **a power cut or electrical failure;** like when all the lights in your house go out suddenly

clutter
n. **mess or litter;** like old magazines that are left in piles on the floor

debris
n. **rubble or ruins;** like pieces of broken concrete and plaster that are left after a building is destroyed

disarray
n. **chaos or confusion;** like a situation where nobody knows what they should be doing

disorder
n. **mess or confusion;** the state that a place gets into when nobody keeps it neat and organized

disturb
v. **to bother or interrupt;** like when you make a noise that stops someone from working

escape
n. **breakout or getaway;** when prisoners run away

explode
v. **to burst or blow up;** like when a bomb goes off and causes a lot of damage

jumble
n. **a mess or mixture;** like a pile of objects that have not been arranged or sorted

muddle
n. **a mess or mix-up;** like a situation where nobody is sure what they are supposed to do

obliterate
v. **to destroy or wipe out;** like a forest fire that leaves nothing behind

or you can try...

overthrow

v. **to defeat and throw out;** like when a group of people take over and force the rulers of their country out

pandemonium

n. **panic and noisy confusion;** like a crowd of angry people screaming and shouting

protest

v. **to complain or object;** like lots of people gathering together to fight for their beliefs

random

adj. **unexpected or not regular;** like when you choose things based on chance rather than for a reason

rebel

n. **someone who breaks the rules;** like a soldier who refuses to follow orders

revolt

n. **a rebellion or revolution;** like when a group of people start fighting against their own government

shambolic

adj. **chaotic or disorganized;** like a show where everything goes wrong

troublemaker

n. **a rebel or stirrer;** someone who deliberately creates trouble for another person

tumult

n. **noise and confusion;** like the sound of a lot of people all shouting at the same time

turmoil

n. **trouble or confusion;** like a situation where nobody feels safe or settled

upheaval

n. **a disruption or disturbance;** like a situation when everything suddenly changes

uproar

n. **noisy protest;** like people shouting because they are angry about something

upsetting

adj. **worrying or disturbing;** like a film about something sad that makes you cry

wreckage

n. **ruins or remains;** like the parts of a car that are scattered around after a bad crash

turn over for fight or battle words >

fight or battle words

v.

ambush

ambushes • ambushing • ambushed

DEFINITION

to make a surprise attack;
like a soldier leaping out suddenly from a hiding place

SAMPLE SENTENCE

Brick wore camouflage and stayed hidden until the moment was perfect to **ambush** his foe.

fight or battle words

v.

bicker

bickers • bickering • bickered

DEFINITION

to argue over silly things;
like sisters arguing about nothing

SAMPLE SENTENCE

The tired, angry politicians **bickered** bitterly about who should be blamed.

fight or battle words

v.

bombard

bombards • bombarding • bombarded

DEFINITION

to attack or overwhelm;
like showering someone with presents on their birthday

SAMPLE SENTENCE

Plato used a huge catapult to **bombard** the enemy with water balloons.

conquer

conquers • conquering • conquered

DEFINITION

to defeat or get control over;
like an army taking over new land

SAMPLE SENTENCE

"One day, I'll **conquer** the world!" cackled the evil baby as he planned to take over the planet.

Action | Character | Emotion | Setting | Taste & Smell | Weather

fight or battle words

n.

feud

DEFINITION

a disagreement or argument that is never settled; like people fighting about the same thing for years

SAMPLE SENTENCE

The family **feud** started with a food fight at a fancy restaurant.

siege

DEFINITION

a blockade or assault;
when an army surrounds a place and does not allow anyone to leave

SAMPLE SENTENCE

The **siege** lasted so long that people died of old age.

or you can try...

Fierce fight or battle words!

ally

***n.* a friend or supporter;** like someone who is fighting on your side in a war

altercation

***n.* an argument or disagreement;** like a noisy fight that breaks out in the street

antagonize

***v.* to annoy or provoke;** like when you deliberately do something to make another person angry

attack

***v.* to act violently or aggressively;** what you do when you run at someone in order to hurt or injure them

brawl

***n.* a fight or scuffle;** like when a lot of people start hitting each other and throwing things

camouflage

***n.* cover or disguise;** like clothes that are the same color as the place where you are hiding

clash

***n.* a fight or conflict;** like when two people get into an argument

conflict

***n.* a battle or war;** like a disagreement between two groups who want different things

defeat

***v.* to beat or conquer;** what the winner of a contest does to the loser

dispute

***n.* an argument or disagreement;** like neighbors arguing about where to put up a fence

hostile

***adj.* unfriendly and aggressive;** like a person who is always unpleasant and tries to start fights

liberate

***v.* to free or release;** what an army does when it rescues people being held prisoner by the enemy

or you can try...

mercy
n. **kindness and forgiveness;** what you show if you choose not to hurt your enemy

prisoner
n. **a captive or inmate;** like a person who is locked up and not allowed to go out

pummel
v. **to beat or pound;** like when someone throws punches one after the other

retreat
v. **to go back or withdraw;** like when an army decides to leave a battle because it is losing

revenge
n. **the act of paying back or getting even;** like when you hurt somebody because they have hurt you

riot
n. **a violent disturbance or uproar;** like when a group of angry people get together and cause chaos

squabble
v. **to argue or quarrel;** like when people get into a fight about something that is not very important

strategy
n. **a plan of action;** like the way you decide to beat your enemy in a war

surrender
v. **to give in or stop fighting;** what an army does when it admits that it has lost and asks for mercy

target
n. **an aim or goal;** like an object you try to hit with an arrow

triumph
v. **to win or come out on top;** like an important battle where you completely defeat your enemy

truce
n. **an agreement to stop fighting;** like when two enemies agree to take a break from fighting for a few days

victim
n. **an injured person or sufferer;** like someone who is wounded

victory
n. **a win or success;** like when you defeat your enemy in a battle

turn over for hard-working words >

hard-working words

adj.

backbreaking

DEFINITION

exhausting or crushing; lifting something so heavy it feels like your back will break

SAMPLE SENTENCE

Oz made a **backbreaking** effort to lift the piano, but it was far too heavy.

hard-working words

adj.

exhausted

DEFINITION

worn out or very tired;
when you are so tired you sleep deeply for hours and hours

SAMPLE SENTENCE

"I can't run any further!" said Plato in an **exhausted** voice.

hard-working words

adj.

grueling

DEFINITION

difficult or draining;
like the effort of carrying a huge bear

SAMPLE SENTENCE

The **grueling** climb was so difficult that Bogart almost gave up.

laborious

DEFINITION

difficult or exhausting; like the job of pushing big, heavy boulders uphill

SAMPLE SENTENCE

Filling the swimming pool one spoonful of water at a time was a **laborious** job.

hard-working words

adj.

overwhelming

DEFINITION

overpowering or immense;
like having to carry a busload of beach equipment on your shoulders

SAMPLE SENTENCE

Oz's emotions were so **overwhelming** that she didn't know whether to laugh or cry.

tedious

DEFINITION

boring or dull;
like having to work through an endless pile of tiresome homework

SAMPLE SENTENCE

Mrs Wordsmith had a **tedious** time in the boring meeting.

or you can try...

Determined, hard-working words!

achievement
n. **a success or positive result;** like something that you have managed to do successfully

assiduous
adj. **careful or thorough;** like cleaning an entire bathroom perfectly using only a toothbrush

competitive
adj. **driven and ambitious;** like someone who always wants to do better than other people

conscientious
adj. **careful and hard-working;** like a decorator who never leaves a job in a mess

determined
adj. **driven or completely set on;** working extra hard to get what you want

diligent
adj. **hard-working and persistent;** like someone who practices a musical instrument every day

efficient
adj. **well-organized and effective;** like someone who can finish a lot of work in a short time

improve
v. **to progress or advance;** what you are doing when the results of your work get better

industrious
adj. **busy and hard-working;** like someone who keeps working at a steady pace for a long time

meticulous
adj. **very careful and precise;** like a librarian who organizes a huge library with a detailed system

motivated
adj. **inspired and determined;** like someone who wants to finish something to get the reward

painstaking
adj. **showing care or being thorough;** like the kind of work it takes to finish a 10,000-piece puzzle

or you can try...

pressure

n. **stress or urgency;** what a baseball player feels the night before the most important game of the year

productive

adj. **effective or getting a lot done;** like someone who achieves a lot in a day

prolific

adj. **producing a lot;** like an author who writes several books every year

resolute

adj. **determined and stubborn;** like someone who keeps trying until they complete a task

rigorous

adj. **thorough and diligent;** like a quiz that asks questions about every single topic

scrupulous

adj. **thorough or detail-oriented;** like someone who writes a diary daily and never leaves out details

sedulous

adj. **careful and dedicated;** like the kind of work and patience it takes to carve a detailed statue

strenuous

adj. **difficult and demanding;** like work that involves lifting heavy objects

stressful

adj. **difficult and worrying;** like a job that involves making lots of important decisions all the time

stubborn

adj. **determined and refusing to change;** like someone who thinks they are right and won't listen to advice

target

n. **an aim or goal;** like the number of cars that a salesperson needs to sell in one month

thorough

adj. **detailed and complete;** like a car mechanic who checks everything that could possibly go wrong

tireless

adj. **hard-working and full of energy;** like someone who can keep working for a long time without stopping

unflagging

adj. **hard-working and tireless;** like someone who never stops trying to help people

turn over for lazy or relaxing words >

lazy or relaxing words

adj.

drowsy

DEFINITION

sleepy or dopey;
how you feel when your alarm clock rings and you want to snooze

SAMPLE SENTENCE

A **drowsy** feeling settled over Armie, and his eyelids seemed to get very heavy.

lazy or relaxing words

v.

lounge

lounges • lounging • lounged

DEFINITION

to lie around or laze;
like someone lying in the sun sipping a cool drink

SAMPLE SENTENCE

Bogart **lounged** luxuriously in the hot bubble bath.

lazy or relaxing words

adj.

pampered

DEFINITION

spoiled or coddled;
like being treated to an indulgent mud bath at a fancy hotel

SAMPLE SENTENCE

Oz had been a **pampered** child who always got what she wanted.

adj.

lazy or relaxing words

sluggish

DEFINITION

slow, lazy, or lifeless;
how you feel when you get up too early in the morning

SAMPLE SENTENCE

The empty chocolate wrapper floated slowly down the **sluggish** river.

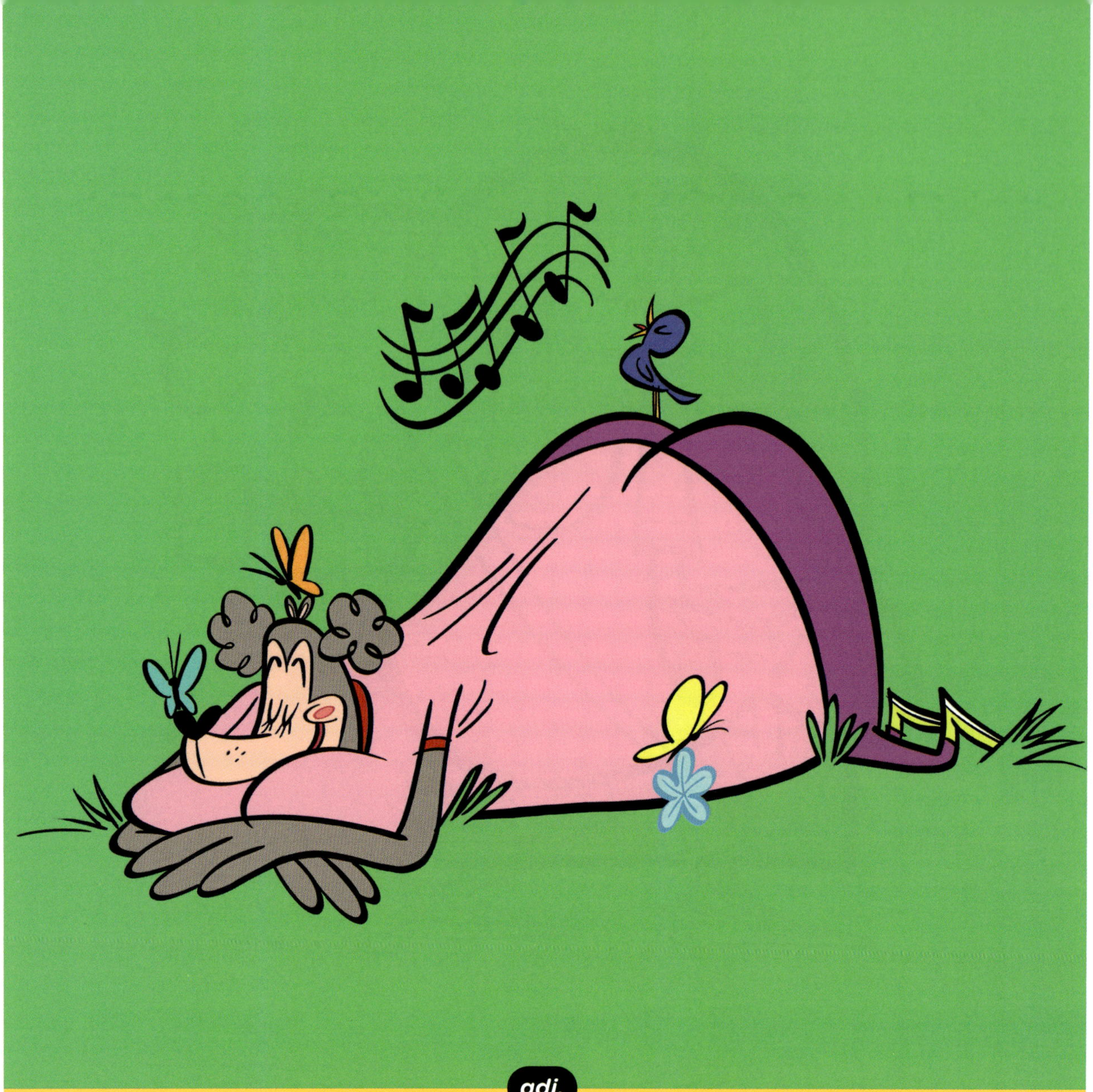

lazy or relaxing words

adj.

soothing

DEFINITION

calming or comforting;
like a sweet song that makes you feel peaceful and sleepy

SAMPLE SENTENCE

Shang High rubbed a **soothing** ointment into his sunburn to stop it from stinging.

lazy or relaxing words

v.

unwind

unwinds • unwinding • unwound

DEFINITION

to rest or relax;
like when you stretch out on the sofa after a long day at work

SAMPLE SENTENCE

Oz needed to completely **unwind** with a long bath at the end of the busy day.

or you can try...

Slow, lazy, or relaxing words!

bask
v. **to lie back and relax;** like an animal that stretches out to enjoy the warm sunshine

calm
adj. **quiet and relaxed;** like a peaceful time when you don't have anything important to do

diversion
n. **a hobby or entertainment;** like a silly game that you play at a party

doze
v. **to sleep or nap;** like when you fall asleep for a short time during the day

flop
v. **to drop or slump;** like the way you let yourself fall down onto a sofa when you are tired

idle
adj. **lazy and not working;** like someone who sits in front of the TV when they have work to do

inactive
adj. **still or lazy;** like someone who likes to sit and watch television rather than play sports

indolence
n. **laziness or idleness;** like that feeling when you don't want to do any work

leisure
n. **relaxation or rest;** time when you don't have to do anything but enjoy yourself

lethargic
adj. **tired and slow;** how you feel when you don't have the energy to do anything

lull
n. **a pause or quiet time;** a time when things come to a stop after being busy

luxuriate
v. **to enjoy or revel in;** like when you take your time having a warm bubble bath

or you can try...

meditative

adj. **thoughtful and calm;** like someone who goes into a deep trance to think about spiritual things

mellow

adj. **relaxed and pleasant;** like a quiet afternoon spent sitting and chatting with your friends

peaceful

adj. **calm and quiet;** like an afternoon spent relaxing in a quiet place

recline

v. **to lie back and rest;** like someone who is stretched out on a towel by the sea

recover

v. **to get better or improve;** like when you rest and get your strength back after an illness

refreshing

adj. **cool and invigorating;** like an iced drink on a hot day

rejuvenate

v. **to refresh or make younger;** like when you decorate a place to make it seem like new again

relaxation

n. **rest or leisure;** like a quiet time to get your strength back after you have been working hard

relief

n. **comfort and relaxation;** a feeling of happiness that something bad has not happened

restorative

adj. **healing and strengthening;** like a vacation that helps you recover from an illness

slothful

adj. **lazy and not active;** like someone who does not do much exercise or work

snooze

v. **to sleep or nap;** like when you lie in bed half asleep in the morning

soporific

adj. **making you sleepy;** like the sound of water in a stream on a warm afternoon

sunbathe

v. **to stretch out in the sun;** like when you lie down on a beach on a hot day

turn over for looking or seeing words >

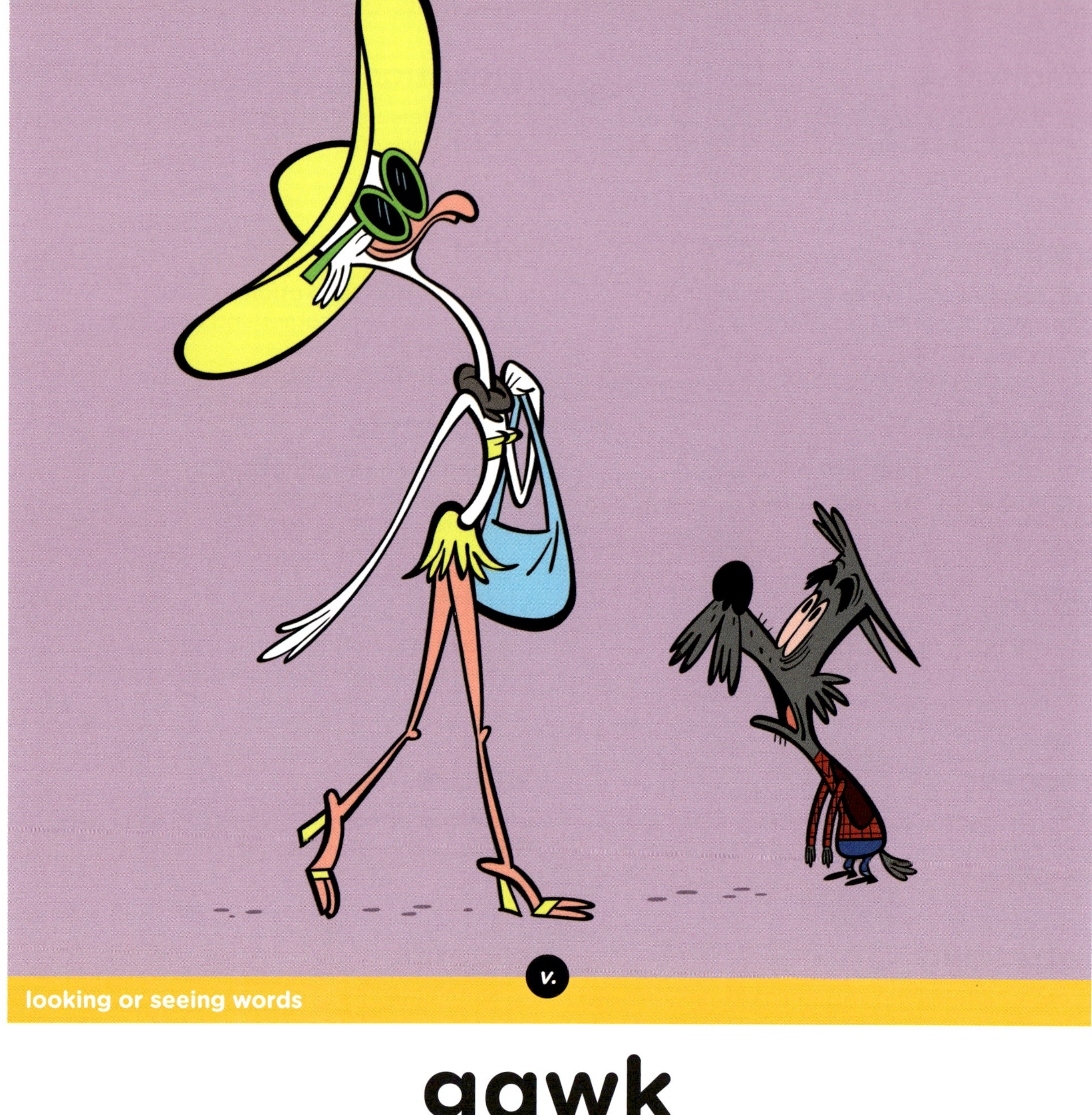

looking or seeing words

v.

gawk

gawks • gawking • gawked

DEFINITION

to gape or goggle;
to look at someone with your eyes popping out of your head

SAMPLE SENTENCE

Bogart **gawked** awkwardly at the actor, too starstruck to think of anything clever to say.

v.

looking or seeing words

gaze

gazes • gazing • gazed

DEFINITION

to stare or look deep in thought; like looking longingly at somebody else's ice cream

SAMPLE SENTENCE

As he thought about his future as an astronaut, Armie **gazed** dreamily up at the moon.

looking or seeing words

v.

glimpse

glimpses • glimpsing • glimpsed

DEFINITION

to spot or get a quick look; like catching sight of a mouse out of the corner of your eye

SAMPLE SENTENCE

The captain of the ship **glimpsed** a light flashing far away in the distance.

v.

looking or seeing words

peer

peers • peering • peered

DEFINITION

to peek or stare;
like looking over your shoulder to see what's going on

SAMPLE SENTENCE

Armie **peered** curiously at the strange beetle in the jar.

looking or seeing words

v.

scrutinize

scrutinizes • scrutinizing • scrutinized

DEFINITION

to inspect or study;
like when you look at something up close and in detail

SAMPLE SENTENCE

Grit **scrutinized** the dog's face, wondering if it might be his long-lost brother.

v.

looking or seeing words

squint

squints • squinting • squinted

DEFINITION

to look through half-closed eyes; like when you shield your eyes from the bright sun

SAMPLE SENTENCE

Even with her sunglasses, the bright light made Mrs Wordsmith **squint** slightly.

or you can try...

Wide-eyed looking and seeing words!

behold

v. **to view or see;** like when you look at an impressive sight

blink

v. **to flutter or wink;** what you do when you quickly close and re-open your eyes

detect

v. **to notice or sense;** what you do when you see something that you were not aware of before

discern

v. **to see something that isn't clear;** like understanding someone's messy handwriting

discover

v. **to find or uncover;** like unexpectedly digging up some ancient coins

distinguish

v. **to recognize something is different;** like noticing a dark figure emerging from fog

eyesight

n. **vision or ability to see;** the power that you have to see the world around you

examine

v. **to inspect or look at closely;** like a doctor looking carefully into your ears

focus

v. **to concentrate or fix on;** what your eyes do when you look at one thing and ignore everything else

gape

v. **to gawk or goggle;** like staring at someone with your eyes wide and your mouth open

image

n. **a picture or representation;** like a photograph or a painting

invisible

adj. **hidden or unseen;** like an insect that you can't see because it is so tiny

or you can try...

magnify

v. **to make bigger or enlarge;** what you do when you zoom in on a picture on a computer screen

notice

v. **to see or observe;** like when you become aware of something interesting or unusual

observant

adj. **watchful and alert;** like someone who sees things that other people don't notice

observe

v. **to watch or view;** what you do when you look at something

perceive

v. **to spot or notice;** like when you see something and realize that it is there

photograph

n. **a picture or image;** an exact representation that you create by using a camera

reflection

n. **an image or likeness;** what you see when you look into a mirror

regard

v. **to view or consider;** the way you look at something when you are forming an opinion about it

scan

v. **to search or study;** like when someone looks at a long list to see if their name is on it

spectacle

n. **a show or performance;** like a colorful firework display that people enjoy watching

survey

v. **to view or examine;** like when you look all around a room to see what is in it

visible

adj. **noticeable or obvious;** like a tower that you can see from miles away

vision

n. **sight or ability to see;** the power you have to see things with your eyes

witness

v. **to see something happen;** like watching bank robbers escape with a bag of money

turn over for running words >

running words

v.

charge

charges • charging • charged

DEFINITION

to run or lunge toward; rushing toward a target as fast as you can

SAMPLE SENTENCE

The horse **charged** forward and leaped across the narrow gap.

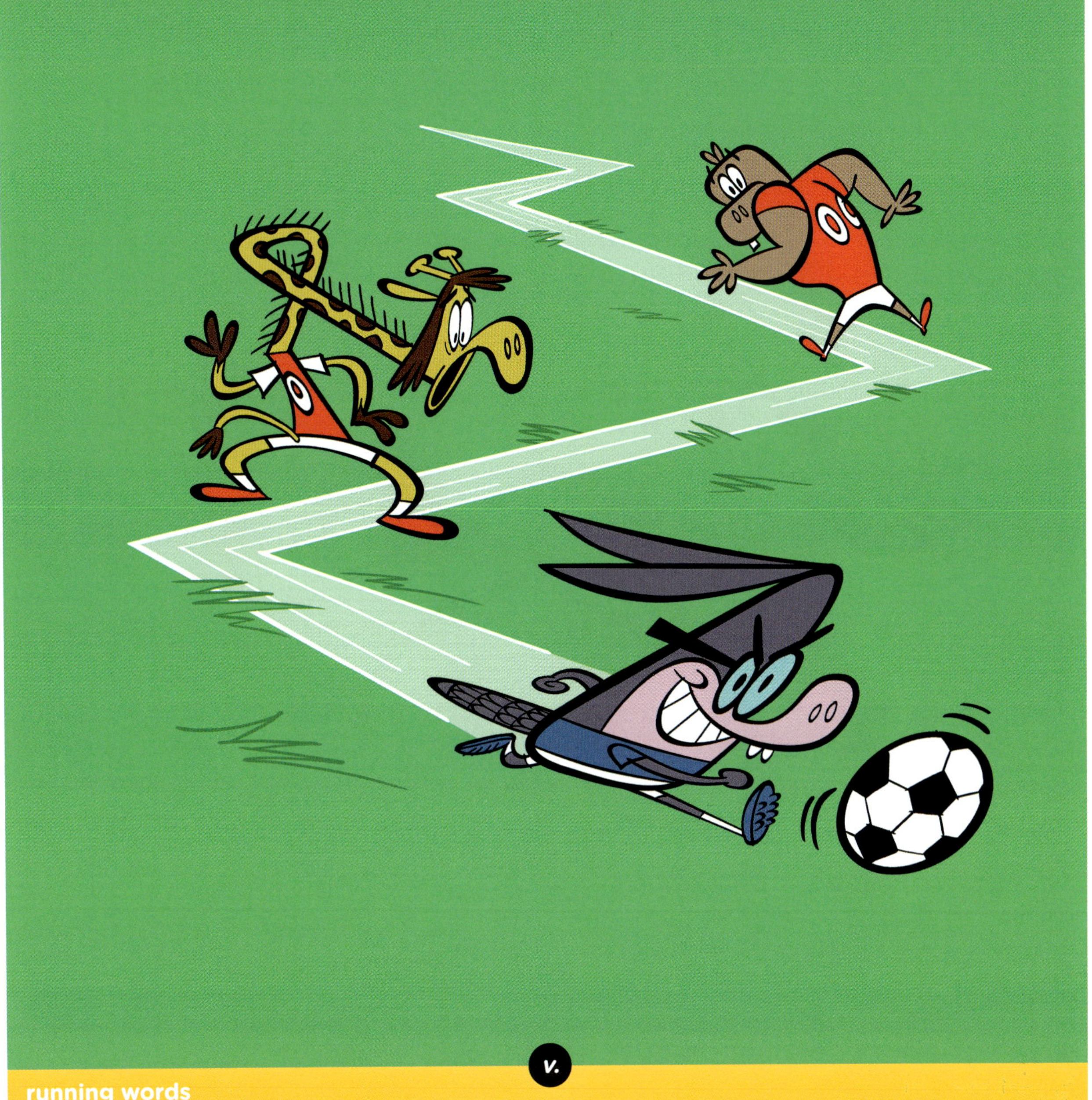

running words

v.

dart

darts • darting • darted

DEFINITION

to sprint or bolt;
running somewhere suddenly and rapidly

SAMPLE SENTENCE

Brick **darted** forward across the starting line when he heard the whistle blow.

running words

n.

dash

DEFINITION

a race or rush;
like a sprinter running at full speed toward the finish line

SAMPLE SENTENCE

"I'm going to be so late!" wailed Armie as he made a wild **dash** for the train.

v.

hurtle

hurtles • hurtling • hurtled

DEFINITION

to rush or move very quickly; like a big asteroid plunging toward Earth

SAMPLE SENTENCE

The movie began with a spaceship **hurtling** through empty space incredibly quickly.

running words

v.

scamper

scampers • scampering • scampered

DEFINITION

to scurry or dash;
how you would run if
you were very excited

SAMPLE SENTENCE

The children heard that dinner was ready and **scampered** inside.

v.

running words

scurry

scurries • scurrying • scurried

DEFINITION

to scamper or scuttle;
like a scared armadillo trying to outrun a huge wave

SAMPLE SENTENCE

The muddy puppy **scurried** away when he realized it was bathtime.

or you can try...

Super-speedy running words!

accelerate

v. **to increase or speed up;** what you do when you run faster than you did before

bolt

v. **to run away or escape;** like a horse that gallops off when it hears a loud bang

bound

v. **to jump or leap;** like a dog springing after a rubber ball

chase

v. **to follow or run after;** like a dog that is trying to catch a rabbit

circuit

n. **a lap or loop;** like a path that leads all the way around a park and back to where you started

escape

v. **to flee or run away;** like when you avoid a person who is chasing you by running faster than them

fitness

n. **health and energy;** the ability to run or walk a long distance

flee

v. **to run away or escape;** like people who are trying not to be captured by enemy soldiers

fly

v. **to run or sprint;** like when someone runs so fast that their feet don't seem to touch the ground

gallop

v. **to rush or sprint;** like a horse moving at top speed

hasten

v. **to hurry or rush;** like when you go somewhere quickly because you are eager to arrive

hurdle

v. **to run and jump;** like a race where you have to jump over obstacles along the way

or you can try...

hurry

v. **to rush or dash;** like someone who is trying to arrive somewhere as quickly as possible

scuttle

v. **to run quickly with short steps;** like a mouse moving quickly across the floor

jog

v. **to run at a steady and gentle pace;** like someone who goes running in the morning to stay fit

speed

v. **to rush or race;** like a police car going as fast as it can to catch a criminal

overtake

v. **to catch up and move past;** like a runner who manages to get ahead of the person they are racing against

sprint

v. **to run or race;** like someone who is running as fast as they can to catch a train

pace

n. **speed or progress;** how quickly you move

track

n. **a path or route;** like a round area used for running races

pitch

v. **to move or fall suddenly;** like someone stumbling down a flight of stairs

train

v. **to exercise or practice;** like a runner who is preparing for the Olympic Games

pursue

v. **to follow or chase;** like a cat that is trying to catch a mouse

trot

v. **to run or jog;** like when you run gently and without using much energy

scramble

v. **to move quickly and awkwardly;** like trying to run over rocks and almost falling over

velocity

n. **speed or pace;** the rate at which a thing moves

turn over for speaking words >

speaking words

v.

blurt

blurts • blurting • blurted

DEFINITION

to cry out or say suddenly; like shouting out when it's someone else's turn

SAMPLE SENTENCE

After Yang accidentally **blurted** out Yin's secret, everyone knew about her crush.

drone

drones • droning • droned

DEFINITION

to hum or make a continuous dull sound; like someone reading out a boring list

SAMPLE SENTENCE

Oz **droned** on and on about herself for so long that everyone fell asleep.

speaking words

v.

protest

protests • protesting • protested

DEFINITION

to disagree or challenge; like refusing to work until someone listens to you

SAMPLE SENTENCE

The whole class vigorously **protested** against losing their lunch breaks.

speaking words

v.

sneer

sneers • sneering • sneered

DEFINITION

to smirk or smile nastily;
like a mean smile that shows you are happy when others make mistakes

SAMPLE SENTENCE

Oz thought Bogart's dancing was awful and **sneered** at him bitterly.

speaking words

v.

squeal

squeals • squealing • squealed

DEFINITION

to wail or yelp; like the high-pitched sound someone makes when they are taken by surprise

SAMPLE SENTENCE

Plato **squealed** in delight because he loved his birthday surprise!

v.

speaking words

whimper

whimpers • whimpering • whimpered

DEFINITION

to whine or sniffle; like a soft crying sound that someone makes when they are in pain or sad

SAMPLE SENTENCE

Oz heard Armie **whimper** softly and found him hiding in the corner.

adj.

walking words

meandering

DEFINITION

wandering or following a winding path; like a sailor roaming across the sea

SAMPLE SENTENCE

Armie wasn't in a hurry so he took a **meandering** route to see more of the scenery.

v.

walking words

skulk

skulks • skulking • skulked

DEFINITION

to creep or prowl;
when you lie low or move carefully to avoid being seen

SAMPLE SENTENCE

The cat **skulked** in the fish market, hanging around until someone gave him scraps.

walking words

v.

stagger

staggers • staggering • staggered

DEFINITION

to stumble or walk unsteadily; how you might walk after being hit over the head with a coconut

SAMPLE SENTENCE

Brick banged his head and **staggered** forward before falling flat on his face.

v.

walking words

swagger

swaggers • swaggering • swaggered

DEFINITION

to strut or stride;
how you walk when you are feeling on top of the world

SAMPLE SENTENCE

Oz **swaggered** confidently into the boss's office, knowing that she would get the job.

walking words

v.

traverse

traverses • traversing • traversed

DEFINITION

to cross or travel through; like a hiker making their way across steep hills

SAMPLE SENTENCE

Grit challenged Shang High to **traverse** the entire globe in eighty days.

v.

walking words

trudge

trudges • trudging • trudged

DEFINITION

to plod or walk slowly with heavy steps; like a tired dog walking out of the sea

SAMPLE SENTENCE

The army **trudged** steadily for days without slowing down.

or you can try...

Leisurely walking words!

amble
***v.* to stroll or walk slowly;** like someone enjoying a leisurely walk in the countryside

approach
***v.* to come near or move toward;** like someone who is getting close to their destination

creep
***v.* to sneak or tiptoe;** like someone trying to go along a hallway without being heard

dawdle
***v.* to walk slowly or linger;** like someone walking slowly on purpose because they don't want to arrive

falter
***v.* to stumble or hesitate;** like someone struggling to walk while carrying a heavy load

follow
***v.* to go after or track;** like a detective who walks behind someone to see where they go

guide
***v.* to lead or escort;** like someone showing you around a museum

hike
***v.* to go on a long walk or trek;** like an explorer marching across wild moorland

hop
***v.* to jump or spring;** like a kangaroo that moves in a series of short leaps

lead
***v.* to guide or show the way;** like a waiter taking you to your table

limp
***v.* to stagger or hobble;** the way you walk when you have hurt one of your legs

lurch
***v.* to stagger or stumble;** like an injured person who sways from side to side as they move

or you can try...

march
***v.* to walk confidently or stride;** like soldiers walking together and keeping a steady rhythm

pace
***v.* to walk impatiently back and forth;** like someone waiting for important news

parade
***v.* to march proudly or strut;** like when a popular soccer team walks together through a cheering crowd

patrol
***v.* to guard and watch over;** like a police officer walking around a town to see what is happening

plod
***v.* to walk slowly and heavily;** like a tired worker going home after a long hard day

promenade
***v.* to walk or stroll;** like people on vacation who take a gentle evening walk around a town

prowl
***v.* to creep or sneak;** like a cat silently hunting for mice

roam
***v.* to wander or ramble;** like a herd of animals wandering through fields aimlessly

saunter
***v.* to wander or stroll;** like a tourist taking their time walking around a marketplace

stride
***v.* to march or walk confidently;** what you do when you walk quickly and with purpose

stroll
***v.* to walk or wander;** like someone who walks around a place without hurrying

traipse
***v.* to walk slowly and trudge;** like someone who has been ordered to go somewhere they don't want to go

trample
***v.* to tread or stomp on;** what you do when you squash things under your feet

tread
***v.* to walk or step;** like walking through a messy room and trying not to step on anything

turn over for wet words >

wet words

v.

douse

douses • dousing • doused

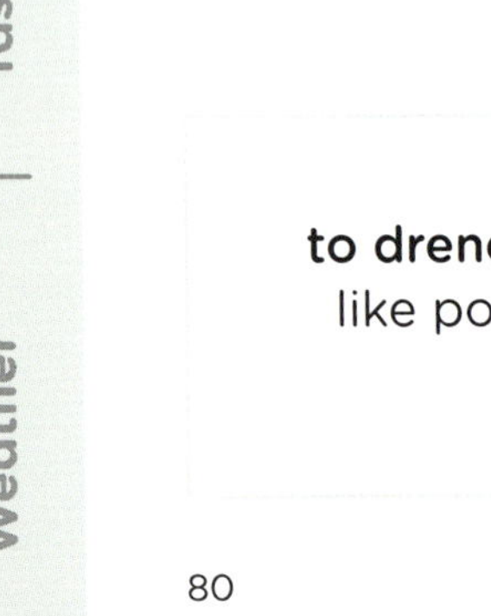

DEFINITION

to drench or put out with water; like pouring a bucket of water over a bonfire

SAMPLE SENTENCE

Plato tried to **douse** the flames with a glass of water, but the fire kept on burning.

wet words

adj.

drenched

DEFINITION

sopping wet or soaked;
like a tiger cub who's had a whole bucket of water thrown over her

SAMPLE SENTENCE

Bearnice's coat was totally **drenched** from the heavy rain.

wet words

v.

immerse

immerses • immersing • immersed

DEFINITION

to dunk or plunge;
like pushing someone right to the bottom of a tank of water

SAMPLE SENTENCE

Brick was only partly **immersed** in the freezing cold water so the waves tickled his belly button.

plunge

plunges • plunging • plunged

DEFINITION

to dive or plummet;
like when you jump off the highest rock into deep water

SAMPLE SENTENCE

Oz **plunged** recklessly into the shark tank.

wet words

v.

squirt

squirts • squirting • squirted

DEFINITION

to spray or splatter;
like making water from a water blaster go in all directions

SAMPLE SENTENCE

Shang High **squirted** ketchup all over his hotdog and the table too.

wet words

adj.

submerged

DEFINITION

completely underwater; like a diver at the bottom of the sea

SAMPLE SENTENCE

Brick put on his diving suit and went in search of the **submerged** shipwreck.

Soaking wet words!

absorb

v. **to take in and soak up;** what a towel does when you use it to mop up water

bathe

v. **to soak or clean;** what you do when you wash with water

bellyflop

v. **to jump and land flat;** like diving into a pool and landing on your stomach

damp

adj. **wet or moist;** like grass after it has been raining

dew

n. **moisture or dampness;** drops of water that settle on surfaces overnight

disperse

v. **to scatter or sprinkle far;** like when a mist spreads out through the air

dissolve

v. **to melt or become liquid;** what happens to a sugar lump when you put it into a cup of hot tea and stir

drought

n. **dryness or shortage of water;** a long period of time when it never rains

flood

n. **a large amount of water;** like a pool of water that completely covers the road after a bad storm

flow

v. **to move or spill;** what a stream of water does when it goes from one place to another

humidity

n. **dampness or moistness;** the amount of water that there is in the air that makes it feel muggy

irrigate

v. **to water or soak;** what farmers do when they supply water to their crops

lather

n. **foam or suds;** like the frothy bubbles that appear when you mix soap with water

moisture

n. **wetness or dampness;** like a small amount of water that stops something from being dry

overflow

v. **to flood or spill over;** like when a river has too much water in it after a bad storm

rivulet

n. **a small river or stream;** like a narrow trickle of water that you can easily jump over

saturated

adj. **soaked and dripping;** like your T-shirt when you get caught in a storm without an umbrella

seep

v. **to ooze or trickle out;** like water gradually getting into a boat through small holes

slosh

v. **to spill or splash;** like water hitting against the sides of a bucket

splash

v. **to spatter or flick;** like kicking your legs really fast in water and getting everything wet

spray

n. **tiny drops blasted into the air;** like the water from a hose flying through the air

sprinkle

v. **to spray or shower;** like when someone waters their plants with a hose

underwater

adj. **submerged or sunken;** like a cave that is hidden below the surface of the sea

waterlogged

adj. **soaked or flooded;** like a field where it has rained so much that there are puddles of water

waterproof

adj. **not letting water in;** like a jacket that keeps your other clothes dry when it rains

watertight

adj. **sealed and waterproof;** like a container that will not let water get out

turn over for action nouns >

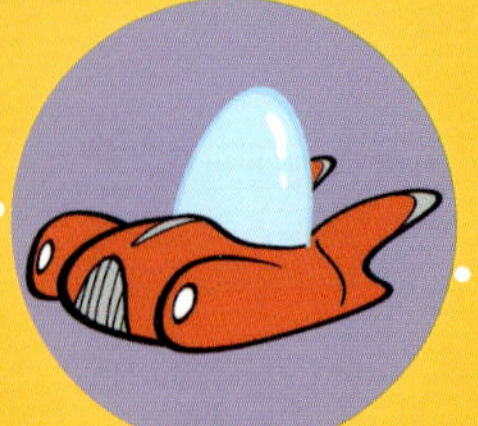

184 astonishing action nouns

Look out below! Drop these nouns and word pairs into your stories with a crash to make your characters panic, investigate, and maybe even fall in love.

missing • private • crashed
n.
airplane
parked • rickety • abandoned
n.
bicycle
giant • airborne • deflated
n.
blimp
magical • runaway • splintered
n.
broomstick
protective • dented • scuffed
n.
bumper
packed • double-decker • jolting
n.
bus
leaky • drifting • capsized
n.
canoe
classic • electric • driverless
n.
car
digital • futuristic • intuitive
n.
dashboard
powerful • purring • turbocharged
n.
engine
overnight • sunken • overloaded
n.
ferry
amazing • enchanted • driverless
n.
flying car
lightweight • crude • motorized
n.
hang glider
dim • blinding • distant
n.
headlights
circling • low-flying • whirring
n.
helicopter
huge • rising • breathtaking
n.
hot air balloon

rented • two-person • powerful
n.
jet ski
private • luxurious • bulletproof
n.
limousine
fast • noisy • turbocharged
n.
motorcycle
torn • built-in • billowing
n.
parachute
electric • folding • compact
n.
scooter
bouncy • plush • ejectable
n.
seats
pirate • sinking • derelict
n.
ship
powerful • elegant • military
n.
speedboat
expensive • imported • stolen
n.
sports car
heated • crooked • leather-clad
n.
steering wheel
spare • screeching • punctured
n.
tire
large • burned-out • clanking
n.
trailer
crowded • superfast • derailed
n.
train
giant • wobbly • lopsided
n.
unicycle
dirty • smashed • bulletproof
n.
windshield
private • cruising • palatial
n.
yacht

skilled • dim-witted • suspected

n.

accomplice

masked • desperate • bumbling

n.

burglar

photographic • solid • forensic

n.

evidence

an object that proves what really happened; like a doughnut forgotten by a criminal during a robbery

single • important • hidden

gruesome • contaminated

n.

clue

n.

crime scene

private • bumbling • cynical

n.

detective

clever • ridiculous • ingenious

n.

disguise

powerful • dim • rechargeable

n.

flashlight

covert • botched • clandestine

n.

operation

deadly • corrosive • radioactive

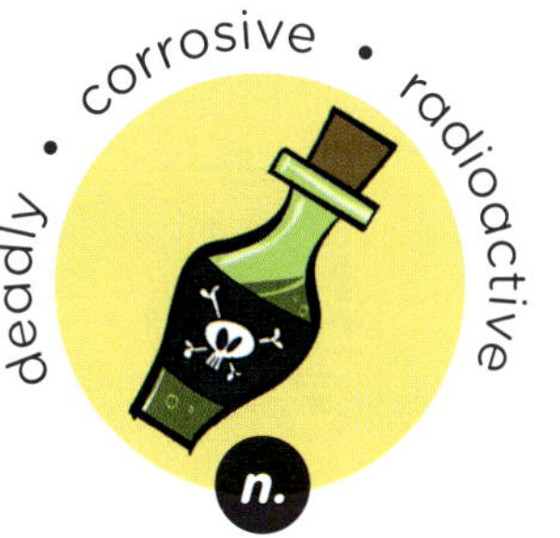

n.

poison

retired • undercover • corrupt

n.

police officer

locked • fireproof • impenetrable

n.

safe

hidden • digital • hacked

n.

security camera

ACTION AND ADVENTURE > THE CRIME

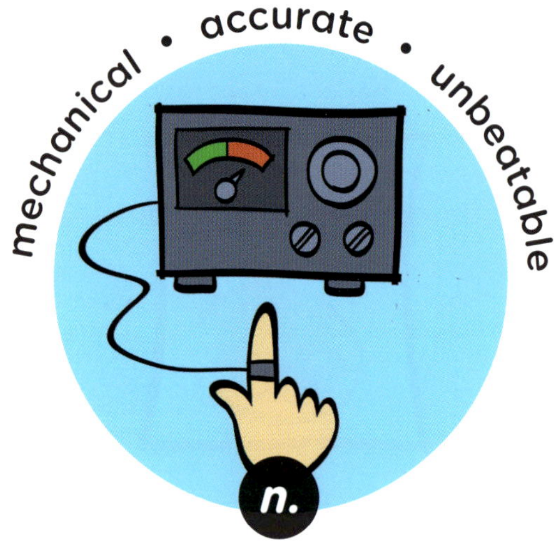

lie detector

a machine that shows if you're lying;
like a thing connected to you that flashes and beeps when you don't tell the truth

ACTION AND ADVENTURE > THE CRISIS

booming • devastating • rapid-fire 
n.
artillery

heavy • razor-sharp • blunt 
n.
axe

sharp • rusty • electrified 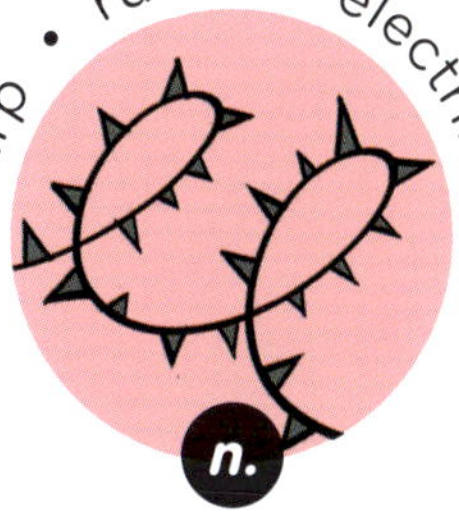
n.
barbed wire

flying • ticking • exploding 
n.
bomb

handmade • flaming • trusty 
n.
bow and arrow

loaded • thundering • belching 
n.
cannon

rusty • concealed • ornate 
n.
dagger

dangerous • spiked • twirling 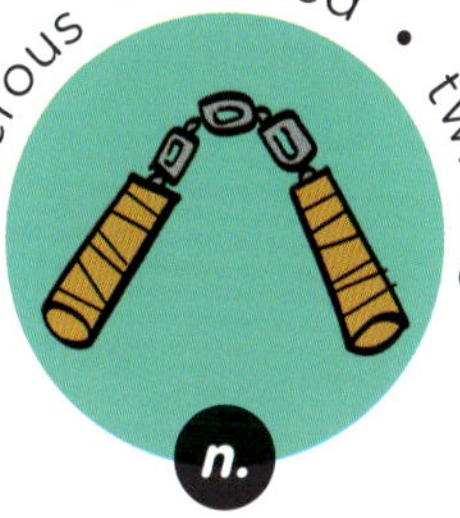
n.
nunchucks

total • mindless • flaming
n.
mayhem

confusion and violent chaos;
like a situation so crazy that everything is destroyed

large • protective • impenetrable
n.
shield

giant • homemade • loaded
n.
slingshot

mighty • flaming • ancient
n.
sword

rolling • camouflaged • derelict
n.
tank

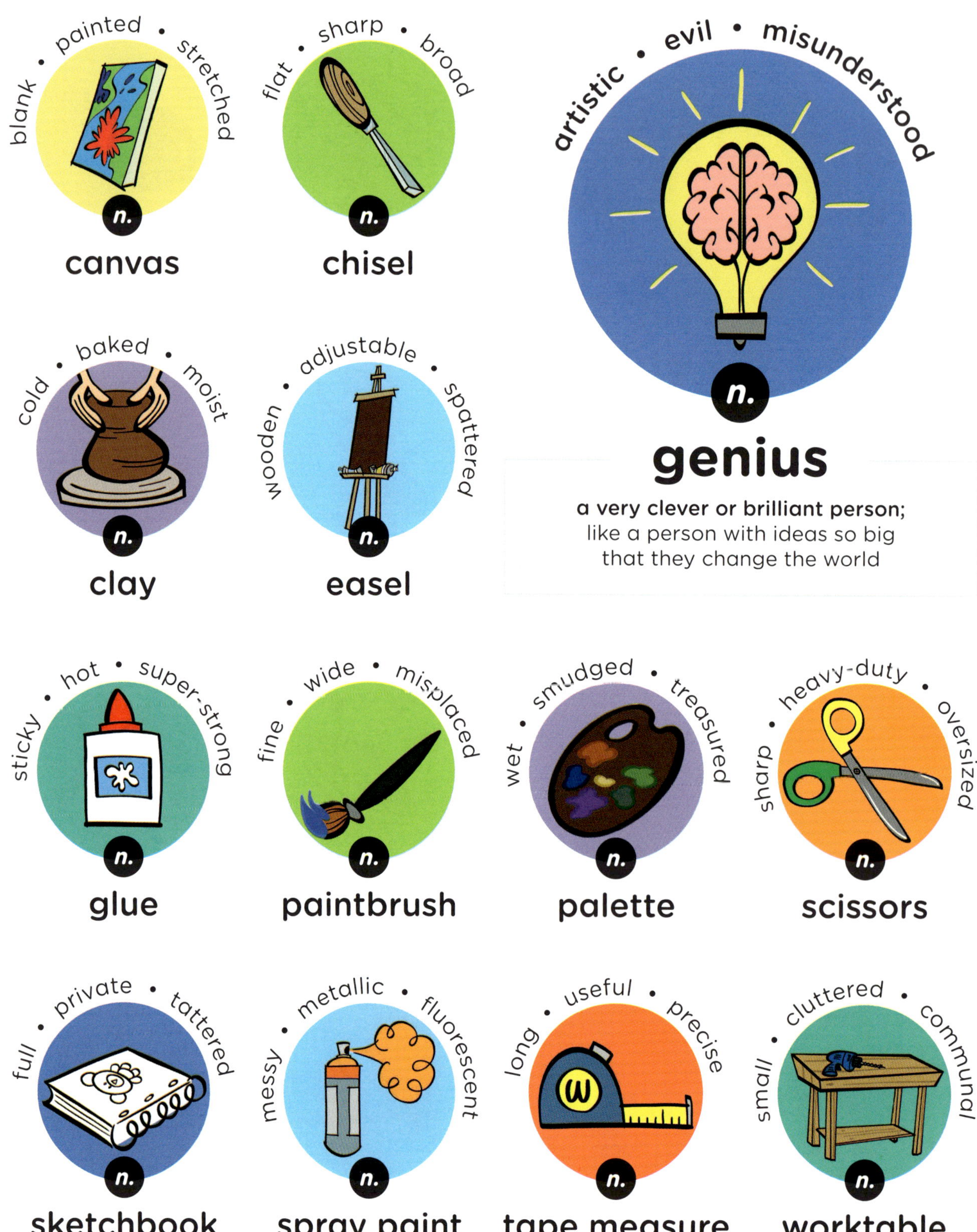
blank • painted • stretched
n.
canvas
flat • sharp • broad
n.
chisel
artistic • evil • misunderstood
n.
genius
a very clever or brilliant person;
like a person with ideas so big
that they change the world
cold • baked • moist
n.
clay
wooden • adjustable • spattered
n.
easel
sticky • hot • super-strong
n.
glue
fine • wide • misplaced
n.
paintbrush
wet • smudged • treasured
n.
palette
sharp • heavy-duty • oversized
n.
scissors
full • private • tattered
n.
sketchbook
messy • metallic • fluorescent
n.
spray paint
long • useful • precise
n.
tape measure
small • cluttered • communal
n.
worktable

harsh • chaotic • deafening

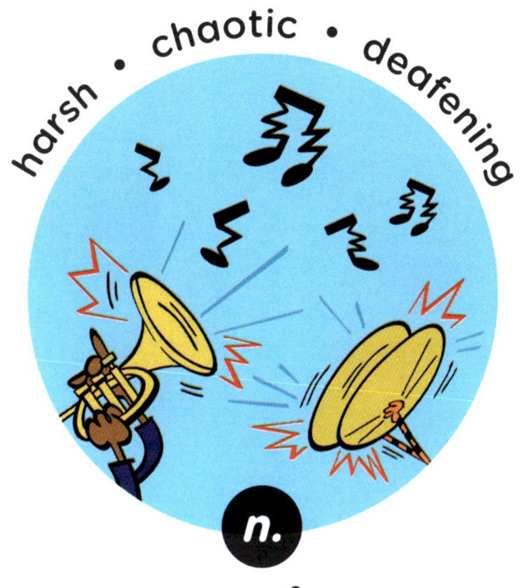

n.

cacophony

lots of horrible, loud noises;
like terrible singing that's so loud you can't ignore it

famous • strict • expressive

n.

conductor

cool • aspiring • legendary

n.

DJ

beating • muffled • thunderous

n.

drums

soft • gentle • shrill

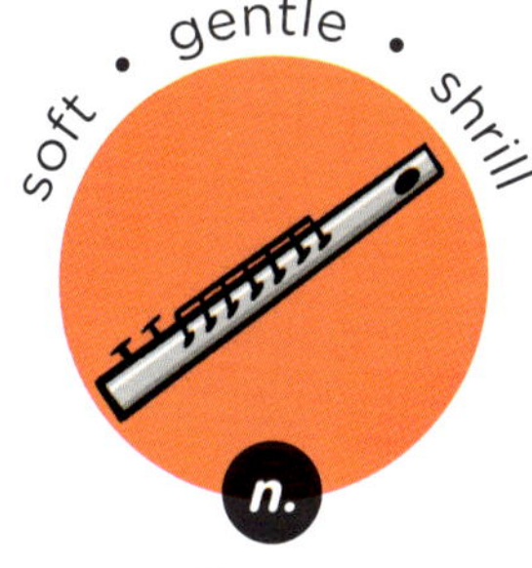

n.

flute

loud • mellow • somber

n.

French horn

wailing • battered • distorted

n.

guitar

wireless • hidden • crackly

n.

microphone

electric • untuned • beloved

n.

piano

talented • inspiring • versatile

n.

singer

futuristic • hypnotic • droning

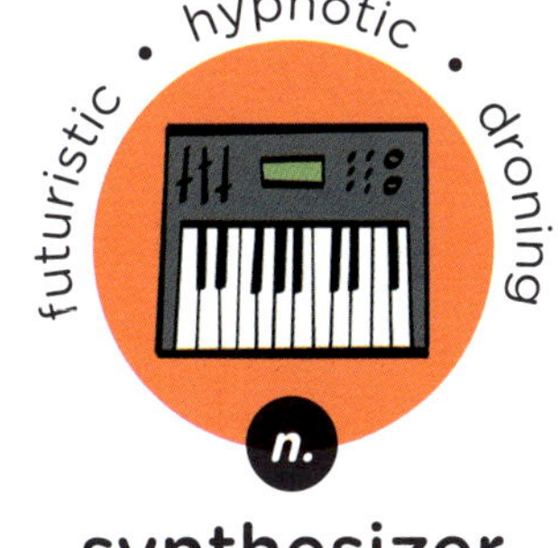

n.

synthesizer

clear • shrill • mournful

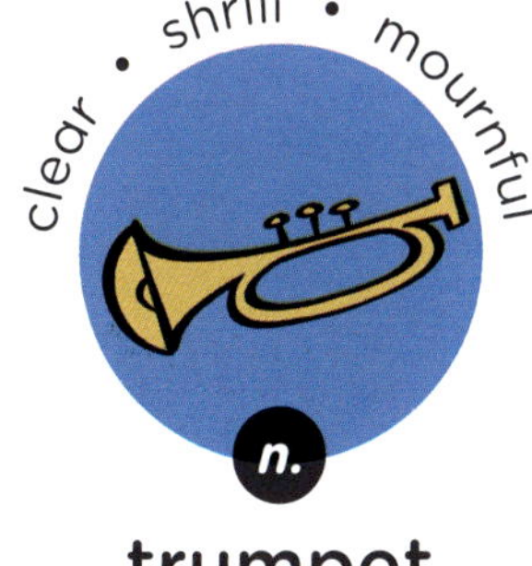

n.

trumpet

sad • screeching • soaring

n.

violin

Action
Character
Emotion
Setting
Taste & Smell
Weather

DRAMA > RELAXATION

DRAMA > ROMANCE

DRAMA > ROMANCE

strong • mysterious • magic

n.

love potion

painful • precious • fond

n.

memories

blind • excessive • unswerving

n.

devotion

deep love and commitment; when you promise your whole heart to something or someone

sweet • subtle • intoxicating

n.

perfume

romantic • bold • unexpected

n.

proposal

SCIENCE AND TECHNOLOGY > CONSTRUCTION

clear • detailed • architectural

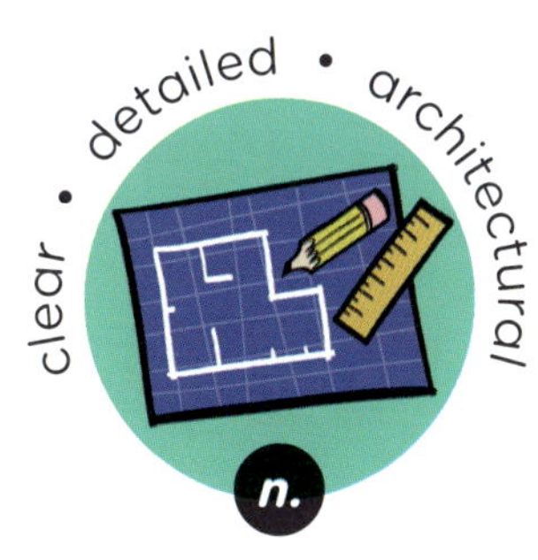

n.

blueprints

gigantic • towering • overhead

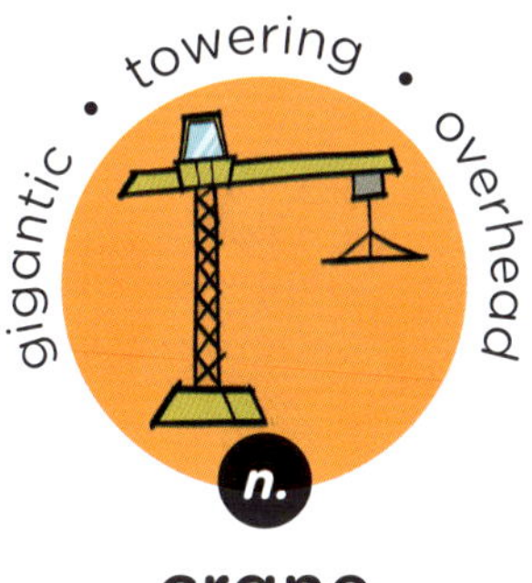

n.

crane

noisy • monstrous • devastating

n.

jackhammer

high-tech • robotic • precise

n.

laser cutter

tiled • solar • corrugated

n.

roofing

temporary • flimsy • lofty

n.

scaffolding

dirty • heavy • bent

n.

shovel

handheld • secure • intrusive

n.

walkie-talkie

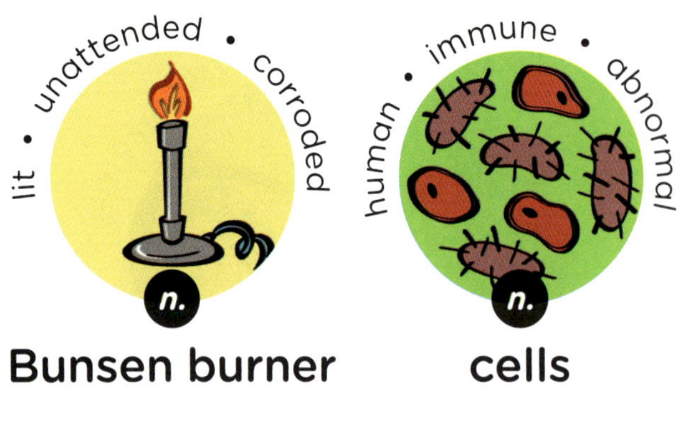

lit • unattended • corroded

n.

Bunsen burner

human • immune • abnormal

n.

cells

scientific • daring • unsuccessful

n.

experiment

a test, trial, or investigation;
like mixing two things to find out what happens

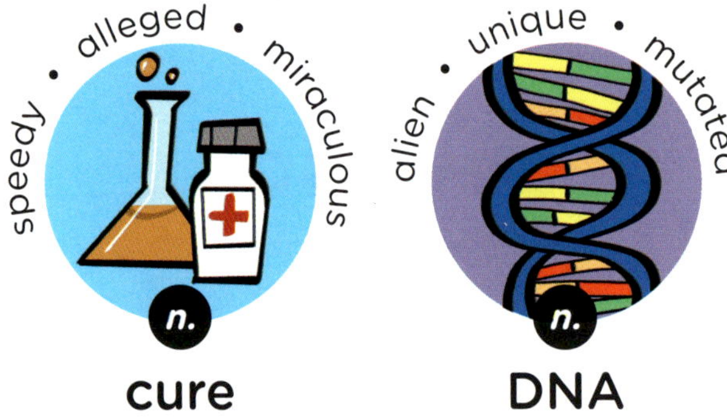

speedy • alleged • miraculous

n.

cure

alien • unique • mutated

n.

DNA

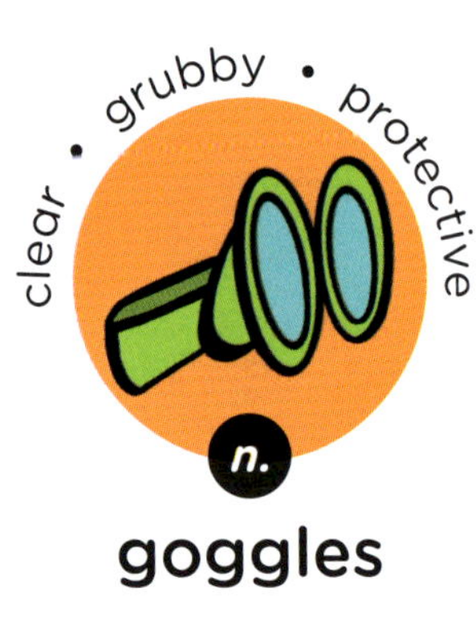

clear • grubby • protective

n.

goggles

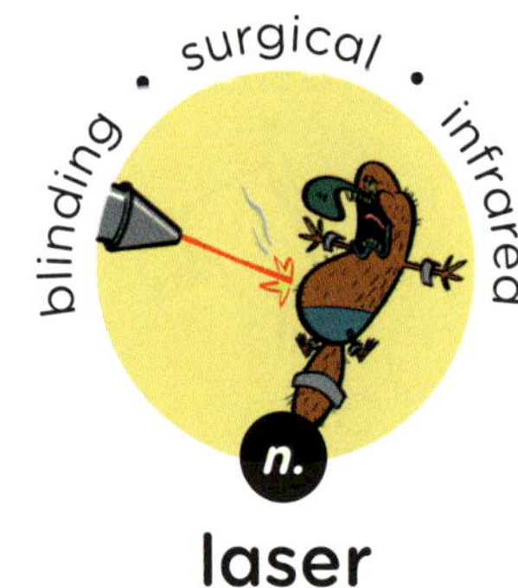

blinding • surgical • infrared

n.

laser

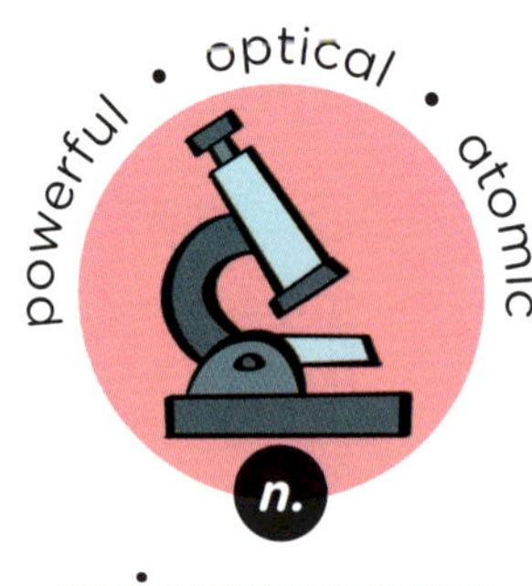

powerful • optical • atomic

n.

microscope

harmful • random • genetic

n.

mutation

collected • random • tainted

n.

sample

escaped • willing • unwitting

n.

test subject

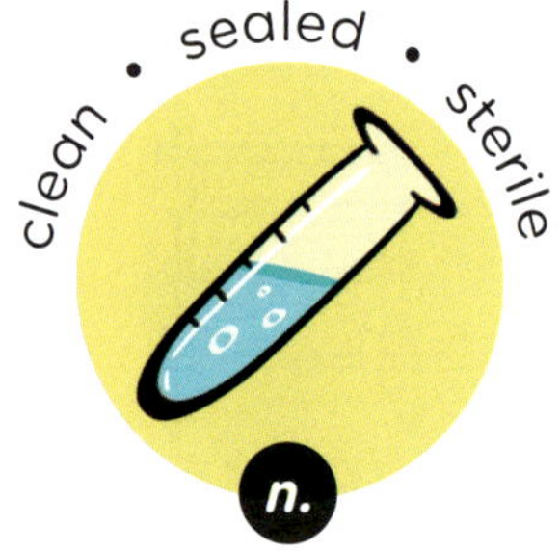

clean • sealed • sterile

n.

test tube

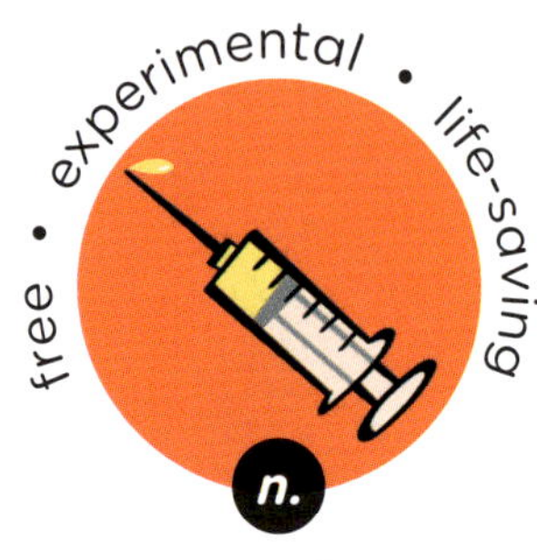

free • experimental • life-saving

n.

vaccine

dead • drained • long-lasting
n.
battery
grubby • wireless • Bluetooth
n.
controller
personal • sensitive • raw
n.
data
powerful • robotic • armored
n.
exosuit
lost • infected • encrypted
n.
flash drive
built-in • reliable • homing
n.
GPS
spare • external • corrupt
n.
hard drive
cheap • expensive • noise-canceling
n.
headphones
advanced • amphibious • military
n.
hovercraft
secret • incorrect • encrypted
n.
password
alien • unmanned • interstellar
n.
probe
fiery • unwieldy • mechanical
n.
rocket boots
expensive • latest • revolutionary
CALL ENDED
n.
smartphone
stylish • dependable • life-changing
n.
smart watch
futuristic • hurtling • sky-piercing
n.
space elevator
massive • doomed • orbiting
n.
space shuttle

SCIENCE AND TECHNOLOGY > TECHNOLOGY

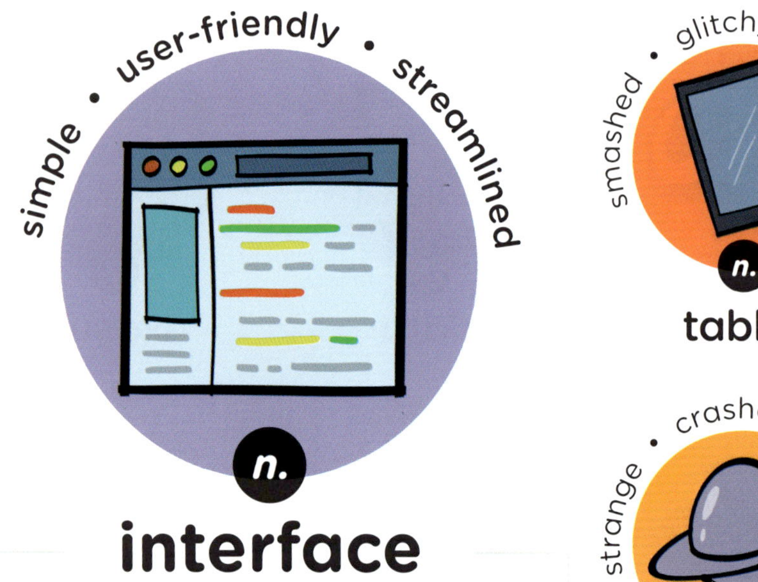

simple • user-friendly • streamlined

n.

interface

the menus and buttons that you see on a screen; like the tools that help you get around a website

smashed • glitchy • waterproof
n. **tablet**

human • broken • interplanetary
n. **teleporter**

strange • crashed • hovering
n. **UFO**

smart • powerful • innovative
n. **wearables**

SPORTS > COMPETITION

gifted • world-class • retired
n. **athlete**

lanky • average • phenomenal
n. **basketball player**

tough • trained • heavyweight
n. **boxer**

respected • livid • legendary
n. **coach**

loyal • die-hard • obsessive
n. **fan**

muscular • talented • aspiring
n. **football player**

competitive • upcoming • pivotal
n. **game**

top • avid • accomplished
n. **golfer**

SPORTS > COMPETITION

SPORTS > EQUIPMENT

The fairy must have blasted it with her weapon. Very **astute**. One less variable in the equation. It was exactly what he himself would have done.

Artemis Fowl by Eoin Colfer

Character

beautiful words

adj.

chiseled

DEFINITION

perfectly carved or sculpted; like the square jaw of a handsome superhero

SAMPLE SENTENCE

Brick thought his **chiseled** chin made him look like a superhero.

adj.

beautiful words

dazzling

DEFINITION

sparkling or amazing; like the glittering lights of a hundred cameras

SAMPLE SENTENCE

The singer flashed a **dazzling** smile at the audience.

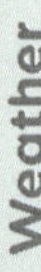

beautiful words

adj.

flawless

DEFINITION

perfect or impeccable;
like a ballet dancer who never makes a single mistake

SAMPLE SENTENCE

Armie had a **flawless** reputation at school because he never did anything wrong.

beautiful words

adj.

impeccable

DEFINITION

elegant and perfect;
like a well-groomed dog

SAMPLE SENTENCE

Oz had **impeccable** taste so she always knew what to wear.

beautiful words

adj.

mesmerizing

DEFINITION

very attractive or bewitching; like something that hypnotizes and distracts you completely

SAMPLE SENTENCE

The screen had such a **mesmerizing** effect on Bearnice that she ignored everything else.

statuesque

DEFINITION

tall, beautiful, and dignified; like someone who looks as impressive as a statue

SAMPLE SENTENCE

The **statuesque** queen made the king look small and ugly in comparison.

or you can try...

Absolutely beautiful words!

alluring
***adj.* attractive or tempting;** like a box of chocolates you would love to eat

angelic
***adj.* beautiful and pure;** like an angel with golden hair and a sweet voice

attractive
***adj.* good-looking or appealing;** like a handsome movie star

breathtaking
***adj.* amazing or astonishing;** like a magic trick that makes you gasp

captivating
***adj.* delightful or charming;** like a beautiful bird that you cannot look away from

celestial
***adj.* pure and heavenly;** like a beautiful sound that seems to come from another world

doll-like
***adj.* beautiful but lifeless;** like a wooden doll with a painted face

elegant
***adj.* graceful and stylish;** like a fashionable, sophisticated outfit

enchanting
***adj.* beautiful and charming;** like the irresistible beauty of a princess in a fairytale

exquisite
***adj.* beautiful, delicate, or perfect;** like a detailed piece of jewelery

fashionable
***adj.* stylish and modern;** like a restaurant that everyone wants to visit

fetching
***adj.* pretty or charming;** like a stylish hat that is very in fashion

or you can try...

glamorous

adj. **stylish and attractive;** like a movie star wearing a fashionable gown on the red carpet

gorgeous

adj. **very beautiful or attractive;** like the stunning view from the top of a mountain

graceful

adj. **charming and elegant;** like a ballerina gliding smoothly across the stage

handsome

adj. **attractive or good-looking;** like a man in a magazine

hypnotic

adj. **making you feel sleepy;** like beautiful, repetitive music that sends you into a trance

intoxicating

adj. **exciting or thrilling;** like a magic potion that makes you feel dizzy

luminous

adj. **bright or shining;** like a single star shining over a desert

magnificent

adj. **grand or impressive;** like a huge palace with many towers and turrets

majestic

adj. **grand or dignified;** like a snow-covered mountain peak

radiant

adj. **bright or shining;** like a smile as bright as the sun

stunning

adj. **beautiful and amazing;** like someone so beautiful that you can't believe it

sublime

adj. **heavenly or glorious;** like a beautiful poem that stays with you forever

timeless

adj. **permanent or unchanging;** like a song that's so good it never gets old

transcendent

adj. **magnificent and heavenly;** like a magical place in another world

turn over for big or fat words >

big or fat words

adj.

bulky

DEFINITION

large, heavily built, or stocky; like someone with a big body and chunky muscles

SAMPLE SENTENCE

There was no way that Brick's **bulky** body would fit into the tiny shorts.

big or fat words

adj.

colossal

DEFINITION

massive or gigantic;
like a huge statue that makes you feel tiny in comparison

SAMPLE SENTENCE

The billionaire kept her **colossal** fortune locked away in the bank.

Action
Character
Emotion
Setting
Taste & Smell
Weather

flabby

DEFINITION

droopy, soft, and floppy; like the wobbly flesh on a hippo's stomach

SAMPLE SENTENCE

The builder's **flabby** arms jiggled as he used the giant drill.

gargantuan

DEFINITION

huge or enormous;
like a giant who towers above you

SAMPLE SENTENCE

Oz began the **gargantuan** task of copying out the dictionary.

Action

Character

Emotion

Setting

Taste & Smell

Weather

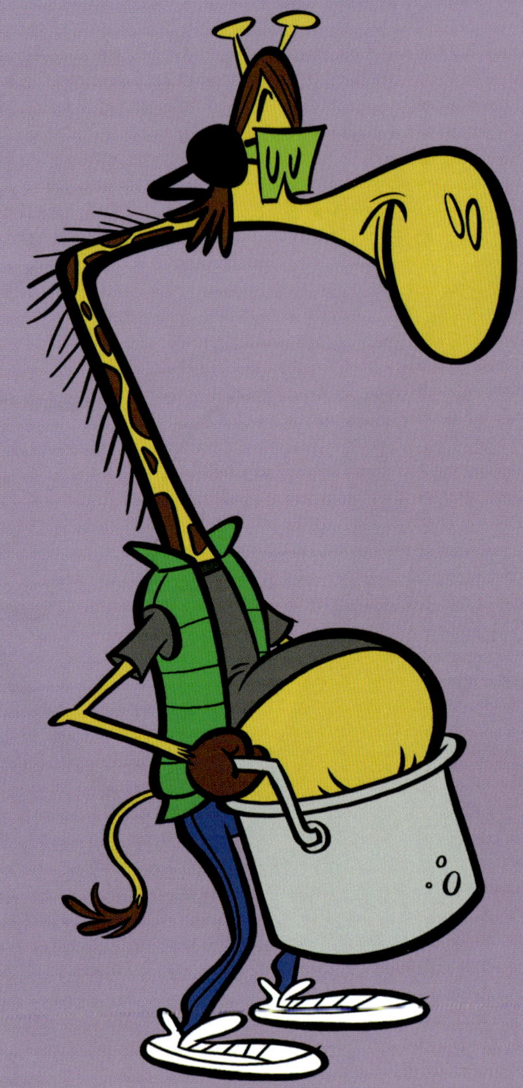

big or fat words

adj.

pot-bellied

DEFINITION

having a round stomach; like someone with a belly that would fit in a pot

SAMPLE SENTENCE

The **pot-bellied** piglet ate so much food that he looked like a football.

big or fat words

adj.

robust

DEFINITION

strong and tough;
like something so hardy
it can't be hurt or broken

SAMPLE SENTENCE

Plato's **robust** health means that he never gets sick.

or you can try...

Big, fat words!

broad
adj. **large and wide;** like a highway with six lanes

bulbous
adj. **large, round, and bulging;** like the eyes of a staring frog

chunky
adj. **solid and heavy;** like a thick winter coat

corpulent
adj. **round or fat;** like a cat that has just eaten five dinners

curvy
adj. **having an attractively round shape;** like the shape of a pear

elephantine
adj. **huge and clumsy;** like a gang of elephants stomping through the jungle

fleshy
adj. **plump and soft;** like the legs of a chubby baby

gigantic
adj. **huge or enormous;** like a giant who is as tall as a skyscraper

herculean
adj. **muscly and strong;** like a giant with huge muscles

hulking
adj. **big and clumsy;** like a huge truck that is difficult to control

immense
adj. **very large or enormous;** like a forest that goes as far as you can see

lumpy
adj. **large and uneven;** like an old pillow with clumped-up pieces of stuffing

or you can try...

massive
adj. **very large or solid;** like an iceberg that's big enough to sink a ship

meaty
adj. **solid or fleshy;** like the hands of a giant

mighty
adj. **strong and powerful;** like the ruler of a great empire

muscular
adj. **strong and well-built;** like someone who spends all their spare time in the gym

obese
adj. **much too heavy;** like a person who is so overweight that it makes them sick

overweight
adj. **too heavy;** like a person who weighs more than is healthy

plump
adj. **fat or round;** like a big, comfortable pillow

protruding
adj. **sticking out or poking out;** like the front teeth of a rabbit

rotund
adj. **fat or round;** like a well-fed turkey with its chest puffed out

solid
adj. **firm and strong;** like the body of a bull

stout
adj. **big and broad;** like a chunky goalie that fills the entire goal

substantial
adj. **large and solid;** like a big slab of chocolate cake

thickset
adj. **heavy or muscular;** like a tough-looking bodyguard

towering
adj. **high or tall;** like a soaring skyscraper with a hundred floors

turn over for clever or sly words >

clever or sly words

adj.

astute

DEFINITION

shrewd or quick-witted;
like someone who understands things quickly and makes smart decisions

SAMPLE SENTENCE

Oz made an **astute** observation that no one else had noticed.

cunning

DEFINITION

sly and crafty;
like someone who cleverly manages to get out of doing their chores

SAMPLE SENTENCE

Bogart's **cunning** plan to take over the world was evil, but brilliant.

devious

DEFINITION

cheating or sly;
like someone who is
busy making evil plans

SAMPLE SENTENCE

Bogart's clever lies and **devious** mind made him an excellent spy.

clever or sly words

adj.

discerning

DEFINITION

clear-sighted or selective; like a judge who is able to decide on the best cupcake

SAMPLE SENTENCE

Shang High was a **discerning** traveler so he only stayed in the best hotels.

clever or sly words

adj.

innovative

DEFINITION

creative or inventive;
like the genius who carved
the first-ever wheel out of stone

SAMPLE SENTENCE

Yang's **innovative** design for a cat toy was unlike anything else that had been seen before.

shrewd

DEFINITION

clever or sharp-witted;
like someone who comes up with a smart plan to make lots of money

SAMPLE SENTENCE

The student's **shrewd** question was so intelligent that it left his teacher speechless.

or you can try...

Clever, sly words!

able
adj. **clever or skillful;** like someone who is very good at their job

academic
adj. **bookish or well-educated;** like an expert who writes very serious books

bookish
adj. **clever or well-educated;** like someone who has read every book in the library

brainy
adj. **clever or intelligent;** like someone who scores 100% on a hard test

bright
adj. **clever or quick to learn;** like a student who understands something the first time it is explained

calculating
adj. **devious or cunning;** like someone who works out how to get other people to do what they want

canny
adj. **clever or shrewd;** like a businessperson who makes a lot of money in every deal

capable
adj. **skillful and effective;** like someone who can be trusted to get a job done

crafty
adj. **sly or cunning;** like someone who bends the rules to get out of a tricky situation

erudite
adj. **educated and wise;** like a professor who can speak fifteen different languages

expert
adj. **skillful or experienced;** like a scientist who knows everything about a complicated subject

gifted
adj. **naturally talented;** like a musician who can play difficult pieces without trying very hard

or you can try...

imaginative

***adj.* creative and full of ideas;** like a writer who invents a whole new world of their own

ingenious

***adj.* clever and creative;** like someone who finds a smart way to solve a tricky problem

intelligent

***adj.* clever or bright;** like someone who is able to solve a difficult puzzle

inventive

***adj.* creative and original;** like someone who is always coming up with new ideas

knowledgeable

***adj.* clever or well-informed;** like an experienced guide who knows every inch of a large city

masterful

***adj.* expert or skillful;** like an artist who can paint perfect portraits

perceptive

***adj.* smart or sensitive;** like someone who notices things that other people don't see

quick-witted

***adj.* clever or smart;** like someone who always comes up with a hilarious joke instantly

sharp

***adj.* clever and alert;** like someone who knows just when to make the winning move in a game

sly

***adj.* cunning and devious;** like someone who tries to swap things around when nobody is looking

smart

***adj.* clever or intelligent;** like a chess player who stays one move ahead of their opponent

talented

***adj.* skillful or gifted;** like someone who has the natural ability to do things that other people can't

wise

***adj.* clever or full of knowledge;** like an old friend who always gives you good advice

witty

***adj.* funny and clever;** like someone who is always saying smart things that make you laugh

turn over for clumsy or silly words >

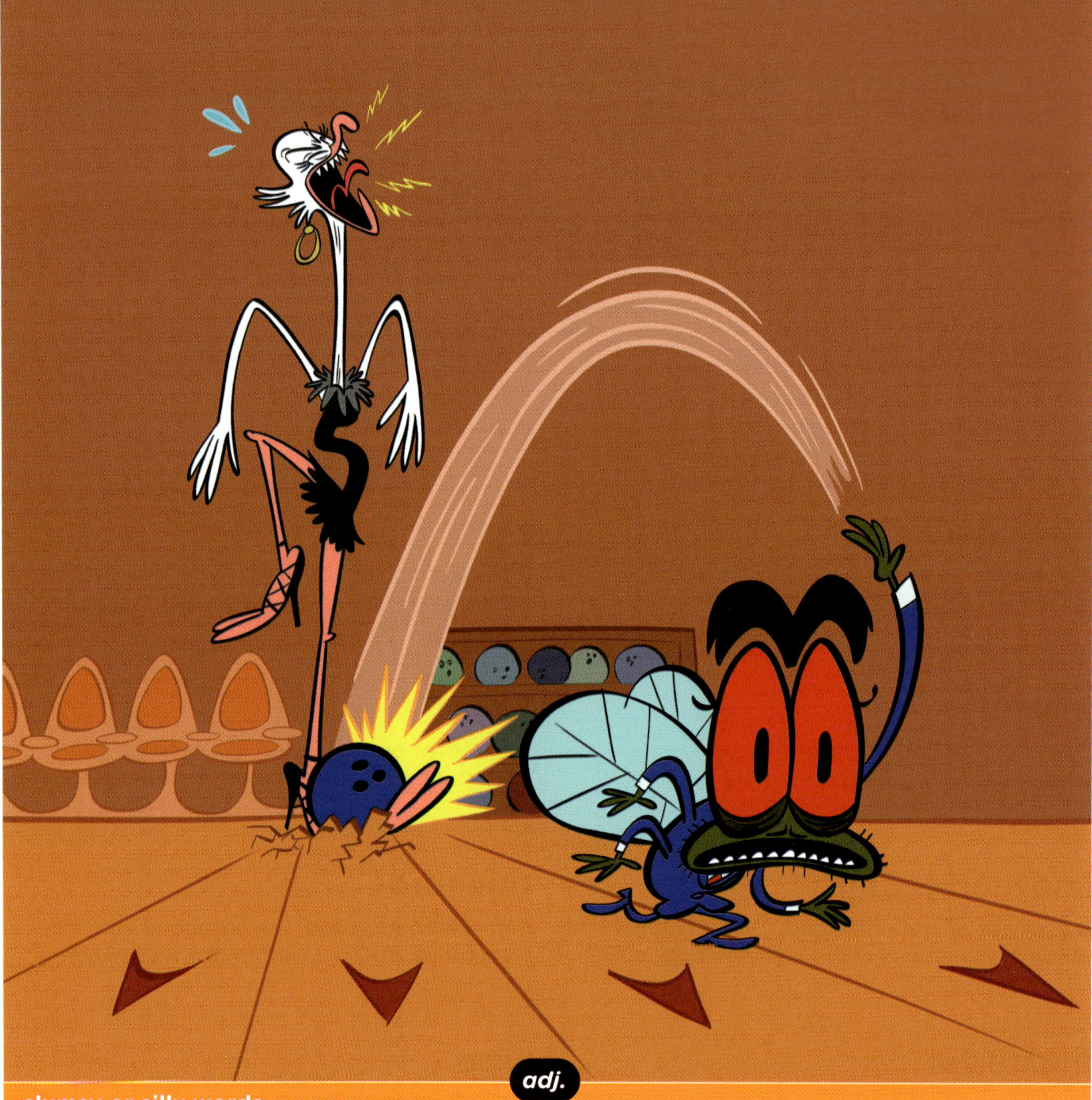

adj.

clumsy or silly words

blundering

DEFINITION

goofy or clumsy;
like accidentally flinging a bowling ball onto somebody's foot

SAMPLE SENTENCE

Bearnice made a **blundering** attempt to fix the table and accidentally broke it in half.

clumsy or silly words

adj.

bumbling

DEFINITION

awkward, clumsy, or useless; like a fisherman who gets tangled up in his own fishing rod

SAMPLE SENTENCE

Armie looked like a **bumbling** buffoon when he tripped over his own legs.

clumsy or silly words

adj.

butterfingered

DEFINITION

clumsy or accident-prone; like someone who constantly drops things

SAMPLE SENTENCE

The **butterfingered** cook dropped his phone in the soup.

clumsy or silly words

adj.

crude

DEFINITION

rude or savage;
like a cavewoman who doesn't care about picking her nose in public

SAMPLE SENTENCE

"Such **crude** manners!" gasped Armie as Grit ate mashed potatoes with his hands.

clumsy or silly words

adj.

daft

DEFINITION

silly or foolish;
like having the idea to catapult
a stone into a beehive

SAMPLE SENTENCE

"These **daft** people will buy anything!"
shouted Bogart as he explained
his idea for a paper frying pan.

adj.

clumsy or silly words

tongue-tied

DEFINITION

speechless or lost for words; when you feel shy and can't think of anything to say

SAMPLE SENTENCE

The **tongue-tied** presenter couldn't pronounce the actor's name.

or you can try...

Clumsy, silly words!

awkward
adj. **clumsy or uncomfortable;** like a bad joke that is made at the most embarrassing moment

bungling
adj. **clumsy or useless;** like a worker who makes a mess of a simple job

careless
adj. **thoughtless or forgetful;** like someone who is always losing their glasses

clownish
adj. **awkward or ridiculous;** like someone who is always making a fool of themselves in public

clunky
adj. **large or awkward;** like an old-fashioned machine that is difficult to use

cumbersome
adj. **big, heavy, and difficult to use;** like a spacesuit you can hardly walk in

foolish
adj. **silly or unwise;** like someone who does not know how little they understand something

fumbling
adj. **clumsy or blundering;** like an inexperienced musician who makes lots of mistakes

goofy
adj. **silly or ridiculous;** like when you make a silly face and grin widely

ham-fisted
adj. **clumsy or unskillful;** like a painter who makes lots of smudges and blotches by accident

imbecilic
adj. **foolish or daft;** like a really bad idea that is certain to fail

incompetent
adj. **unskilled or not able;** like a mechanic who is not able to fix a car

or you can try...

inelegant
adj. **clumsy or ungraceful;** like an elephant trying to tap dance

inept
adj. **clumsy or useless;** like a magician whose tricks all go wrong

irrational
adj. **foolish or not sensible;** like a fear of something that you know is not there

irresponsible
adj. **careless or unreliable;** like spending all of your money on chocolate instead of healthy food

laughable
adj. **ridiculous or absurd;** like a silly idea that everybody makes fun of

ludicrous
adj. **ridiculous or absurd;** like an unrealistic excuse that cannot possibly be true

nonsensical
adj. **ridiculous or silly;** like a song with words that have no meaning

oafish
adj. **bad-mannered and stupid;** like someone who talks noisily in a theater instead of watching the play

preposterous
adj. **ridiculous or outrageous;** like a lie that nobody would ever believe

scatterbrained
adj. **careless or forgetful;** like someone who gets off a train and leaves their bag behind

sloppy
adj. **careless or messy;** like a worker who makes a lot of silly mistakes

uncouth
adj. **rude and bad-mannered;** like someone who picks their nose at the dinner table

ungainly
adj. **awkward and ungraceful;** like a horse whose legs seem to go in different directions

unwise
adj. **foolish or not sensible;** like someone who believes everything they hear

turn over for confident words >

Action
Character
Emotion
Setting
Taste & Smell
Weather

adj.

confident words

assertive

DEFINITION

forceful or self-confident; like someone who always manages to get their way

SAMPLE SENTENCE

Mrs Wordsmith's **assertive** personality made it difficult to say no to her.

audacious

DEFINITION

bold and daring;
like someone brave enough
to dive into a pool full of sharks

SAMPLE SENTENCE

In an **audacious** move,
Armie fired his own boss.

confident words

adj.

brazen

DEFINITION

bold and shameless;
like stealing a police officer's wallet in plain sight

SAMPLE SENTENCE

Bogart's **brazen** lie was so obvious that he was surprised that anyone believed him.

confident words

adj.

conceited

DEFINITION

vain or proud;
like someone who is constantly taking selfies

SAMPLE SENTENCE

Bogart had a **conceited** attitude and thought he already knew everything.

confident words

adj.

presumptuous

DEFINITION

overconfident, arrogant, or rude; like someone who starts celebrating before they actually win

SAMPLE SENTENCE

Oz walked straight into the VIP room because of her **presumptuous** attitude.

unflappable

DEFINITION

cool, calm, or unworried; when you're so chilled out that nothing can upset you

SAMPLE SENTENCE

The actor held his **unflappable** composure even as the audience hissed and booed.

or you can try...

Brave, confident words!

arrogant

***adj.* proud and boastful;** like a boxing champion who says that nobody can possibly beat them

assured

***adj.* calm and confident;** like a singer who feels totally comfortable in front of an audience

bold

***adj.* brave or daring;** like a soldier who charges into battle against a thousand enemies

brave

***adj.* daring or courageous;** like a firefighter who goes into a burning house to rescue someone

certain

***adj.* sure or confident;** like someone who knows they are doing the right thing

composed

***adj.* calm or controlled;** like someone who doesn't panic when everybody else does

convinced

***adj.* sure or certain;** like someone who won't ever change their mind about something

cool-headed

***adj.* calm or unemotional;** like a football player who makes the winning kick despite the crowd's boos

courageous

***adj.* brave or fearless;** like someone who faces their fears boldly

fearless

***adj.* brave or daring;** like a diver who jumps off the highest board without getting scared

gallant

***adj.* brave and heroic;** like the knight in a fairytale who saves the day

gutsy

***adj.* brave and plucky;** like someone who stands up to a bully

or you can try...

heroic

adj. **admirably brave or gallant;** like someone who saves other people from danger

hubristic

adj. **too proud or confident;** like a swaggering general who does not see the danger ahead

intrepid

adj. **brave or adventurous;** like an explorer entering an unknown jungle

nonchalant

adj. **cool or casual;** like a tennis player who makes a difficult shot look easy

plucky

adj. **brave or courageous;** like someone who chases after a thief

poised

adj. **calm and composed;** like someone who manages to keep control in a tricky situation

reckless

adj. **careless or rash;** like a daredevil who jumps out of a plane without thinking twice

resolute

adj. **determined and decided;** like someone who knows what they believe and stands by it

self-assured

adj. **confident or assertive;** like someone who knows they have the talent to succeed

strong-willed

adj. **determined or stubborn;** like someone who only wants to do things their way

undaunted

adj. **brave or persistent;** like someone who keeps on trying in spite of many failures

unperturbed

adj. **unworried or untroubled;** like someone who isn't bothered when everything falls apart

valiant

adj. **brave or fearless;** like a soldier who marches confidently into battle

turn over for eye words >

Action | Character | Emotion | Setting | Taste & Smell | Weather

adj.

eye words

bloodshot

DEFINITION

red and sore;
how your eyes look when you haven't had nearly enough sleep

SAMPLE SENTENCE

The tired train driver examined his **bloodshot** eyeballs in the mirror.

bulging

DEFINITION

swollen or sticking out;
how your eyes look when you stare at something in amazement

SAMPLE SENTENCE

The **bulging** vein on the teacher's forehead was an angry, purple color.

eye words

adj.

expressive

DEFINITION

showing your thoughts or feelings; like the look in someone's eyes that tells you how they feel

SAMPLE SENTENCE

Armie's **expressive** eyebrows showed how surprised he was at the news.

eye words

adj.

fiery

DEFINITION

hot-tempered or furious; like someone who has lost their temper

SAMPLE SENTENCE

Mrs Wordsmith had a **fiery** look in her eyes because she was angry.

eye words

adj.

steely

DEFINITION

cold and determined;
like that look in someone's eyes that makes them seem as tough as steel

SAMPLE SENTENCE

Brick fixed a **steely** gaze upon his opponent that showed how serious he was about chess.

eye words

vacant

DEFINITION

empty or without emotion; like eyes that have a blank and lifeless look

SAMPLE SENTENCE

Armie's **vacant** eyes showed that he was in the middle of a daydream.

or you can try...

Watchful eye words!

all-knowing
adj. **very wise and intelligent;** like a goddess watching over her creation

almond-shaped
adj. **oval, with one pointed end;** like eyes in the shape of almonds

beady
adj. **small, bright, and round;** like the mean eyes of a greedy bear

bewitching
adj. **charming or attractive;** like the eyes of a beautiful witch who is casting a spell on you

bug-eyed
adj. **having large, staring eyes;** like an insect whose eyes take up most of its face

cloudy
adj. **dull or hazy;** like the eyes of a person in a trance

commanding
adj. **confident and powerful;** like a warrior queen ordering her soldiers to attack

compassionate
adj. **kind and understanding;** like the eyes of a friend who helps you with all your problems

darting
adj. **making short, fast movements;** like someone's eyes watching twenty television screens at the same time

drooping
adj. **tired and heavy;** like the eyelids of a dog who has not slept for two days

elongated
adj. **long or stretched;** like the long, thin eyes carved on a stone statue

fluttering
adj. **blinking quickly or trembling;** like the eyes of a person coming out of a cave into bright sunshine

or you can try...

focused

***adj.* concentrating or thoughtful;** like a chess player thinking about his next move

gentle

***adj.* soft and kind;** like the eyes of a friendly puppy

glazed

***adj.* blank and expressionless;** like someone whose eyes have been replaced by a sheet of glass

honest

***adj.* truthful or genuine;** like someone who would never tell a lie

languid

***adj.* slow or lazy;** like a cat resting by the fireplace

laughing

***adj.* jolly or cheerful;** like the eyes of a person who always sees the funny side of things

mysterious

***adj.* secretive or puzzling;** like someone who is hiding something about themselves

sorrowful

***adj.* sad and full of regret;** like a mother hen who has lost all her chicks

soulful

***adj.* full of emotion and meaning;** like the eyes of someone singing a sad song

twinkling

***adj.* glistening or flickering;** like a shiny star in the night sky

watery

***adj.* damp or tearful;** like the eyes of someone who is about to start crying

weary

***adj.* tired or worn out;** like a traveler at the end of a long journey

wide-set

***adj.* far apart;** like a frog whose eyes are on either side of its head

wild

***adj.* out of control or fierce;** like a charging bull

turn over for shy or uncertain words >

Action
Character
Emotion
Setting
Taste & Smell
Weather

shy or uncertain words

adj.

diffident

DEFINITION

modest or shy;
like someone who doesn't expect to be noticed

SAMPLE SENTENCE

Armie's **diffident** manner made him seem nervous.

shy or uncertain words

adj.

hesitant

DEFINITION

nervous or uncertain;
like someone afraid to
jump off a diving board

SAMPLE SENTENCE

The **hesitant** student knew the answer, but someone else spoke up first.

shy or uncertain words

adj.

insecure

DEFINITION

anxious or self-conscious; like someone who feels exposed in public

SAMPLE SENTENCE

The **insecure** teenager couldn't stop thinking about the enormous zit on his nose.

shy or uncertain words

adj.

introverted

DEFINITION

shy or reserved;
like someone who dreads going to parties and hides in a corner

SAMPLE SENTENCE

The **introverted** artist preferred to work alone as it helped her focus.

adj.

shy or uncertain words

sheepish

DEFINITION

shy, ashamed, or uncomfortable; the way you feel when you've done something silly or stupid

SAMPLE SENTENCE

The magician stood in **sheepish** silence when the rabbit stayed stuck in his hat.

adj.

wary

DEFINITION

careful or cautious;
like a fly who is afraid of getting zapped

SAMPLE SENTENCE

The chickens walked at a **wary** distance from the hungry fox.

or you can try...

Worried, shy, and uncertain words!

anxious

adj. **nervous or worried;** like someone who thinks they are going to fail a math test

apprehensive

adj. **worried or nervous;** like someone who is about to visit the dentist

bashful

adj. **shy or self-conscious;** like someone who does not dare to ask for something that they want

cowardly

adj. **scared or not brave;** like someone who will not stand up for what is right

demure

adj. **shy and modest;** like a sweet child who would never dream of doing anything wrong

doubtful

adj. **unsure or suspicious;** like someone who doesn't think they have much chance of succeeding

faint-hearted

adj. **nervous or easily scared;** like someone who is not prepared to take a risk

faltering

adj. **hesitant or unsteady;** like someone who is trying hard not to fall over

inhibited

adj. **shy or uneasy;** like a singer who is too frightened to perform in public

jittery

adj. **nervous and shaky;** like an actor who is worried before his first-ever performance

meek

adj. **shy or quiet;** like someone who never gets involved in an argument

modest

adj. **humble or not proud;** like someone who never boasts about what they have done

or you can try...

mousy

***adj.* shy or quiet;** like a hard-working person who never complains

neurotic

***adj.* unhealthily nervous;** like someone who worries about everything

reluctant

***adj.* unwilling or not interested;** like someone who does not want to answer a question

reserved

***adj.* shy or private;** like someone who never talks about themselves or their problems

reticent

***adj.* shy and quiet;** like someone who likes to keep their opinions to themselves

retiring

***adj.* shy or unassertive;** like a creature that lives out of sight in a remote jungle

self-effacing

***adj.* modest or humble;** like someone who plays down their own achievements

skittish

***adj.* nervous or easily scared;** like a deer that runs away at the slightest sound

tentative

***adj.* hesitant or uncertain;** like someone slowly dipping a toe into a bath to see how hot the water is

timid

***adj.* fearful or shy;** like someone who is worried about making a mistake

timorous

***adj.* nervous or fearful;** like a terrified kitten who hides under the bed

unassuming

***adj.* modest or not showing off;** like someone who does not draw attention to themselves

uneasy

***adj.* nervous or uncomfortable;** like a king who thinks his sons may be plotting against him

withdrawn

***adj.* shy and quiet;** like someone who stays in their bedroom and never talks

turn over for small or thin words >

Action

Character

Emotion

Setting

Taste & Smell

Weather

small or thin words

adj.

emaciated

DEFINITION

skeletal or very thin;
like a prisoner who is being starved in a dungeon

SAMPLE SENTENCE

The man's **emaciated** body was so thin that you could see his ribs.

small or thin words

adj.

lanky

DEFINITION

tall, thin, and ungraceful; like a giraffe trying to roller skate for the first time

SAMPLE SENTENCE

The **lanky** teenager's jeans were too short for him.

adj.

small or thin words

scrawny

DEFINITION

thin and bony;
like a wet dog who is
all skin and bones

SAMPLE SENTENCE

Brick's finger was the same size as Bogart's **scrawny** arm.

small or thin words

adj.

shriveled

DEFINITION

wrinkled or shrunken;
like hippo skin that has been in the bath too long

SAMPLE SENTENCE

The brown, wrinkly, **shriveled** apple was the last one left in the bowl.

small or thin words

adj.

squat

DEFINITION

short and stubby;
like a body that looks as if it has been squashed down

SAMPLE SENTENCE

The **squat** man was so short that he couldn't reach the door handle.

small or thin words

adj.

willowy

DEFINITION

tall, slender, and graceful; like the branches of a drooping willow tree

SAMPLE SENTENCE

The **willowy** dancer was much taller and thinner than the rest of the performers.

or you can try...

Small, thin words!

compact
adj. **small and closely packed;** like an umbrella that folds up until it's really small

dainty
adj. **delicate and elegant;** like a light and tasty little cake

delicate
adj. **fragile or elegant;** like a cup made from fine china

frail
adj. **weak or fragile;** like a stray kitten who hasn't had a good meal in a long time

gangly
adj. **tall and thin;** like a person with very long arms and legs

gaunt
adj. **thin and unhealthy;** like the face of someone who is sick

hollow-cheeked
adj. **having thin, sunken cheeks;** like someone who has not eaten for days

lean
adj. **thin and healthy;** like the long, strong body of a tiger

lightweight
adj. **thin and delicate;** like a jacket that will not keep out the cold

miniature
adj. **little or tiny;** like a very small painting

miniscule
adj. **little or tiny;** like a single crumb of cake left on a plate

narrow
adj. **tight or close together;** like a tiny crack that you can only just squeeze through

or you can try...

nimble
adj. **light and quick;** like a runner who dodges out of the way to avoid an obstacle

pencil-thin
adj. **thin or narrow;** like a wooden stick that you can snap easily

petite
adj. **small and delicate;** like someone who looks little next to other people

puny
adj. **small and weak;** like a tiny raft about to be smashed by a giant wave

shrunken
adj. **small or shriveled;** like the body of someone who has grown smaller with age

sinewy
adj. **slim and muscly;** like a lightweight boxer who is stronger than he looks

skeletal
adj. **thin and bony;** like an unhealthy person whose bones show through their skin

skinny
adj. **thin or bony;** like a baby animal that is not yet fully grown

slender
adj. **thin and graceful;** like the neck of a swan

slim
adj. **slender or gracefully thin;** like a long-distance runner who trains a lot

spindly
adj. **thin or fragile;** like the legs of a giraffe

starved
adj. **hungry or thin;** like an Arctic explorer who has run out of food

toned
adj. **firm, strong, and shapely;** like the body of someone who works out in a gym

trim
adj. **slim or neat;** like a well-groomed athlete in a stylish tracksuit

turn over for voice words >

voice words

adj.

abrasive

DEFINITION

harsh and grating;
like a horrible noise that makes your hair stand on end

SAMPLE SENTENCE

Grit's **abrasive** manner made him difficult to get to know.

voice words

adj.

gruff

DEFINITION

rough or husky;
like a growling cowboy

SAMPLE SENTENCE

Brick's **gruff** tone
scared Oz into hiding.

voice words

adj.

hollow

DEFINITION

empty or not solid;
like the sound made when you shout into an empty tree trunk

SAMPLE SENTENCE

"I'm not afraid of ghosts," lied Yang with a **hollow** laugh.

voice words

adj.

nasal

DEFINITION

whiny or from your nose;
like a voice that sounds like you're talking through your nose

SAMPLE SENTENCE

Brick's nose was blocked so his deep laugh was turned into a **nasal** whine.

voice words

adj.

shrill

DEFINITION

sharp or high-pitched;
like the sound of a giant whistle

SAMPLE SENTENCE

The baby's **shrill** cry was so high-pitched that all the dogs on the street started barking.

voice words

adj.

velvety

DEFINITION

smooth and silky;
like a voice so lovely it feels like velvet on your ears

SAMPLE SENTENCE

The singer's deep, **velvety** voice sent a shiver up Bogart's spine.

164 clever character nouns

Use these nouns and word pairs to give your characters glamorous gowns and slippery slime.

ARCHETYPES - HERO OR VILLAIN?

unlikely • unsung • valiant 
n.
hero

secret • jealous • faithful 
n.
lover

wise • lifelong • spiritual 
n.
mentor

old • arch • vengeful 
n.
nemesis

bitter • longtime • formidable 
n.
rival

sly • charming • lovable 
n.
rogue

mighty • corrupt • oppressive 
n.
ruler

young • loyal • annoying 
n.
sidekick

cowardly • suspected • filthy
n.
traitor

professional • cunning • devious
n.
trickster

frightened • innocent • unsuspecting
n.
victim

evil • scheming • treacherous
n.
villain

clear • scrappy • lovable
n.
underdog

someone who isn't expected to win;
like a tiny boxer facing the heavyweight champion

body type or build; like the size and shape of a person's body

THE BODY > GROSS STUFF

THE BODY > HAIRSTYLES

THE BODY > HANDS

THE BODY > INSIDES

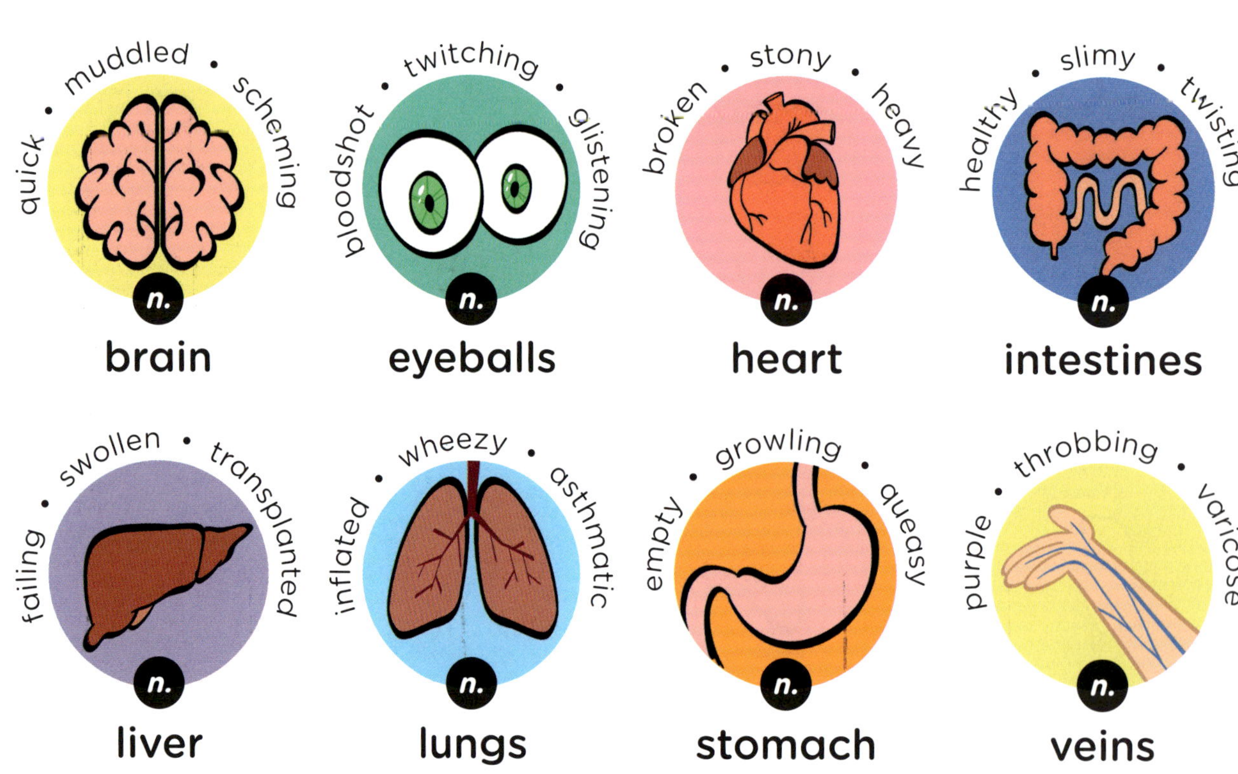

bushy • bristly • grizzly

n.

beard

purple • unique • blotchy

n.

birthmark

fresh • severe • first-degree

n.

burn

high • sculpted • defined

n.

cheekbones

deep • charming • angelic

n.

dimples

thick • wire-framed • tinted

n.

glasses

strong • rounded • chiseled

n.

jawline

dark • hairy • fake

n.

mole

thick • groomed • drooping

n.

mustache

fresh • jagged • prominent

n.

scar

huge • hairy • unsightly

n.

wart

kind • faint • deep-set

n.

wrinkles

stiff • upright • correct

n.

posture

position or stance; like the way a person holds themselves when they're standing or sitting

CLOTHING > DRESSING UP

CLOTHING > SHOES

CLOTHING > SUMMER CLOTHES

CLOTHING > WINTER CLOTHES

CLOTHING > WINTER CLOTHES

CREATURES > CREATURE FEATURES

sharp • stubby • spiraling
n.
horns
mighty • clenched • gaping
n.
jaws
broad • pointed • velvety
n.
muzzle
muddy • nimble • oversized
n.
paws
huge • crushing • unforgiving
n.
pincer
slimy • coarse • glistening
n.
scales
protective • outer • fragile
n.
shell
rubbery • greasy • shriveled
n.
skin
slippery • toxic • oozing
n.
slime
sharp • bristly • bony
n.
spines
striped • deadly • fearsome
n.
stinger
bushy • stumpy • curly
n.
tail
powerful • menacing • fierce
n.
talons
long • writhing • venomous
n.
tentacle
sensitive • bristly • twitching
n.
whiskers
flapping • outspread • clipped
n.
wings

MONSTROUS CREATURES > MONSTERS

SCI-FI CHARACTERS

We are just like the Mafia, once you cross us we bear a **grudge** all our lives.

The Secret Diary of Adrian Mole, Aged 13¾
by Sue Townsend

Emotion

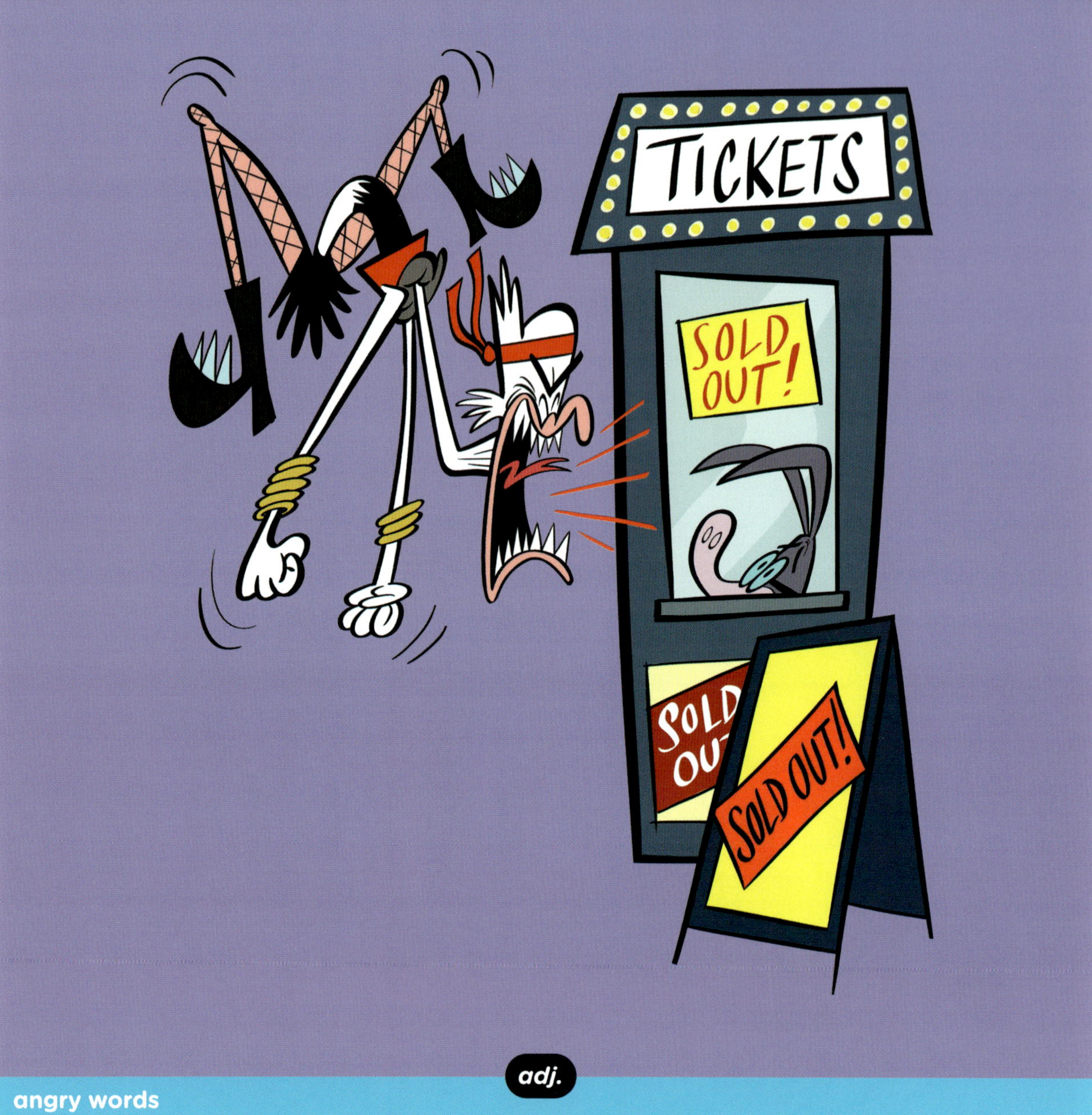

angry words

adj.

furious

DEFINITION

very angry or enraged;
how you would feel if all the tickets to your favorite band were sold out

SAMPLE SENTENCE

A **furious** customer started throwing fries at Plato, angry at how soggy they were.

grudge

DEFINITION

hatred or bitterness;
when you stay angry with someone and refuse to forgive them

SAMPLE SENTENCE

After arguing for days, Yin and Yang agreed to bury their **grudge** and be friends again.

adj.

angry words

irritated

DEFINITION

annoyed or peeved;
like when a stupid song you hear over and over again makes you grumpy

SAMPLE SENTENCE

Armie let out an **irritated** sigh, annoyed to be repeating his instructions yet again.

adj.

angry words

livid

DEFINITION

raging or furious;
how you feel when you
lose a video game

SAMPLE SENTENCE

Grit flew into a **livid**
fury and almost turned
purple with anger.

angry words

adj.

raging

DEFINITION

furious or fuming;
like an angry bull
on a rampage

SAMPLE SENTENCE

Grit's **raging** temper
meant that even the smallest
problem made him angry.

angry words

adj.

spiteful

DEFINITION

hateful or mean;
like purposefully spilling paint on someone's work just to ruin it

SAMPLE SENTENCE

Oz thought the newspapers were full of **spiteful** gossip that was cruel and untrue.

or you can try...

Fuming anger words!

aggravated

***adj.* angry or annoyed;** the way you feel when someone has treated you unfairly

aggressive

***adj.* angry and forceful;** like someone who reacts more violently than they need to

annoyed

***adj.* angry or upset;** the way you feel when someone has an irritating habit

antagonized

***adj.* annoyed or provoked;** like someone who is teased until they get really angry

cantankerous

***adj.* bad-tempered and argumentative;** like someone who never says anything nice to anyone

displeased

***adj.* disappointed or annoyed;** like a teacher when someone in their class is really naughty

fractious

***adj.* grumpy or argumentative;** like someone who is always making enemies and upsetting people

fuming

***adj.* angry or furious;** like someone who feels like they have been punished for something they didn't do

galled

***adj.* annoyed or irritated;** like someone who feels they had lots of unfair bad luck

hostile

***adj.* unfriendly and aggressive;** like someone who is always unpleasant and tries to start fights

incensed

***adj.* angry or enraged;** like someone who loses their temper after they have been tricked

infuriated

***adj.* annoyed or enraged;** like someone who feels angry when other people cut in line

or you can try...

irate
adj. **angry or furious;** like someone who has waited over an hour to be served at a restaurant

seething
adj. **filled with intense anger;** like someone who is upset because they have been betrayed

irked
adj. **annoyed or irritated;** the way you feel if someone is rude to you for no reason

stroppy
adj. **bad-tempered and argumentative;** like someone who is grumpy if they don't get their own way

moody
adj. **grumpy and unpredictable;** like someone who keeps getting upset for no good reason

testy
adj. **easily irritated or grumpy;** like a soccer coach who gets very angry when their team loses

peeved
adj. **annoyed or irritated;** the way you feel if you think you should have won first place in a competition

tetchy
adj. **bad-tempered or cranky;** like someone who gets annoyed about every little thing

piqued
adj. **annoyed or resentful;** the way you feel if someone behaves coldly toward you

vengeful
adj. **unforgiving and wanting revenge;** like a victim who wants the person who harmed them to be punished

ratty
adj. **cross or bad-tempered;** like someone who gets angry very easily

vexed
adj. **annoyed or frustrated;** the way you feel when you can't find something

resentful
adj. **bitter or full of anger;** like someone who stays angry for a long time because they have been hurt

wrathful
adj. **full of anger or rage;** like a powerful ruler who punishes anyone who disobeys them

turn over for feeling bad words >

feeling bad words

adj.

deflated

DEFINITION

feeling hopeless or let down;
like when you feel as sad and empty as a ball with the air let out

SAMPLE SENTENCE

Brick's pride was **deflated** after the baby beat him in an arm wrestle.

feeling bad words

adj.

desperate

DEFINITION

anxious, frantic, or despairing; how you feel when you can't wait to go to the bathroom

SAMPLE SENTENCE

In his **desperate** efforts to put out the fire, all Plato could think to do was pee on it.

feeling bad words

adj.

disheartened

DEFINITION

sad, crushed, or disappointed; the feeling you might have after dropping your ice cream

SAMPLE SENTENCE

The scientist was **disheartened** by the result of his failed experiment.

envious

DEFINITION

jealous or resentful;
when you want something that someone else has

SAMPLE SENTENCE

Brick cast an **envious** glance over at Grit's mouthwatering steak.

feeling bad words

adj.

humiliated

DEFINITION

ashamed or embarrassed; how you feel if someone pulls down your pants as a joke

SAMPLE SENTENCE

The basketball team was **humiliated** when they were beaten by some toddlers.

snubbed

DEFINITION

ignored or rejected;
how you feel if someone rudely turns away when you bring them flowers

SAMPLE SENTENCE

Armie's great idea was **snubbed** by his boss, who never listened to anyone but himself.

or you can try...

Horrible feeling bad words!

abandoned

adj. **left behind or deserted;** like a sailor who is left on an island when their ship sails off

awkward

adj. **embarrassed or uncomfortable;** like someone who does not know how to act when they meet their hero

belittled

adj. **mocked or humiliated;** the way you feel when people make fun of your ideas and achievements

betrayed

adj. **cheated by someone you trust;** like a criminal who is handed over to the police by one of his friends

burdened

adj. **weighed down or bothered;** like someone who has a lot to worry about so they can't do what they want

defeated

adj. **beaten and sad;** like someone who is unhappy because they keep trying but they never win

defenseless

adj. **helpless or unprotected;** like someone who can't protect themselves from a hungry wild animal

discontented

adj. **unhappy or not satisfied;** like someone who thinks things could be better

discouraged

adj. **sad or disheartened;** like someone who has lost confidence and stops trying

disgruntled

adj. **unhappy and annoyed;** like someone who is grumpy because they think they've been treated badly

dissatisfied

adj. **disappointed or not content;** like when you look forward to a meal and then it is not as good as you had hoped

frustrated

adj. **unsuccessful and annoyed;** like someone who has failed a lot of times and gets upset

or you can try...

hopeless

adj. **despairing or without hope;** like someone who thinks their problems are too difficult to solve

patronized

adj. **spoken down to or dismissed;** the way you feel when people treat you as though you are unimportant

inadequate

adj. **not good enough;** like someone who feels worse when they compare themselves to others

self-conscious

adj. **uncomfortable and embarrassed;** like someone who thinks everybody else in the room is looking at them

indecisive

adj. **uncertain or hesitating;** like someone who keeps changing their mind about what to wear

spurned

adj. **rejected or turned down;** the way you feel if you ask someone to be your friend and they say no

isolated

adj. **lonely or separate;** how you feel when you don't have anyone to talk to

troubled

adj. **worried or anxious;** the way you feel when you keep thinking something will go wrong

lonely

adj. **separate or alone;** how you feel if you don't have anyone to talk to about things

unappreciated

adj. **ignored or unnoticed;** the way you feel when you do someone a favor but they don't say thanks

misunderstood

adj. **feeling separate or not understood;** like a dog that has a nasty reputation but really just wants to play

uncertain

adj. **unsure or not confident;** like someone who doesn't know if they are doing the right thing or not

neglected

adj. **ignored or not looked after;** like someone whose family and friends never visit them

wretched

adj. **sad or miserable;** the way you feel when you realize you have hurt someone's feelings by mistake

turn over for happy words >

happy words

adj.

contented

DEFINITION

satisfied and comfortable;
like feeling so relaxed and happy that you sleep soundly

SAMPLE SENTENCE

Yin and Yang lived a happy, **contented** existence of sleeping, eating, and playing.

ecstatic

DEFINITION

blissful or thrilled; how you would feel if you won an award

SAMPLE SENTENCE

After Oz's incredible performance, the audience rose in **ecstatic** applause.

exhilarated

DEFINITION

excited or thrilled;
how you feel when you ride a rollercoaster

SAMPLE SENTENCE

Grit jumped out of bed on his birthday in an **exhilarated** mood.

happy words

adj.

gleeful

DEFINITION

cheerful or merry;
when you feel full of joy

SAMPLE SENTENCE

Yin and Yang's **gleeful** laughter echoed around the corridors as they tickled each other.

Action | Character | Emotion | Setting | Taste & Smell | Weather

adj.

happy words

light-hearted

DEFINITION

carefree and happy;
so pleased you could jump for joy

SAMPLE SENTENCE

Brick thought the disco was **light-hearted** fun, but Shang High took music very seriously.

overjoyed

DEFINITION

delighted and gleeful;
like when you feel like partying

SAMPLE SENTENCE

Brick's parents were **overjoyed** when he said his first words.

or you can try...

Grinning happy words!

animated

***adj.* lively and enthusiastic;** like someone who is talking about something that they find very exciting

beaming

***adj.* smiling or grinning;** like someone who is so happy that they can't help but show it

blissful

***adj.* extremely happy or full of joy;** how you feel when you watch a beautiful sunset over the sea

carefree

***adj.* relaxed and unworried;** like someone who does not have any problems to think about

cheerful

***adj.* happy and jolly;** like someone who always seems pleased to see you

chirpy

***adj.* happy and lively;** like someone who is in a good mood and makes lots of jokes

content

***adj.* happy and satisfied;** like someone who does not want to change their life at all

delighted

***adj.* happy or thrilled;** like someone who has just found out that they did well on a test

delirious

***adj.* thrilled or excited;** like someone who has just won a million dollars in the lottery

elated

***adj.* thrilled or overjoyed;** like someone who is so happy they feel they are walking on air

euphoric

***adj.* joyful and excited;** like an Olympic athlete who has just won a gold medal

exultant

***adj.* happy and celebratory;** like someone who has just won a difficult contest

or you can try...

flattered
adj. **complimented and pleased;** like when you hear something nice about yourself that you didn't expect

glad
adj. **happy or pleased;** like someone who has just heard some good news

jovial
adj. **cheerful or jolly;** like someone who is always telling jokes

joyous
adj. **joyful or cheerful;** like time spent celebrating with your friends and family

jubilant
adj. **thrilled or triumphant;** like a group of protesters who finally succeed after a long campaign

merry
adj. **cheerful or jolly;** like a lively party that everyone is enjoying

mirth
n. **fun or laughter;** like the pleasant atmosphere when everyone is enjoying a funny joke

radiant
adj. **glowing and joyful;** like someone who is so happy that it shows in everything they do

rapturous
adj. **joyful or ecstatic;** like the loud applause when a famous singer appears on stage

reassured
adj. **comforted and encouraged;** how a patient feels when a doctor tells them they will get better soon

relieved
adj. **comforted and reassured;** like the way you feel when you find your missing keys

satisfied
adj. **happy or contented;** like someone who thinks they have done a good day's work

triumphant
adj. **elated and victorious;** like a team that has just won the world championship

untroubled
adj. **calm or peaceful;** like a period when everything goes according to plan

turn over for hopeful words >

auspicious

DEFINITION

hopeful or encouraging;
like getting a sign that everything is going to turn out well

SAMPLE SENTENCE

After an **auspicious** beginning, Plato's career took a turn for the worse.

hopeful words

adj.

encouraging

DEFINITION

positive or motivating;
like someone who cheers you on

SAMPLE SENTENCE

Mrs Wordsmith's **encouraging** words convinced Armie that he could be an astronaut.

hopeful words

adj.

idealistic

DEFINITION

very optimistic and unrealistic; like someone who dreams of creating a perfect world

SAMPLE SENTENCE

Bearnice's "Free Doughnuts for All" campaign was dismissed as a silly, **idealistic** dream.

optimistic

DEFINITION

hopeful and positive;
like being certain that the weather is going to get better

SAMPLE SENTENCE

Brick's **optimistic** outlook always cheered his friends up.

hopeful words

adj.

promising

DEFINITION

hopeful or encouraging;
like a baby rocket scientist

SAMPLE SENTENCE

Bogart's **promising** career as a taxi driver was ruined after he lost his driver's license.

hopeful words

adj.

sanguine

DEFINITION

optimistic and cheery;
like when you feel happy even though things are going wrong

SAMPLE SENTENCE

Some people thought Mrs Wordsmith's **sanguine** prediction was too optimistic.

or you can try...

Upbeat, hopeful words!

aspirational

adj. **hoping for a better life;** like someone who wants to be more successful and have more money

assured

adj. **sure or confident;** like someone who is positive that everything will go well

belief

n. **faith or confidence in something;** like the feeling you have when you are sure that something is true

buoyant

adj. **cheerful or optimistic;** like the mood you are in when everything seems to be going well

confident

adj. **certain or positive;** like someone who thinks they are likely to be successful

conviction

n. **confidence or certainty;** the feeling you have when you are totally sure that you know something

daydream

n. **a fantasy or distracting thoughts;** like imagining that you will be the first person on Mars

dreamy

adj. **pleasant and unreal;** like someone who daydreams about nice things all the time

emboldened

adj. **given courage and confidence;** like someone who has a small success and so then tries to achieve more

enthusiastic

adj. **eager and interested;** like someone who really cares about trying their best

expectant

adj. **waiting and hopeful;** the way you feel when you think you are going to get a birthday present

fortunate

adj. **lucky or favorable;** like when you happen to get good weather for a day out

or you can try...

forward-looking

adj. **ambitious and thinking about the future;** like someone who makes plans that will help them succeed later on

heartened

adj. **comforted or encouraged;** like the way you feel when someone promises to help you with a difficult task

inspired

adj. **excited and motivated;** like when you want to learn an instrument after someone else plays it beautifully

positive

adj. **hopeful or optimistic;** like someone who only thinks about the good side of what is happening

potential

n. **talent or promise;** what you say someone has if you think they might be successful in the future

rose-tinted

adj. **too hopeful or too optimistic;** like someone who only sees the positives and ignores anything bad

rosy

adj. **looking hopeful or promising;** like a view of the future that makes everything look great

secure

adj. **confident, safe, or certain;** like someone who feels sure that their good situation is not going to change

sunny

adj. **pleasant or optimistic;** like a person who always brightens up a room

trusting

adj. **believing or not doubting;** like someone who thinks that other people will always behave kindly and fairly

unrealistic

adj. **silly or not likely to happen;** like a hopeful plan that probably won't work

upbeat

adj. **cheerful and optimistic;** like someone who acts as though everything is going to go perfectly

utopian

adj. **impossibly ideal or visionary;** like trying to create a perfect world where everyone is happy all the time

wannabe

n. **a person who pretends to be someone they're not;** like someone who acts like they're a pop star

turn over for love and hate words >

love and hate words

n.

disgust

DEFINITION

a strong dislike or repulsion;
like when you find a fly in your food

SAMPLE SENTENCE

Grit couldn't hide his intense **digust** at Bearnice's moldy sandwich platter.

fixated

DEFINITION

obsessed or focused;
like a hungry tiger cub that can't take her eyes off the goldfish bowl

SAMPLE SENTENCE

Bearnice was so **fixated** on her favorite actor that she didn't blink for the whole movie.

love and hate words

adj.

infatuated

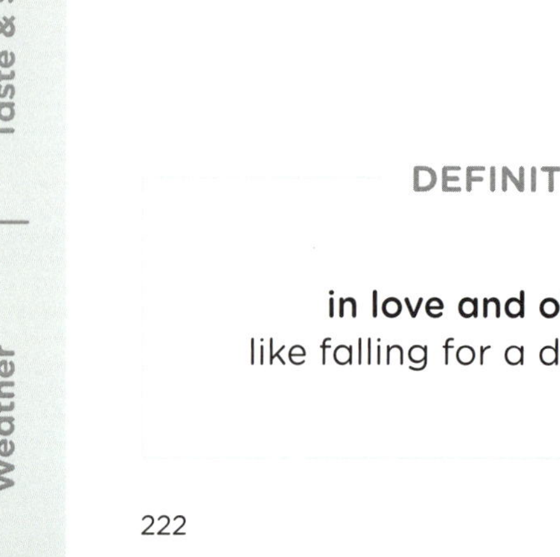

DEFINITION

in love and obsessed;
like falling for a dreamy singer

SAMPLE SENTENCE

Oz was so **infatuated** with her boyfriend that she didn't notice that he smelled like rotten eggs.

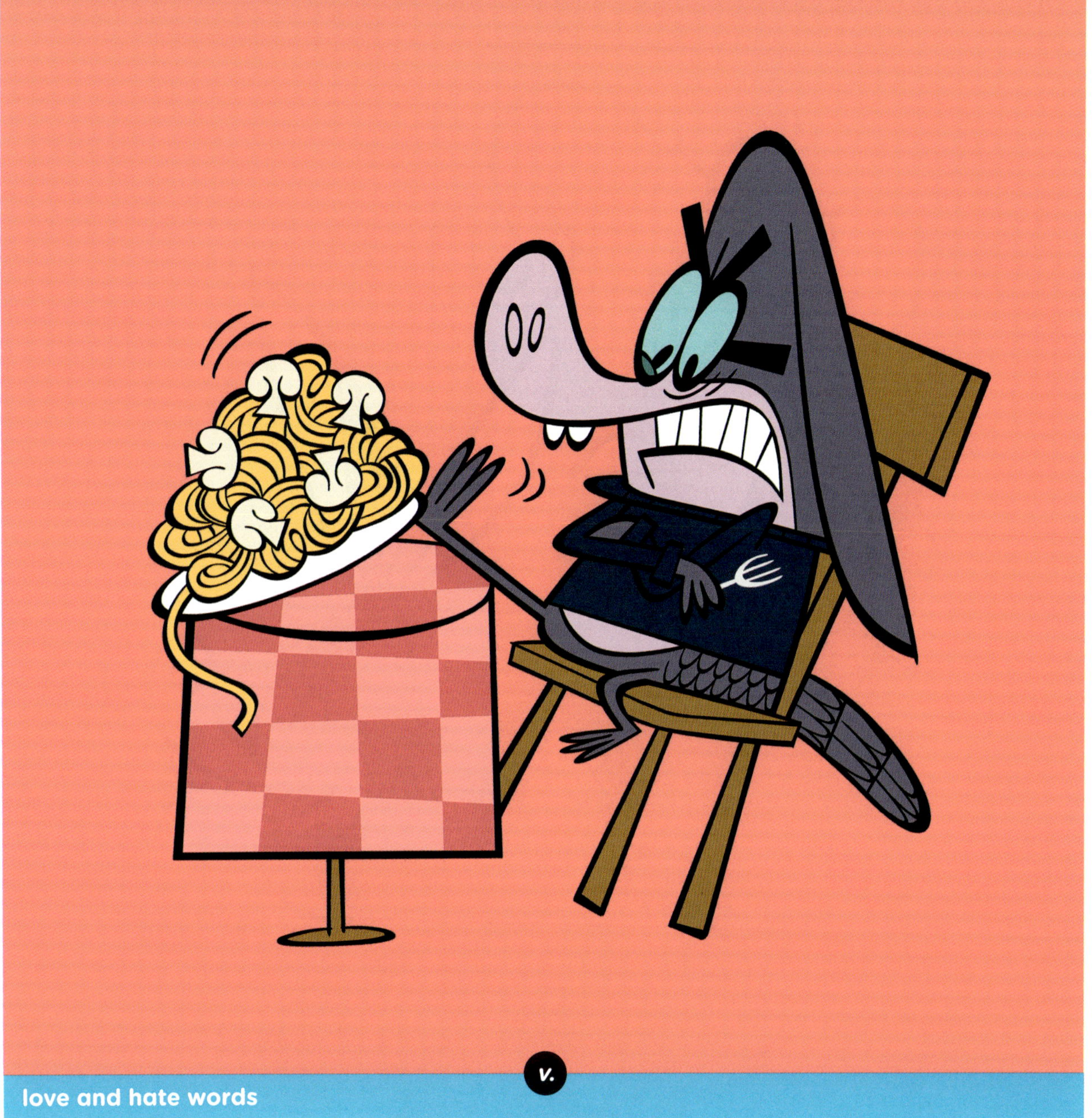

v.

loathe

loathes • loathing • loathed

DEFINITION

to hate or dislike intensely; like how you feel about your least favorite food

SAMPLE SENTENCE

After eating fifteen hamburgers in fifteen minutes, Bearnice **loathed** the sight of sliced cheese.

love and hate words

n.

scorn

DEFINITION

dislike and contempt;
what an environmentalist feels when they see someone littering

SAMPLE SENTENCE

Grit felt so much **scorn** for pop music that he threw his radio into the lake.

n.

love and hate words

yearning

DEFINITION

a strong desire or longing;
like a prisoner who misses her friends

SAMPLE SENTENCE

Bearnice had a strange **yearning** for a doughnut and cheese sandwich.

Action | Character | Emotion | Setting | Taste & Smell | Weather

sad words

adj.

desolate

DEFINITION

miserable, depressed, and lonely; how you feel when you lose everything and are all alone

SAMPLE SENTENCE

There were no signs of life in the **desolate** wasteland.

sad words

adj.

glum

DEFINITION

sad or gloomy;
when you feel like you're walking around with a little black cloud over your head

SAMPLE SENTENCE

Yin sat in **glum** silence, refusing to join in the fun until Yang came home.

sad words

adj.

heartbroken

DEFINITION

miserable or crushed;
how you feel when you sob on the sofa eating ice cream all day

SAMPLE SENTENCE

Shang High's mother was **heartbroken** when he wouldn't wear the scarf she knitted for him.

inconsolable

DEFINITION

very unhappy or broken-hearted; like feeling so sad that it's impossible to cheer you up

SAMPLE SENTENCE

Grit's **inconsolable** grief meant even his favorite food couldn't make him happy.

sad words

adj.

melancholy

DEFINITION

depressed or gloomy;
like someone who walks around despairing about everything

SAMPLE SENTENCE

The **melancholy** tune filled Mrs Wordsmith with sadness.

sad words

adj.

wistful

DEFINITION

sad, longing, or nostalgic;
like the sad feeling you get when you look back on good memories

SAMPLE SENTENCE

Oz gave a **wistful** smile to her sweetheart, who stood waving on the platform as the train left.

or you can try...

Gloomy, sad words!

blue
***adj.* sad and depressed;** like someone who is unhappy because they are away from their family

crestfallen
***adj.* sad and disappointed;** like a team who has just lost a big game

dejected
***adj.* sad and disappointed;** like a soccer fan whose team has just been knocked out of the World Cup

despondent
***adj.* hopeless and discouraged;** like a prisoner who worries that they will never be released

disconsolate
***adj.* sad or wretched;** like when you feel so bad that you can't be comforted

dismal
***adj.* gloomy or depressed;** like your mood when you are unhappy and can't see things getting better

doleful
***adj.* sad-looking or gloomy;** like someone who has a very unhappy expression on their face

downcast
***adj.* unhappy or depressed;** like someone who has had to cancel their vacation

empty
***adj.* numb or feeling nothing;** like someone who doesn't feel sad but also doesn't feel happy

forlorn
***adj.* sad and lonely;** like someone who is standing alone and crying

gloomy
***adj.* unhappy or depressed;** like someone who is worried that their life is going to get worse

grief-stricken
***adj.* desperately sad or grieving;** like someone who has been told that their pet has died

or you can try...

hangdog

adj. **ashamed or guilty-looking;** like the look on someone's face that tells you they have behaved badly

heartsore

adj. **sad and aching;** like someone who is feeling pain after a great tragedy

joyless

adj. **serious and depressing;** like someone who is very strict and doesn't want other people to have fun

lonesome

adj. **sad and lonely;** like someone who is all on their own in an unfamiliar city

melancholic

adj. **sad and gloomy;** like someone who is always thinking about sad things

miserable

adj. **sad or despairing;** like someone who has been sent away to a school that they hate

morose

adj. **gloomy or sulky;** like someone who is bad-tempered and never joins in with other people

mournful

adj. **sad and sorrowful;** like someone who is thinking about happier times in the past

pining

adj. **sad and longing;** like someone who is missing old friends who have gone away

somber

adj. **sad and serious;** like the mood after something really sad happens

sorrowful

adj. **sad or regretful;** how you feel when you lose something very important to you

subdued

adj. **quiet and sad;** like when you're so unhappy that you talk less than you normally do

tearful

adj. **crying or close to tears;** like someone who starts to cry during a sad movie

woeful

adj. **sad or unhappy;** like a story with a tragic ending

turn over for stressed and scared words >

stressed and scared words

adj.

anxious

DEFINITION

worried or nervous;
how you feel when you panic about a test at school

SAMPLE SENTENCE

For one **anxious** moment, Armie panicked that he had forgotten his underwear.

apprehensive

DEFINITION

nervous or afraid;
like when you feel worried about a big decision that you've made

SAMPLE SENTENCE

Yin shared an **apprehensive** glance with Yang after they had broken their neighbor's window.

stressed and scared words

adj.

distressed

DEFINITION

worried and upset;
you might get all sweaty and bite your nails

SAMPLE SENTENCE

"Where did I leave my keys?" cried Mrs Wordsmith in a **distressed** voice.

stressed and scared words

adj.

exasperated

DEFINITION

annoyed or frustrated;
when you feel like screaming because you can't have what you want

SAMPLE SENTENCE

Oz was such a wild teenager that she drove her **exasperated** parents crazy.

stressed and scared words

adj.

flustered

DEFINITION

nervous, muddled, and unsettled; the way you act when you forget your homework

SAMPLE SENTENCE

Bogart made a **flustered** attempt to close the door, but his butterfly collection still escaped.

petrified

DEFINITION

terrified or horrified;
like being so frightened
that you turn into stone

SAMPLE SENTENCE

Oz stood still in **petrified**
astonishment as the alien
spaceship landed in her garden.

or you can try...

Trembling stress and fear words!

agitated
adj. **worried or nervous;** like someone who feels upset because they have to take a test

anguished
adj. **miserable or wretched;** like someone who feels tormented because they have done something very bad

daunted
adj. **frightened and intimidated;** like someone who has been given a task that they think they cannot do

dismayed
adj. **disappointed and upset;** the way you feel if you get a bad grade for a piece of work

distraught
adj. **shocked and upset;** like someone who has made a serious mistake and feels terrible about it

frantic
adj. **worried and panicking;** like a parent whose child has gone missing

frightened
adj. **afraid or scared;** how you feel after someone tells a ghost story

harassed
adj. **troubled and pestered;** like a celebrity who is followed by photographers wherever they go

hassled
adj. **troubled, nagged, or pestered;** how you feel when someone keeps asking if you've done your homework

horrified
adj. **frightened and surprised;** like someone who has just been told a terrifying secret

intimidated
adj. **frightened and threatened;** the way you feel when someone acts like a scary bully

jittery
adj. **nervous and shaky;** like someone who feels anxious before an important test

or you can try...

jumpy

***adj.* on edge or nervous;** like someone who is always worried that something bad is about to happen

overburdened

***adj.* given too much to do;** like someone who is weighed down by doing three jobs at once

overstretched

***adj.* busy and overwhelmed;** like someone who has taken on too much work and can't get it all done

overwhelmed

***adj.* stressed and defeated;** like someone who has so many problems that they don't know what to do

panicky

***adj.* frightened and anxious;** like someone who jumps whenever they hear a noise

pressured

***adj.* persuaded or forced;** like someone who feels they have to do something they don't want to do

rattled

***adj.* nervous and frightened;** like someone who is worried that their guilty secret is going to be found out

shaky

***adj.* trembling or unsteady;** like someone who is so worried that they start to shake

spooked

***adj.* frightened or terrified;** like a horse that panics when it hears a sudden noise

strained

***adj.* tense and uncomfortable;** like the stressful silence after something worrying happens

terrified

***adj.* frightened or scared;** how you feel when you watch a really scary movie

terrorized

***adj.* threatened and scared;** like someone who is bullied until they are full of fear

timorous

***adj.* unconfident or easily scared;** like a nervous little kitten hiding under a bed

unnerved

***adj.* frightened or disturbed;** how you feel if you hear a scary noise in the dark

turn over for surprised words >

adj.

surprised words

alarmed

DEFINITION

frightened, startled, or disturbed; how you feel when you get woken up suddenly by a loud noise

SAMPLE SENTENCE

"There's a fly in my soup!" said Bogart, with an **alarmed** glance at the waiter.

astonished

DEFINITION

surprised or amazed;
like when you've seen something so incredible that you can't believe it

SAMPLE SENTENCE

The **astonished** audience was amazed by the acrobat's incredible tricks.

surprised words

adj.

flabbergasted

DEFINITION

shocked or amazed;
like how you would feel
if you won the lottery

SAMPLE SENTENCE

The **flabbergasted** onlookers gasped as Brick started climbing the building to rescue the baby.

surprised words

speechless

DEFINITION

dumbstruck or lost for words; how you feel when someone hangs up the phone on you

SAMPLE SENTENCE

Brick sat in **speechless** amazement as the magician pulled a coin from his ear.

surprised words

adj.

startled

DEFINITION

surprised or frightened;
like the feeling you get when someone jumps out at you

SAMPLE SENTENCE

Shang High awoke with a **startled** expression as the mouse ran up his pajama pants.

surprised words

adj.

stunned

DEFINITION

amazed or stupefied;
like being so surprised
you instantly freeze

SAMPLE SENTENCE

The **stunned** crowd remained
quiet as Shang High performed
his break dance.

or you can try...

Shocking surprised words!

aghast
adj. **shocked or horrified;** like someone who arrives home to see their house is on fire

amazed
adj. **surprised or astonished;** like someone who discovers that they have magic powers

astounded
adj. **shocked or amazed;** like an author whose book becomes an unexpected bestseller

awed
adj. **amazed and filled with wonder;** like someone who watches a magician perform impossible tricks

bemused
adj. **confused or bewildered;** like when you see something that you just can't explain

bewildered
adj. **confused or puzzled;** like a pop star who can't understand why nobody likes their new album

confounded
adj. **surprised and annoyed;** the way you feel when something unexpected ruins your plans

dazed
adj. **stunned or dizzy;** like someone who has witnessed a tragedy and doesn't know what to do

dumbfounded
adj. **amazed or astonished;** like when you are so surprised by something that you can't speak

dumbstruck
adj. **speechless or tongue-tied;** like someone who is so surprised that they can't manage to speak

floored
adj. **shocked and confused;** like when you're so surprised that you don't know what to say or do

flummoxed
adj. **confused or baffled;** how you feel when you try to solve a puzzle but can't work it out

or you can try...

incredulous

***adj.* shocked and unbelieving;** like when you can't really believe what someone is telling you

jolted

***adj.* shocked or startled;** like someone who is so surprised that they actually jump slightly

nonplussed

***adj.* surprised or stunned;** like when someone says something strange and you don't know how to react

open-mouthed

***adj.* surprised or gaping;** like people watching a spaceship arrive on Earth

overcome

***adj.* overwhelmed or stunned;** like someone who is feeling very strong emotions and cannot speak or move

puzzled

***adj.* confused or baffled;** the way you feel when you see something unexpected that doesn't make sense

shell-shocked

***adj.* shocked and dazed;** like someone who has just been fired from their job

shocked

***adj.* surprised and disturbed;** the way you feel when you get news that you were not expecting at all

stupefied

***adj.* stunned or dazed;** like when you are so surprised that your mind goes blank

thunderstruck

***adj.* shocked or amazed;** like when you are so surprised that you can't do anything for a moment

unanticipated

***adj.* unexpected or surprising;** like winning a soccer match that everybody thought you would lose

unexpected

***adj.* surprising or not predicted;** like a visit from a friend you thought was in a different country

unforeseen

***adj.* unexpected or surprising;** like something that you didn't plan for because you didn't think it would happen

wide-eyed

***adj.* surprised and staring;** like someone who opens a box and finds it is full of gold coins

turn over for trying hard words >

adj.

trying hard words

ambitious

DEFINITION

determined to achieve big things; like someone who has plans to rule the world

SAMPLE SENTENCE

Shang High's **ambitious** vision for his future was to be seen as the world's greatest DJ.

adj.

trying hard words

committed

DEFINITION

completely loyal and dedicated; like two people who have promised to stay together forever

SAMPLE SENTENCE

The **committed** fan watched his favorite team play despite the weather.

trying hard words

adj.

dedicated

DEFINITION

committed or devoted;
when you care about something so much nothing can stop you

SAMPLE SENTENCE

The café hired a **dedicated** team to keep up with Bearnice's appetite for cheeseburgers.

adj.

trying hard words

determined

DEFINITION

driven or completely set on; like working extra hard to get what you want

SAMPLE SENTENCE

With a **determined** expression on his face, Brick lifted the heaviest weight at the gym.

trying hard words

v.

persevere

perseveres • persevering • persevered

DEFINITION

to keep going or carry on; like running all the way to the end of a marathon

SAMPLE SENTENCE

Plato **persevered** resolutely as he tried to build a sandcastle in the rain.

adj.

trying hard words

tenacious

DEFINITION

determined or strong-willed;
like refusing to let go of something

SAMPLE SENTENCE

Oz's **tenacious** grip on her handbag meant the thief wasn't strong enough to steal it from her.

or you can try...

Gritty trying hard words!

concentrate

v. **to focus or direct your attention;** when you give all of your attention to one thing

conscientious

adj. **careful and thorough;** like someone who is determined to do their job as well as they can

diligent

adj. **hard-working and careful;** like an artist who draws every single nose hair in a portrait

dogged

adj. **determined and stubborn;** like someone who keeps working hard without any encouragement

earnest

adj. **serious and sincere;** like someone who takes everything very seriously

enduring

adj. **tough or long-lasting;** like a boxer who gets hit but never falls down

engrossed

adj. **completely focused or fascinated;** like someone who is enjoying a book and can't think about anything else

focus

v. **to pay a lot of attention or concentrate;** like when you think about one thing and nothing else

hard-working

adj. **committed or enthusiastic;** like someone who always turns up and does their best

incentive

n. **reason or motivation;** like a prize that you will be given if you do something well

indomitable

adj. **determined and unbeatable;** like someone who keeps going even when things get really tough

inflexible

adj. **fixed or stubborn;** like someone who will not change the way that they do something

or you can try...

motivated

adj. **inspired and determined;** like someone who wants to finish something to get the reward

obsessive

adj. **loving in an unhealthy way;** like someone who can't get their favorite pop star out of their head

persistent

adj. **determined and steady;** like a runner who keeps going even when they're tired

purposeful

adj. **driven and determined;** like someone who knows what they want and how to achieve it

pushy

adj. **forceful and ambitious;** like a worker who keeps asking their boss for a promotion

resolved

adj. **determined and decided;** like someone who has made a decision and will not change their mind

single-minded

adj. **concentrating on one thing;** like an athlete who is completely focused on their training program

steadfast

adj. **steady and dependable;** like someone who keeps going when things get difficult

strong-willed

adj. **stubborn and determined;** like someone who has fixed opinions and will not change their mind

studious

adj. **bookish and hard-working;** like someone who works carefully so they don't make any mistakes

tireless

adj. **determined and full of energy;** like someone who never stops trying

undeterred

adj. **tireless and unstoppable;** like someone who is not put off when they encounter a problem

unwavering

adj. **steady and resolved;** like someone who never changes their mind when things get difficult

unyielding

adj. **firm or inflexible;** like a team that's losing but refuses to give up or give in

turn over for setting >

Someone... something was approaching.
It was shrouded in a **murky** green mist,
but as it got closer, the Campers
and Hunters gasped.

Percy Jackson and the Titan's Curse
by Rick Riordan

Setting

city words

adj.

affluent

DEFINITION

rich or wealthy;
like a neighborhood where everyone lives in fancy houses

SAMPLE SENTENCE

Bogart hoped to marry into an **affluent** family with lots of money.

bustling

DEFINITION

crowded or lively; like a busy market full of shoppers

SAMPLE SENTENCE

Bearnice walked around the **bustling** town, weaving her way through the crowded streets.

city words

adj.

diverse

DEFINITION

mixed or varied;
like a group of people who are all very different from each other

SAMPLE SENTENCE

Shang High played a **diverse** mix of music at the party, everything from jazz to techno.

hectic

DEFINITION

very busy or manic;
how your day is when you have to do everything quickly

SAMPLE SENTENCE

Oz had a very **hectic** day, packed with meetings all over the city.

adj.

city words

imposing

DEFINITION

grand or impressive;
like a building so big and important it towers over you

SAMPLE SENTENCE

The enormous statue of Oz was an **imposing** structure that nobody could ignore.

city words

adj.

polluted

DEFINITION

dirty or foul;
like smelly air that you try not to breathe in

SAMPLE SENTENCE

Armie spent the summer cleaning up the **polluted** environment of the nearby beaches.

or you can try...

Busy city words!

ancient
adj. **old or from a long time ago;** like a city that was built three thousand years ago

central
adj. **in the middle;** like the exciting area at the heart of a city

cosmopolitan
adj. **multicultural and varied;** like a city where the people come from all over the world

crowded
adj. **busy or full of people;** like a street where there are so many people that it's hard to move

district
n. **an area or region;** like a part of a city that has its own name and character

downtown
adj. **in the busiest part of a city;** like a street that has all of the main shops and cafés on it

expanding
adj. **growing or spreading;** like a city where new houses are being built on the surrounding countryside

genteel
adj. **rich, elegant, and respectable;** like a placewhere everyone is very fancy and sophisticated

historic
adj. **old and important;** like cities where people go to visit castles and museums

impoverished
adj. **poor or in need;** like a part of town where people do not have enough food to eat

industrial
adj. **full of factories;** like the part of a city where lots of things get made

lively
adj. **busy and exciting;** like a city where the cafés and shops are always full of visitors

or you can try...

metropolis
n. **a very big city;** an important or main city that covers a large area

romantic
adj. **idealistic or dreamy;** like a place where people might meet and fall in love

modernized
adj. **rebuilt and improved;** like a city where old houses have been replaced by new ones

skyline
n. **a city's outline or silhouette;** the shape that tall buildings make against the sky

neglected
adj. **ignored or not well cared for;** like a place where all the buildings need to be repaired and painted

suburban
adj. **at the edge of a city;** like the quieter areas of the city outside of the center

neighborhood
n. **an area or community;** like a part of town where people know each other and live side by side

touristy
adj. **popular with visitors or crowded;** like a place where a lot of people go when they are on vacation

pedestrianized
adj. **designed for walking;** like a street that cars are not allowed to enter

underdeveloped
adj. **poor and not built on;** like a part of a country where there are not many houses or businesses

quarter
n. **an area or neighborhood;** a part of a city that has a particular atmosphere or culture

vast
adj. **huge or enormous;** like a city that stretches for miles and miles in every direction

residential
adj. **designed for living in;** like a quiet area that has lots of homes but not many shops or offices

vibrant
adj. **lively and exciting;** like a city where there is always a lot going on

turn over for countryside words >

countryside words

adj.

idyllic

DEFINITION

ideal or perfect;
like a beautiful place where you can relax in the sun

SAMPLE SENTENCE

Armie strolled around the **idyllic** island, wondering how it could be so perfect.

adj.

countryside words

lush

DEFINITION

rich, flourishing, or overgrown; like a garden full of big, healthy plants

SAMPLE SENTENCE

The cow looked so happy munching on the **lush**, green grass that Grit had a nibble himself.

rolling

DEFINITION

rippling, wavy, or tumbling; like gentle hills that rise and fall like endless waves

SAMPLE SENTENCE

Shang High watched the **rolling** waves of the blue ocean rise and fall.

countryside words

adj.

scenic

DEFINITION

beautiful and picturesque;
like a postcard of the countryside

SAMPLE SENTENCE

Armie thought the ugly supermarket ruined an otherwise **scenic** landscape.

adj.

countryside words

secluded

DEFINITION

quiet or remote;
like a place where you can be completely alone

SAMPLE SENTENCE

Grit discovered a **secluded** village that was untouched by the outside world.

countryside words

adj.

verdant

DEFINITION

green and leafy;
like a lush valley where
sheep graze on the grass

SAMPLE SENTENCE

Bogart dressed entirely in
green so he would be fully
hidden in the **verdant** forest.

or you can try...

Peaceful countryside words!

abundant
adj. **rich or fruitful;** like land where it's easy to grow lots of plants for food

agricultural
adj. **used for farming;** like land that is used for growing crops and keeping animals

arable
adj. **fertile or productive;** like land that is perfect for growing crops

arid
adj. **dry or barren;** like a part of the world where it hardly ever rains

backwoods
n. **remote or isolated countryside;** like an area where there are not many people or houses

breathtaking
adj. **impressive or stunning;** like a view that is so beautiful it makes you gasp

bucolic
adj. **pleasant and rustic;** like the lovely countryside scene of a shepherd watching over his sheep

cultivated
adj. **farmed or used for growing plants;** like land that farmers plow and plant with crops

desolate
adj. **wild, remote, and bleak;** like a faraway place where no one goes and no plants grow

enchanting
adj. **delightful or charming;** like countryside with beautiful lakes and castles

expansive
adj. **wide or sweeping;** like rolling hills that go on for miles and miles

farmland
n. **fields or pastures;** land that is used for growing crops and keeping animals

or you can try...

fertile
adj. **rich or fruitful;** like healthy soil where plants will grow well

landscape
n. **scenery or countryside;** like the woods, fields, and hills in a painting of the countryside

low-lying
adj. **flat and easily flooded;** like marshy land next to a river or sea

manicured
adj. **trimmed and tidy;** like the neat grass on the putting greens at a golf course

moor
n. **a high-up, flat, and open area of land;** like a stretch of wild countryside covered in rough grass

outback
n. **remote or isolated country;** like the parts of Australia that are a long way from any big cities

pastoral
adj. **rural, peaceful, and idealized;** like a perfect country scene with fields of sheep or goats

pasture
n. **meadows or farmland;** like fields where cows can feed on grass

protected
adj. **guarded or kept safe;** like a place where no one is allowed to harm the wildlife

provincial
adj. **local or regional;** like the parts of a country that are outside the capital city

undulating
adj. **going up and down;** like land where there are lots of small, rolling hills

unspoiled
adj. **natural or untouched;** like beautiful countryside that nobody has built houses on

vale
n. **a valley or dale;** an area of low ground between hills

wooded
adj. **tree-covered or forested;** like a valley where there are many trees growing together

turn over for house words >

house words

adj.

cluttered

DEFINITION

messy or littered;
like a room with clothes and toys thrown all over the place

SAMPLE SENTENCE

Grit couldn't find anything underneath all the junk in his **cluttered** room.

house words

adj.

dilapidated

DEFINITION

run-down or shabby;
like a dirty, messy house with broken windows and leaky ceilings

SAMPLE SENTENCE

The **dilapidated** school had a leaking roof and a single window with glass left in it.

house words

adj.

immaculate

DEFINITION

perfect or spotless;
like a house that is so clean it shines and glitters

SAMPLE SENTENCE

Oz had a detailed beauty routine to keep her appearance looking so **immaculate**.

palatial

DEFINITION

vast or splendid;
like a mansion where you live in the lap of luxury

SAMPLE SENTENCE

Plato dreamed of building a giant, **palatial** house with six bathrooms and a swimming pool.

house words

adj.

poky

DEFINITION

tiny or cramped;
like a cupboard under the stairs where there is barely room to squeeze inside

SAMPLE SENTENCE

Plato's **poky** lodgings barely had space for his bed.

house words

adj.

sparse

DEFINITION

scarce or few;
like a big, empty room
with hardly any furniture

SAMPLE SENTENCE

Grit's lawn had so many holes
that it was really just a few
sparse clumps of grass.

or you can try...

Cozy house words!

ancestral

***adj.* old and inherited;** like a grand house that is passed down from generation to generation

authentic

***adj.* genuine or not copied;** like furniture that was definitely made at a specific time in history

cavernous

***adj.* huge and vast;** like a building with large rooms and high ceilings

contemporary

***adj.* modern or current;** like a stylish house that has been built in the last few years

cozy

***adj.* warm and comfortable;** like a cottage with an open fire

derelict

***adj.* abandoned and run-down;** like a house that has not been lived in for a long time

elegant

***adj.* stylish or graceful;** like a fancy house with a beautiful garden

high-rise

***adj.* tall or towering;** like a block of apartments with twenty floors

labyrinthine

***adj.* twisting or maze-like;** like a set of hallways and passages that make it easy to get lost

lofty

***adj.* tall and impressive;** like a palace with many high towers

minimalistic

***adj.* simple and stylish;** like a room that only has a few, carefully chosen pieces of furniture

open-plan

***adj.* without walls;** like a large building that is not divided into separate rooms or offices

or you can try...

ornate
adj. **fancy and detailed;** like a grand building with beautifully carved columns and doorways

period
adj. **old and historic;** like a house that has been kept in the style of the original builders

rambling
adj. **large and spread out;** like a building with many hallways and staircases

redecorated
adj. **fixed or restored;** like a house that has been painted in a new color

ruined
adj. **destroyed or wrecked;** like an old house with a collapsed roof and holes in the walls

snug
adj. **small, cozy, and comfortable;** like a little cottage that stays warm through the winter

spacious
adj. **large and open;** like a house where lots of people can live comfortably together

sprawling
adj. **large and spread out;** like a mansion with many long hallways where you can easily get lost

stark
adj. **harsh and bare;** like an ugly house with sharp corners and no decorations

tumbledown
adj. **old and uncared for;** like a house with crumbling walls and flaking paint

unfurnished
adj. **empty or bare;** like a new house before any furniture is put in it

unoccupied
adj. **empty or vacant;** like a house that nobody lives in

vaulted
adj. **arched or curved;** like an underground room with pointed ceilings and sloped walls

well-appointed
adj. **well-furnished and convenient;** like a house that contains all the things you might possibly need

turn over for mountain words >

n.

mountain words

crevasse

DEFINITION

a crack or deep hole;
a huge pit that you can fall into and never climb out of again

SAMPLE SENTENCE

Brick had to walk around the narrow **crevasse** because he was too big to squeeze through it.

mountain words

precipitous

DEFINITION

steep or dangerously high; like the edge of a very scary mountain

SAMPLE SENTENCE

Oz skied so well that even the most **precipitous** slope didn't scare her.

mountain words

adj.

rugged

DEFINITION

rough, uneven, or craggy; like a stretch of coast full of big, jagged rocks

SAMPLE SENTENCE

The landscape had a **rugged** beauty, with sharp rocks and wind-beaten trees.

mountain words

adj.

steep

DEFINITION

sharp and vertical; like the big, snowy drop beneath a ski lift

SAMPLE SENTENCE

Yin and Yang rolled down the **steep** hillside at incredible speed.

summit

DEFINITION

top or peak;
the very highest point of a mountain, where you can plant your flag

SAMPLE SENTENCE

Ascending the mountain's **summit** was hard, but Oz was determined to get to the top!

mountain words

adj.

towering

DEFINITION

extremely tall;
like a mountain looming over you

SAMPLE SENTENCE

Bearnice looked up at the **towering** peak that seemed to almost touch the clouds.

or you can try...

Rugged mountain words!

alpine
adj. **on high mountains;** like a plant that only grows in very high places

ascent
n. **the climb or trek up;** like the final stretch before you reach the top of a mountain

avalanche
n. **a landslide or deluge;** a sudden heavy fall of snow down a mountain

bleak
adj. **cold, bare, and miserable;** like the top of a mountain where there is no shelter from the wind

craggy
adj. **rocky and jagged;** like a barren island with dangerous cliffs

dizzying
adj. **confusing or making you woozy;** like when you're very high up and you feel faint when you look down

foothill
n. **a small hill;** a low hill around the edge of a group of high mountains

forested
adj. **tree-covered or wooded;** like hills where pine trees grow close together

formidable
adj. **large and intimidating;** like a high mountain peak that few people have ever managed to climb

gradual
adj. **slow and regular;** like a gentle slope

highland
adj. **mountainous or hilly;** like the parts of Scotland where there are high hills

inaccessible
adj. **remote or out of reach;** like a valley that is surrounded by high mountains on all sides

or you can try...

jagged
adj. **pointed, spiky, or uneven;** like the top of a mountain that has lots of sharp peaks

sacred
adj. **holy or blessed;** like a mountain that people think is the home of gods or spirits

lofty
adj. **high and impressive;** like a huge mountain that reaches up into the clouds

sheer
adj. **steep or sharp;** like a path that goes straight down from the top of a cliff to the ground

lunar
adj. **like the moon;** like a dusty, empty landscape that looks like the surface of the moon

snow-capped
adj. **topped with snow;** like a very high mountain where the snow at the top never melts

majestic
adj. **magnificent and impressive;** like a huge mountain that towers over the countryside

snowfield
n. **a permanently snowy area;** a large expanse that is completely covered by snow

mountaineer
n. **a climber or explorer;** someone who climbs up and down mountains for fun

terrace
n. **a flat or level area;** like a flattened piece of land on the side of a mountain

perilous
adj. **dangerous or risky;** like a narrow path where you can easily slip and hurt yourself

tundra
n. **icy or frozen land;** like plains where it's too cold for trees to grow

rocky
adj. **hard and stony;** like a mountain that is not covered with grass or trees

volcano
n. **a mountain with a hole at the top;** a mountain that occasionally spews out molten lava

turn over for night words >

night words

n.

dusk

DEFINITION

twilight or nightfall; the time just before the sun goes down when the evening sky is glowing

SAMPLE SENTENCE

Grit wandered into the deepening **dusk** and soon vanished into the night.

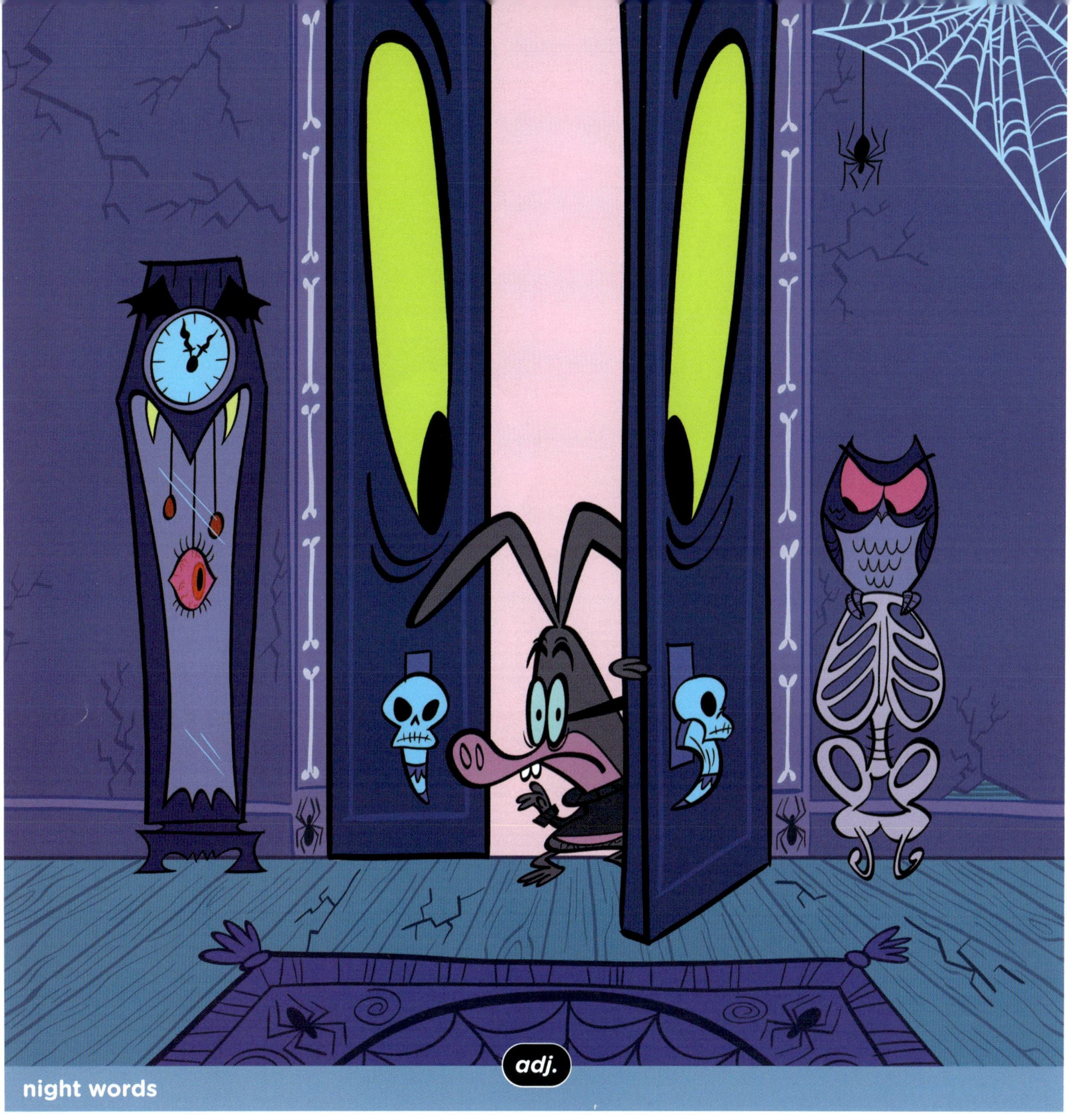

eerie

DEFINITION

weird, ghostly, or creepy; like a dark, spooky room full of skeletons and cobwebs

SAMPLE SENTENCE

Bogart found the **eerie** silence in the temple creepy so he hummed nervously to himself.

night words

adj.

moonlit

DEFINITION

lit up by the moon;
like a bright night sky

SAMPLE SENTENCE

The silvery light made Grit's **moonlit** stroll even more beautiful.

night words

adj.

nocturnal

DEFINITION

nightly or active at night; like bats and owls that come out to hunt when it gets dark

SAMPLE SENTENCE

Armie's sleepwalking meant that he went on many **nocturnal** adventures.

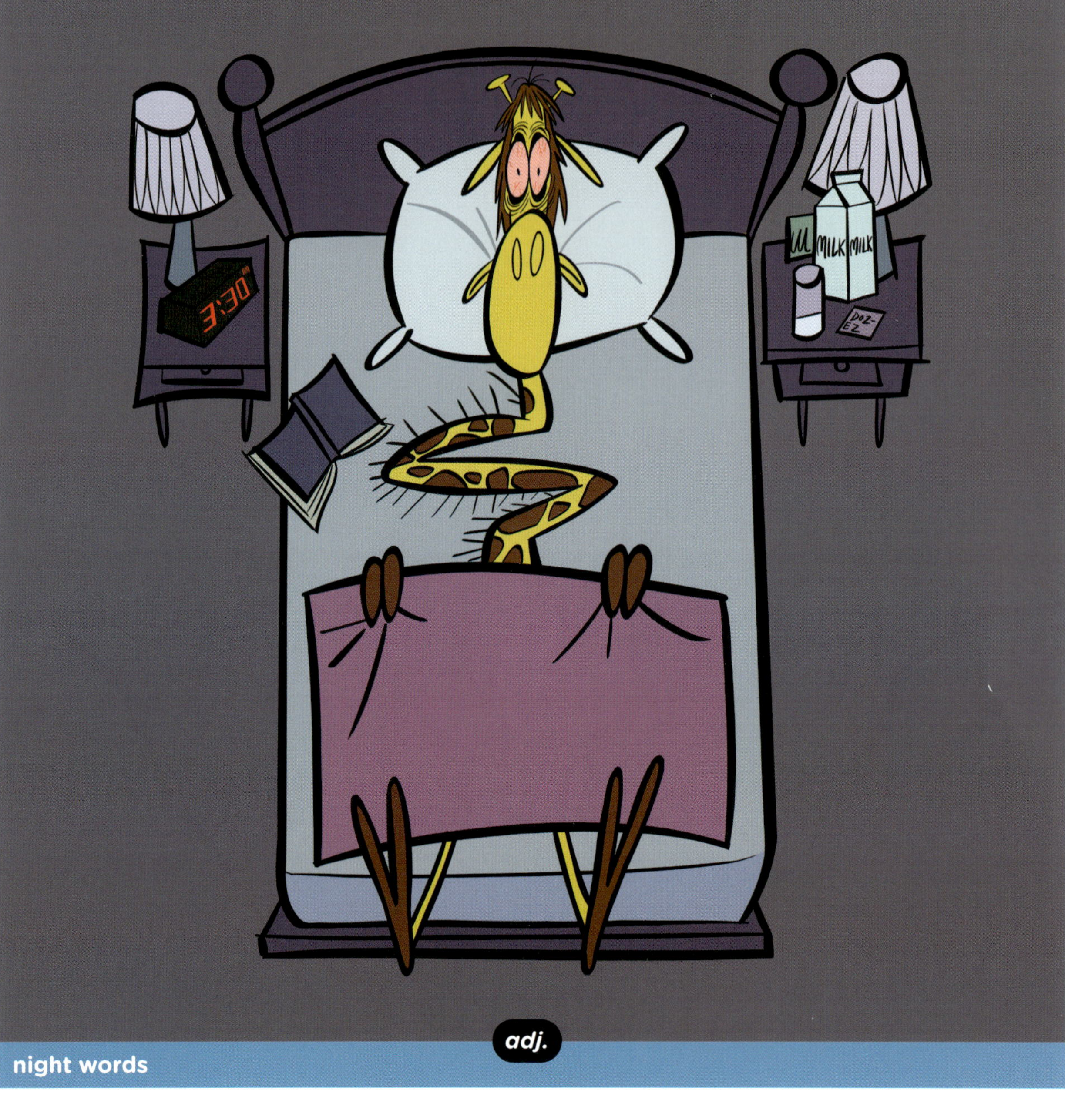

adj.

night words

sleepless

DEFINITION

wide awake and disturbed; like one of those nights when you can't get a wink of sleep

SAMPLE SENTENCE

When Bearnice threw a party, her neighbors were kept awake for eight **sleepless** hours.

twilight

DEFINITION

dusk or early evening; the soft light of evening that is too dim to read by

SAMPLE SENTENCE

Oz loved the summer, when long **twilights** meant that the sun took a long time to disappear.

or you can try...

Moonlit night words!

dim
adj. **dark or badly lit;** like a room where there is not much light and you can't see very well

dismal
adj. **dark and gloomy;** like a rainy night in winter that makes you feel miserable

dusky
adj. **dim or in twilight;** like the light in the sky as the day turns into night

evening
n. **nightfall or dusk;** the time toward the end of the day when it starts to get dark

ghostly
adj. **strange, eerie, or unnatural;** like a mysterious sound you hear in the middle of the night

ghoulish
adj. **unpleasant or creepy;** like a dark night when everything seems spooky

gloomy
adj. **dark and dismal;** like a basement without any windows where you don't want to spend any time

haunted
adj. **cursed or spooky;** like a house where people think they see ghosts

inky
adj. **as dark as ink;** like a completely dark sky when there are no stars or street lights

jet-black
adj. **dark or pitch-black;** the color of the night sky when there is no moon

midnight
n. **twelve o'clock at night;** a point about halfway between the start and the end of the night

murky
adj. **dim or cloudy;** like a dark evening when it is difficult to see clearly

or you can try...

mysterious

adj. **strange or odd;** like hearing noises when it's too dark to know where they came from

nightfall

n. **darkness or dusk;** the time at the start of the night when it first gets dark

nightmare

n. **a bad dream;** like a scary dream about being chased by monsters

obscurity

n. **darkness or shadow;** like a place where something is hidden from sight

semi-darkness

n. **twilight or dimness;** when you can't see clearly and can only make out vague shapes

shadowy

adj. **dark or shady;** like a gloomy alleyway that you can barely see the end of

silent

adj. **quiet or without sound;** like a night so still that you can't hear a thing

sinister

adj. **scary or threatening;** like hearing a door creak open in the middle of the night

spooky

adj. **weird or frightening;** like a dark shape that you think might be a ghost

starless

adj. **dark or pitch-black;** like a night when you cannot see anything at all

still

adj. **quiet and calm;** like the middle of the night when everyone is asleep

sundown

n. **sunset or dusk;** at the end of the day when the sun disappears and it starts to get dark

uncanny

adj. **strange or mysterious;** like an unsettling feeling that you can't explain

unlit

adj. **dark or dim;** like a hallway where there are no electric lights to help you see the way

turn over for noise words >

noise words

adj.

blaring

DEFINITION

loud or booming;
like huge speakers pumping out music so loud that they shake

SAMPLE SENTENCE

The **blaring** music from Shang High's room kept everyone awake.

deafening

DEFINITION

very loud or noisy;
like the sound of an
airplane taking off

SAMPLE SENTENCE

The lion tamer's instructions were lost in the **deafening** roar.

adj.

noise words

ear-splitting

DEFINITION

loud or piercing;
like someone playing a
flute right into your ear

SAMPLE SENTENCE

Brick heard Yang's **ear-splitting** shriek from the other side of the playground.

noise words

adj.

grating

DEFINITION

harsh and annoying;
like the sound of sharp nails scraping a blackboard

SAMPLE SENTENCE

Bogart's **grating** voice was the last straw for Brick.

noise words

adj.

muffled

DEFINITION

hushed or stifled;
like the sound made when you speak into a pillow

SAMPLE SENTENCE

Brick hit the pile of pillows with a **muffled** thud.

noise words

adj.

reverberating

DEFINITION

echoing and vibrating;
like the clashing sound of cymbals that shakes your whole body

SAMPLE SENTENCE

The **reverberating** crash of the collapsed bookshelf echoed around the library.

outdoor words

adj.

barren

DEFINITION

empty or bare;
like a lonely desert where nothing can grow

SAMPLE SENTENCE

Grit strode across the **barren** earth, hoping that he'd see some signs of life soon.

outdoor words

adj.

impenetrable

DEFINITION

dense or inaccessible; like a forest with so many trees that you can't find a way to walk through it

SAMPLE SENTENCE

The thick trees made the forest practically **impenetrable**.

outdoor words

adj.

overgrown

DEFINITION

wild or tangled;
like a jungle with plants growing on top of each other, everywhere

SAMPLE SENTENCE

The abandoned house became an **overgrown** ruin, with vines growing through its windows.

outdoor words

adj.

tangled

DEFINITION

twisted or snarled;
like a fly trapped
in a spiderweb

SAMPLE SENTENCE

Bearnice had to be rescued after she got stuck in the jungle's **tangled** undergrowth.

Action | Character | Emotion | **Setting** | Taste & Smell | Weather

outdoor words

adj.

teeming

DEFINITION

full or crowded;
like a park that is overflowing with birds, insects, and animals

SAMPLE SENTENCE

The **teeming** wildlife made the jungle floor look like it was constantly moving.

adj.

village words

deprived

DEFINITION

poor or needy;
like children who have
no home, food, or clothes

SAMPLE SENTENCE

Armie made a pie for the **deprived** family, knowing they didn't have enough to eat.

adj.

village words

picturesque

DEFINITION

attractive or scenic; like a village so pretty it could be on a postcard

SAMPLE SENTENCE

The tiny, **picturesque** town looked like a perfect painting of simple country life.

quaint

DEFINITION

charming or picturesque;
like a pretty, old-fashioned cottage

SAMPLE SENTENCE

The **quaint** street had pretty cobbled roads and charming little shops.

village words

adj.

remote

DEFINITION

far away and alone;
like an island where one
person lives all by himself

SAMPLE SENTENCE

Yin and Yang got lost in
a **remote** part of the countryside
far away from the campsite.

rural

DEFINITION

rustic or natural;
like being in the countryside

SAMPLE SENTENCE

Oz wanted to live in a **rural** area, but she was worried about getting bored in the countryside.

or you can try...

Charming village words!

abandoned
adj. **empty or deserted;** like a car that's been left for good by the side of the road

charming
adj. **attractive and pretty;** like a small village with old stone cottages and bridges

cobbled
adj. **made of round stones;** like a street with a bumpy surface that was built before cars were invented

deserted
adj. **empty or abandoned;** like a village where all the people have left

flourishing
adj. **successful and growing;** like a place where people have plenty of money and there is a lot to do

hamlet
n. **a village or settlement;** like a small group of houses with no shops or traffic lights

isolated
adj. **far away or remote;** like a place that is many miles away from the next village or town

lazy
adj. **quiet and relaxed;** like a place where everything happens very slowly

local
adj. **nearby or within reach;** like the shops that people can easily go to from their homes

medieval
adj. **from the Middle Ages;** like a village with a castle and old stone walls

old-fashioned
adj. **old and out-of-date;** like a village where it seems that nothing has changed for the last fifty years

parochial
adj. **local or inward-looking;** like the issues that are talked about by a town council

or you can try...

peaceful
adj. **quiet and friendly;** like a village where the people get along with each other

pleasant
adj. **attractive or charming;** like a place you can enjoy walking around

prosperous
adj. **rich or wealthy;** like a place where all the people have plenty of money to spend

rustic
adj. **simple and unsophisticated;** like something that is typical of old-fashioned country ways

seaside
adj. **by the sea;** like a village that sits right next to the water

sleepy
adj. **peaceful but dull;** like a place where nothing interesting ever happens

thriving
adj. **busy and successful;** like a place where the people have plenty of money to spend

traditional
adj. **in an old style;** like a place where everything looks the same as it did a hundred years ago

tranquil
adj. **calm or peaceful;** like a place where there are no noisy activities going on

typical
adj. **normal or standard;** like a village that looks exactly as you would expect a village to look

unchanged
adj. **the same or identical;** like a place where things are just as they used to be in the past

undisturbed
adj. **peaceful and unchanged;** like a place that is not often visited by travelers

untouched
adj. **unspoiled or not damaged;** like a beautiful village that has not been affected by the modern world

welcoming
adj. **pleasant and friendly;** like a place where travelers can enjoy rest and refreshments

turn over for water words >

water words

adj.

choppy

DEFINITION

rough or stormy;
like the sea when it is full of small, bumpy waves

SAMPLE SENTENCE

Armie felt sick as the **choppy** water tossed the boat from side to side.

water words

adj.

frothy

DEFINITION

foaming or bubbly; like a coffee covered in whipped cream

SAMPLE SENTENCE

Plato gulped his milkshake all at once and ended up with a **frothy** milk mustache.

adj.

water words

murky

DEFINITION

dark, muddy, or cloudy; like water that's so dirty you can barely see through it

SAMPLE SENTENCE

The crocodile hid in the **murky** pool, waiting for careless travelers to step into his open mouth.

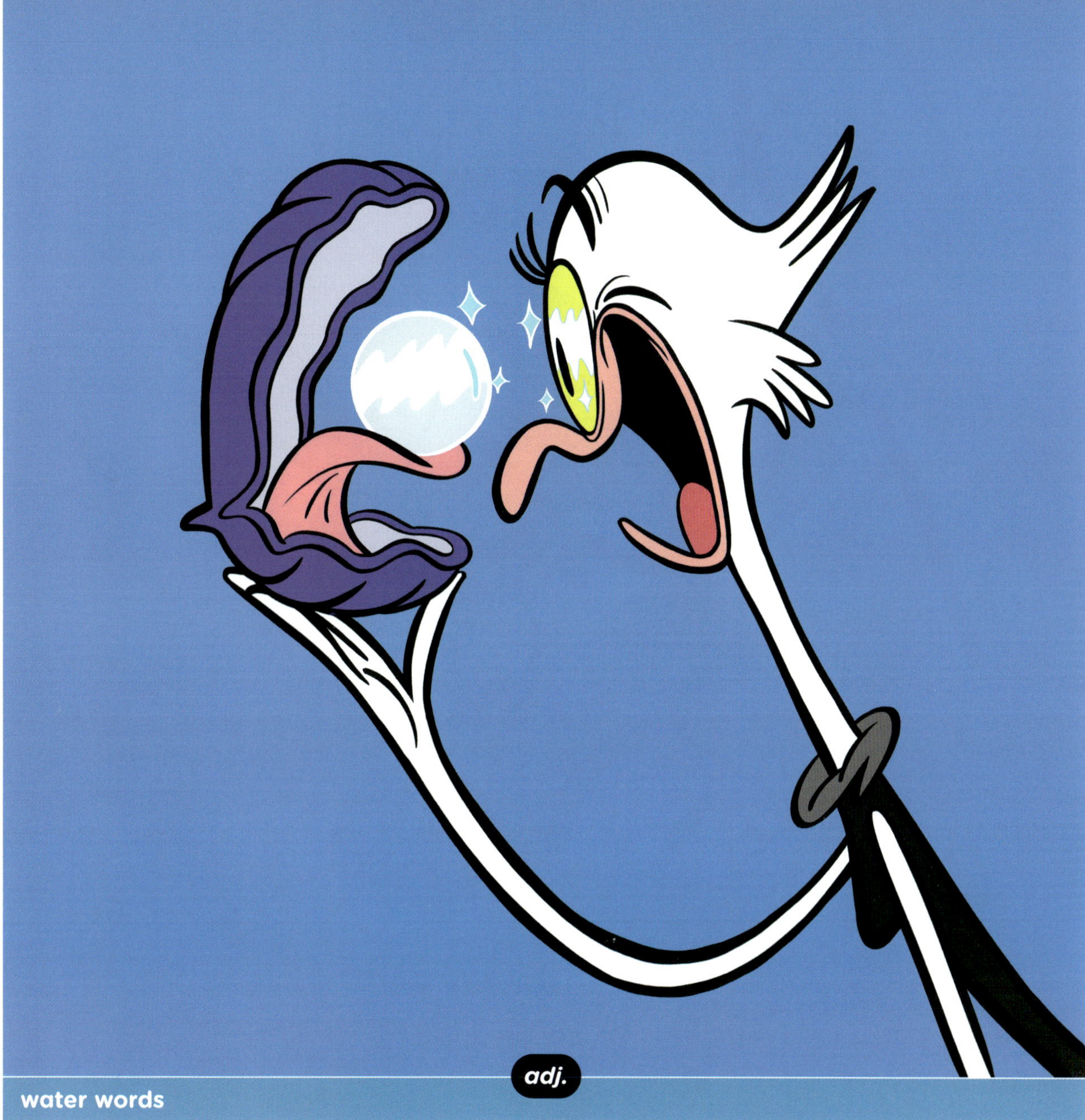

shimmering

DEFINITION

gleaming or glistening;
like a precious pearl
when it catches the light

SAMPLE SENTENCE

Plato gazed out at the **shimmering** sea, hypnotized by the reflection of the moon.

water words

adj.

stagnant

DEFINITION

stale or motionless;
like a dirty pond where nothing is living or moving

SAMPLE SENTENCE

Stinky fumes rose from the **stagnant** swamp as everything continued to rot.

water words

adj.

treacherous

DEFINITION

dangerous or unsafe;
like terrifying rapids that might throw you out of your boat

SAMPLE SENTENCE

Bogart's boat tour was canceled due to dangerous, **treacherous** conditions at sea.

or you can try...

Wet water words!

aquatic
adj. **watery or marine;** like an animal that lives entirely in the water

brackish
adj. **slightly salty;** like a mixture of fresh river water and sea water

briny
adj. **salty or tasting of the sea;** like sea water

calm
adj. **smooth or still;** like the surface of a lake when there is no wind

channel
n. **a passage or length of water;** like a narrow stretch of water between two countries

crystalline
adj. **like crystals or sparkling;** like the surface of water when it reflects the sun

eddying
adj. **swirling and spinning;** like a fast-flowing river that bubbles and twists when it passes over rocks

fetid
adj. **stinking or smelly;** like a pool of still water that has been there for a long time and smells rotten

floodplain
n. **a low-lying and flat area;** land that floods easily

fountain
n. **a jet of liquid or a spring;** a stream of water that shoots up out of the ground

freshwater
adj. **living in water that is not salty;** like a fish that lives in ponds or rivers but not in the sea

glistening
adj. **shining or gleaming;** like the sparkly surface of water in sunlight

or you can try...

harbor

n. **a port or dock;** a place on the shore where ships can be tied up safely

marine

adj. **of the sea;** like animals that live in the ocean

maritime

adj. **seaside or coastal;** like a part of a country that is next to the sea

navigable

adj. **able to be sailed on;** like a river that you can sail a boat along safely and easily

quay

n. **a dock or harbor;** a place where people unload goods from ships and load goods onto them

reservoir

n. **a lake or pool;** a place that has been specially built to store water to send to people's houses

seeping

adj. **leaking or trickling;** like seawater that gradually gets into a ship through small holes

swollen

adj. **made bigger or increased;** like a river that has more water in it than usual after heavy rains

tidal

adj. **affected by tides;** like a river where the water level rises and falls at different times of day

tidemark

n. **a line left by the sea;** like the change in color on a beach at the furthest place the tide has reached

torrent

n. **a strong stream or flood;** like a swollen river that rushes down a hillside after a storm

turbulent

adj. **rough or violent;** like a fast-flowing river that creates bubbles and foam as it crashes against rocks

uncharted

adj. **unknown or undiscovered;** like an unexplored island that does not appear on any map

violent

adj. **rough and powerful;** like a fast-flowing current of water that washes away everything in its path

turn over for setting nouns >

373 serene setting nouns

Take a tour of these wild nouns and word pairs, and set your story in its own living, breathing universe.

busy • congested • international
n.
airport

dark • narrow • winding
n.
alley

local • family-owned • artisan
n.
bakery

well-run • reputable • profitable
n.
bank

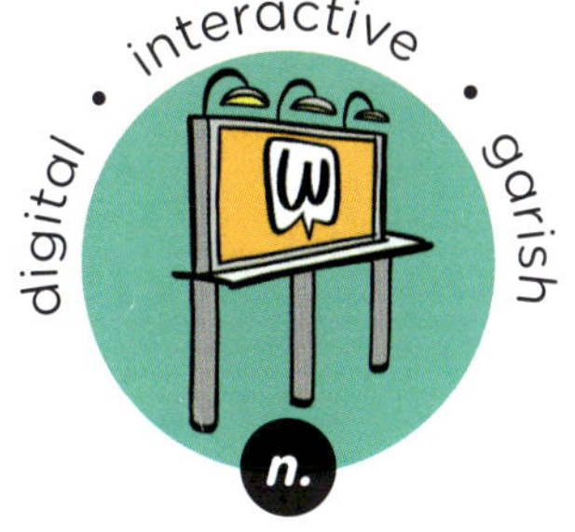

digital • interactive • garish
n.
billboard

local • organic • award-winning
n.
butchershop

passing • honking • available
n.
cab

friendly • handy • late-night
n.
convenience store

wide • faded • unlit
n.
crosswalk

noisy • dense • bustling
n.
crowd

run-down • automated
n.
factory

colorful • spray-painted • rude
n.
graffiti

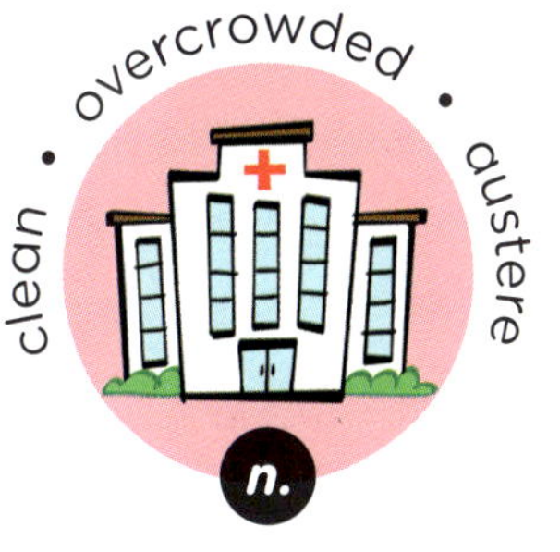
clean • overcrowded • austere
n.
hospital

five-star • trendy • charming
n.
hotel

flashing • blinking • buzzing
n.
neon sign

deep • dangerous • gaping
n.
pothole

icy • narrow • coastal

important • confusing • well-lit

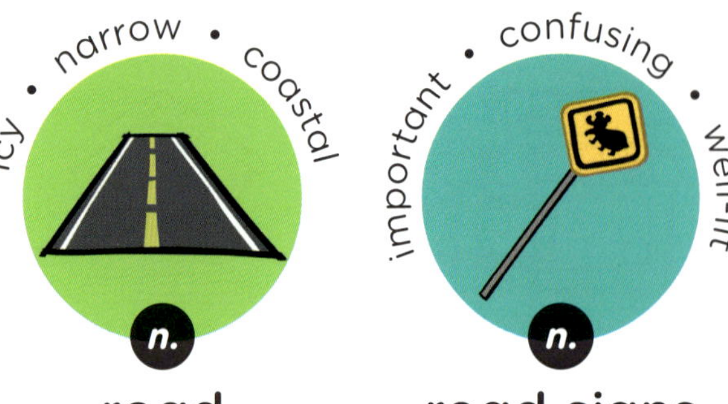

n. **road**

n. **road signs**

stinking • blocked • overflowing

n. **sewer**

crowded • high-end • abandoned

n. **shopping mall**

uneven • slippery • littered

n. **sidewalk**

towering • iconic • futuristic

n. **skyscraper**

famous • life-size • headless

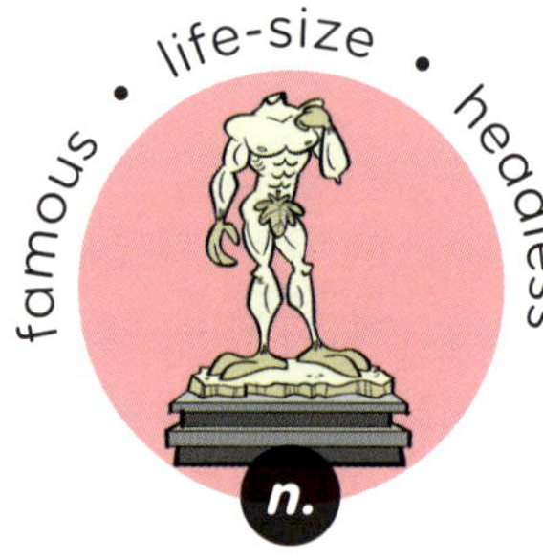

n. **statue**

bright • flickering • crooked

n. **streetlamp**

general • excited • big-city

n. **hubbub**

a lot of noise caused by people talking over each other; like two basketball teams arguing about the referee

local • self-service • ransacked

n. **supermarket**

eager • countless • stranded

n. **tourists**

heavy • slow-moving • oncoming

n. **traffic**

noisy • bustling • underground

n. **train station**

CITIES > JUNKYARD

CITIES > PARK

CITIES > PARK

DRAMATIC > DANGER ZONE

DRAMATIC > SAFE HAVEN

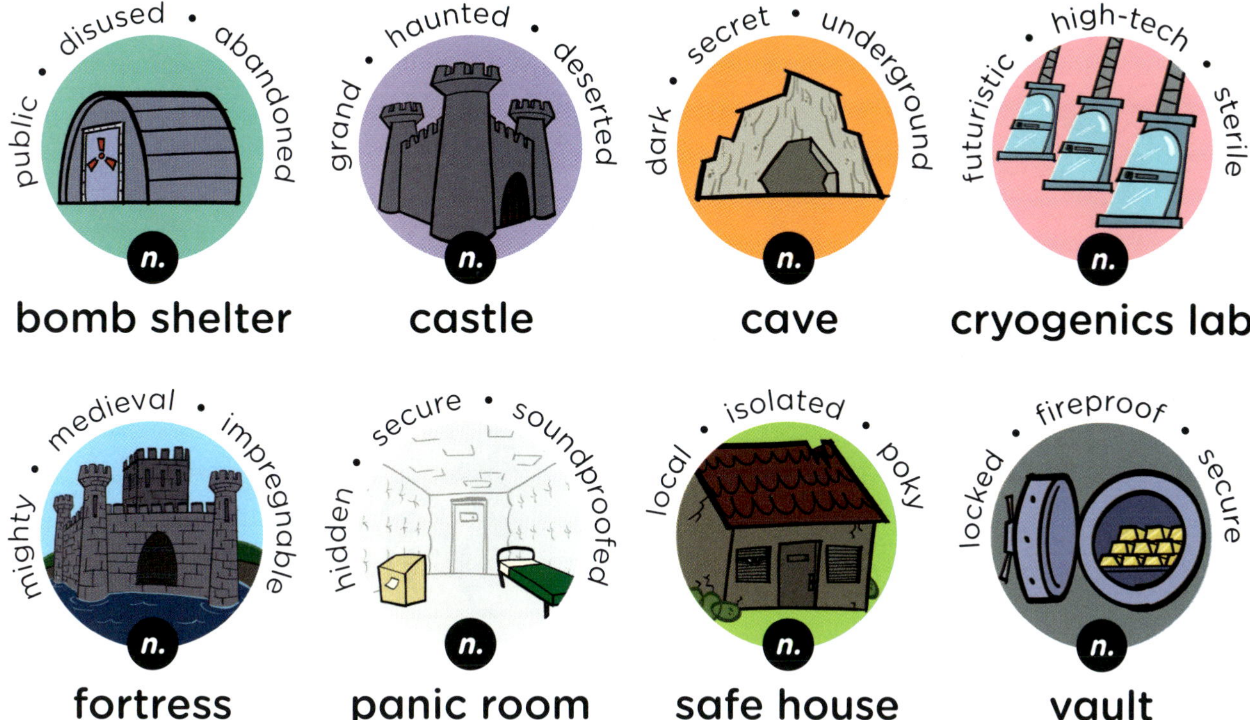

FARM > FARMYARD

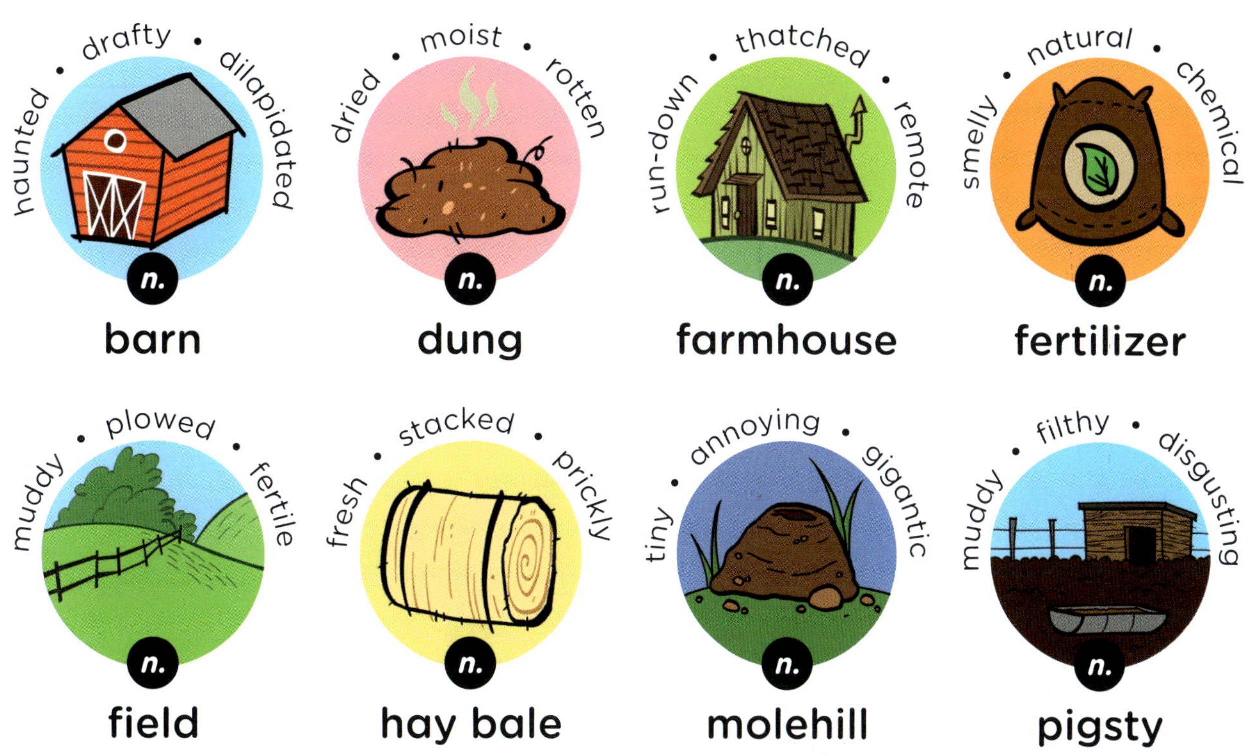

FARM > FARM ANIMALS

HOME > GARDEN

HOME > GARDEN

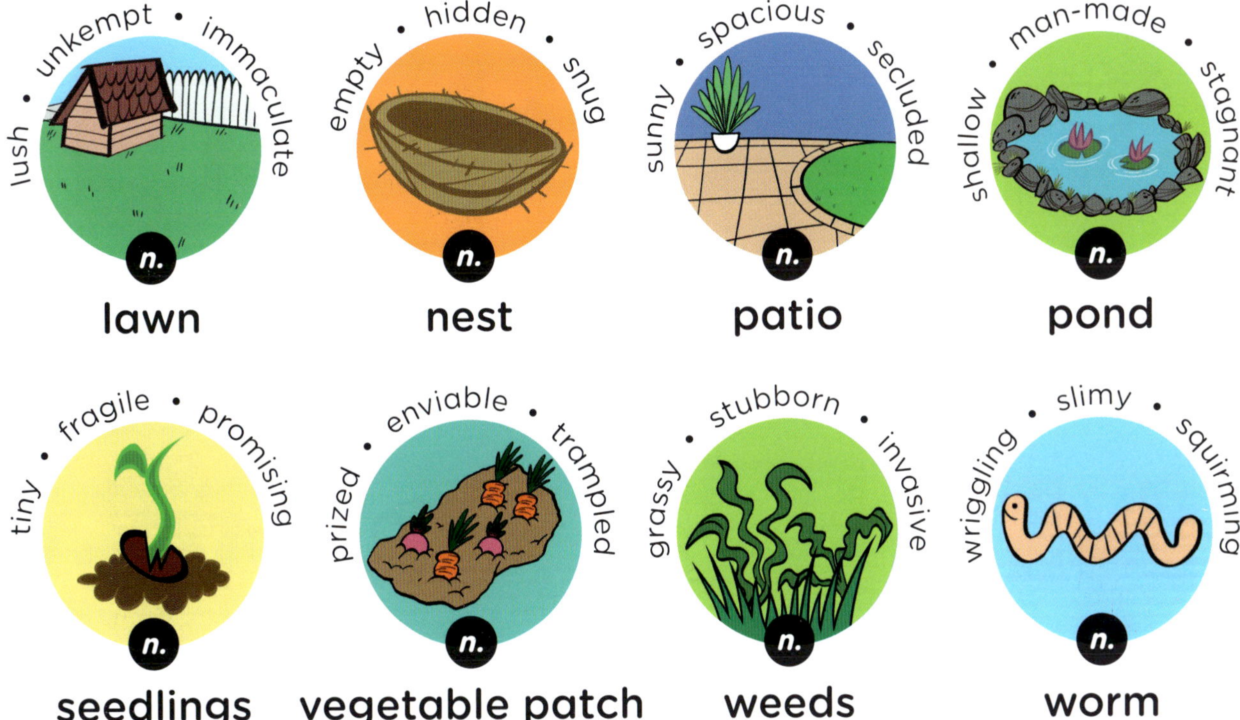

HOME > GEEK'S DEN

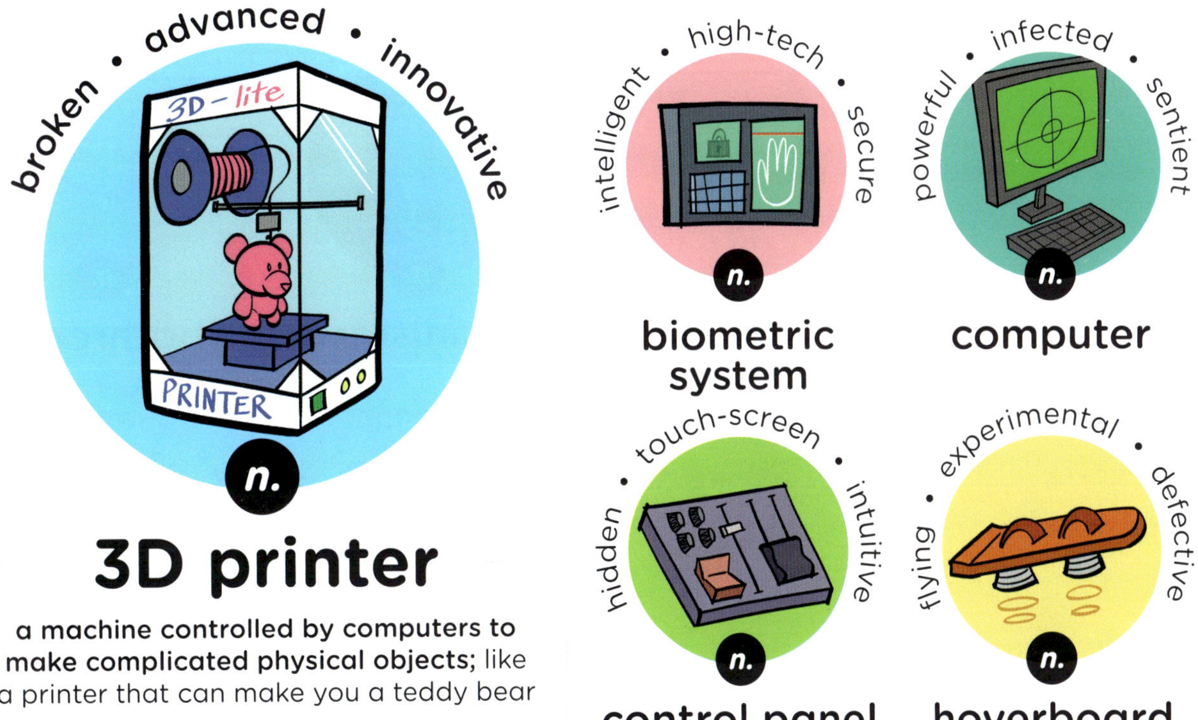

3D printer

a machine controlled by computers to make complicated physical objects; like a printer that can make you a teddy bear

Action | Character | Emotion | Setting | Taste & Smell | Weather

HOME > GEEK'S DEN

HOME > INTERIORS AND EXTERIORS

solid • crumbling • exposed
n.
bricks
locked • trophy • overhead
n.
cabinet
thick • stained • threadbare
n.
carpet
secret • damp • vast
n.
cellar
glittering • antique • ornate
n.
chandelier
smoky • blackened • crooked
n.
chimney
walk-in • mirrored • overstuffed
n.
closet
glass • stylish • antique
n.
coffee table
heavy • drawn • gaudy
n.
curtains
spacious • welcoming • elegant
n.
dining room
formal • elegant • communal
n.
dinner table
open • creaky • revolving
n.
door
dusty • roaring • wood-burning
n.
fireplace
empty • enormous • saltwater
n.
fishtank
wooden • carpeted • creaky
n.
floor
filthy • underground • cluttered
n.
garage

unlocked • cast-iron • imposing
n.
gate
quiet • private • disorganized
n.
home office
expensive • luxury • immersive
n.
home theater
basic • open-plan • immaculate
n.
kitchen
hanging • dimmed • ornamental
n.
lamp
cozy • inviting • contemporary
n.
living room
locked • rusty • stuffed
n.
mailbox
firm • lumpy • stained
n.
mattress
polished • full-length • shattered
n.
mirror
empty • adorable • chaotic
n.
nursery
famous • abstract • exquisite
n.
painting
open • walk-in • overstocked
n.
pantry
hard • plump • downy
n.
pillow
rusty • clogged • burst
n.
pipes
messy • beloved • high-tech
n.
playroom
front • shady • ivy-covered
n.
porch

roof *n.* — leaky • tiled • thatched

rug *n.* — thick • bearskin • shaggy

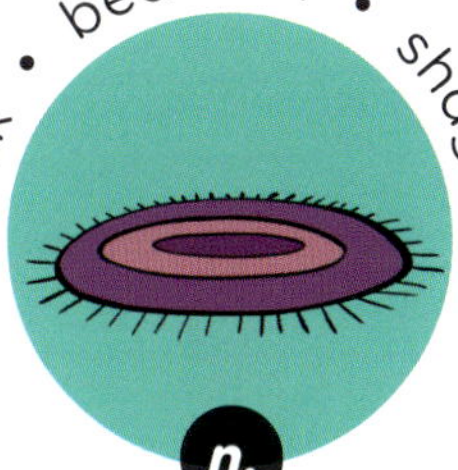

shower *n.* — ice-cold • steamy • invigorating

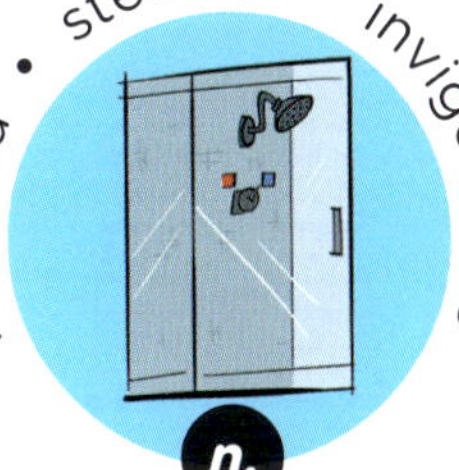

sofa *n.* — plush • sagging • threadbare

solar panels *n.* — modern • built-in • roof-mounted

solarium *n.* — bright • airy • leafy

staircase *n.* — secret • spiraling • creaky

stool *n.* — three-legged • sturdy • wobbly

dated • quirky • opulent

décor *n.*

the things in a room that make it comfortable and look nice; like furniture, pictures, wallpaper, and ornaments

tiles *n.* — square • hand-painted • cracked

toilet *n.* — stinking • outdoor • unflushed

wallpaper *n.* — patterned • floral • peeling

windows *n.* — broken • grimy • shuttered

new • humble • temporary
n.
abode
empty • high-rise • cramped
n.
apartment
charming • detached • squat
n.
bungalow
dark • lakeside • remote
n.
cabin
romantic • alpine • luxurious
n.
chalet
seaside • quaint • whitewashed
n.
cottage
large • communal • unpatrolled
n.
dormitory
grand • vacant • dilapidated
n.
house
floating • moored • ramshackle
n.
houseboat
mud • beachside • primitive
n.
hut
wooden • safari • exclusive
n.
lodge
red-brick • grand • restored
n.
manor
elegant • aristocratic • opulent
n.
mansion
royal • vast • enchanted
n.
palace
stylish • luxurious • sprawling
n.
penthouse
private • princely • spacious
n.
residence

HOME > TYPES OF HOUSE

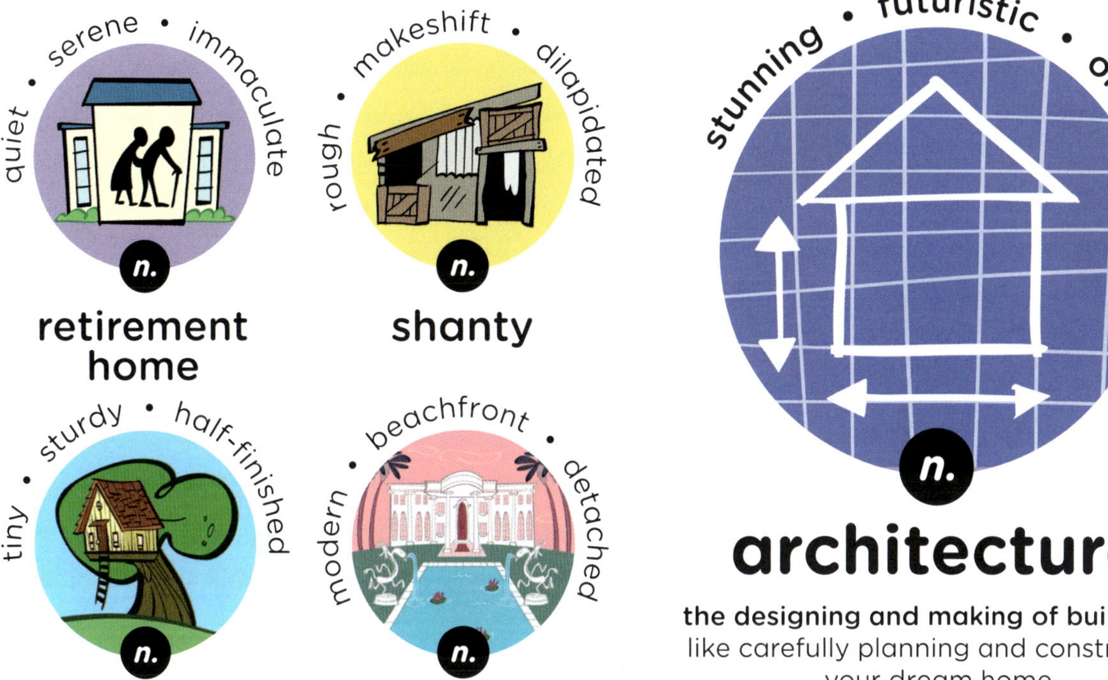

the designing and making of buildings; like carefully planning and constructing your dream home

LANDSCAPES > COUNTRYSIDE

LANDSCAPES > COUNTRYSIDE

LANDSCAPES > DESERT

LANDSCAPES > DESERT

distant • cruel • shimmering

n.

mirage

an optical illlusion caused by bending light rays; like when you're lost in the desert and think you can see water in the distance

leafy • pleasant • welcome

n.

shade

hairy • motionless • gargantuan

n.

tarantula

slow • wise • sacred

n.

tortoise

rolling • blazing • bedraggled

n.

tumbleweed

LANDSCAPES > MOUNTAINS

falling • jagged • immense

n.

boulder

rocky • bottomless • breathtaking

n.

canyon

steep • coastal • overhanging

n.

cliff

wild • bleak • windswept

n.

highland

snow-capped • rugged • majestic

n.

mountain

open • volcanic • desolate

n.

plateau

snowy • distant • volcanic

n.

peak

stony • downward • precipitous

n.

slope

playful • majestic • elusive
n.
arctic fox
floating • enormous • submerged
n.
iceberg
melting • immense • advancing
n.
glacier
a huge mass of moving ice;
like a slow-moving, frozen river
polar • thawing • colossal
n.
icecap
cozy • hidden • abandoned
n.
igloo
howling • shaggy • gaunt
n.
husky
horned • gigantic • mysterious
n.
narwhal
friendly • waddling • comical
n.
penguin
mighty • playful • endangered
n.
polar bear
swimming • curious • lovable
n.
puffin
stray • harnessed • timid
n.
reindeer
wooden • loaded • overturned
n.
sled
fat • enormous • beached
n.
walrus

shallow • secluded • picturesque
n.
bay
sandy • pebbly • pristine
n.
beach
colorful • bouncing • deflated
n.
beach ball
soaked • faded • garish
n.
beach towel
deep-water • jagged • precious
n.
coral
friendly • beady-eyed • scuttling
n.
crab
inflatable • drifting • upturned
n.
dinghy
trained • muscular • responsible
n.
lifeguard
calm • choppy • tempestuous
n.
ocean
seaside • crowded • rickety
n.
pier
rocky • sunken • treacherous
n.
reef
golden • damp • scorching
n.
sand
tall • collapsed • elaborate
n.
sand castle
hungry • squawking • thieving
n.
seagull
spiral • fragile • brittle
n.
seashells
plastic • gleaming • custom-made
n.
surfboard

LANDSCAPES > TROPICAL

LANDSCAPES > UNDER THE SEA

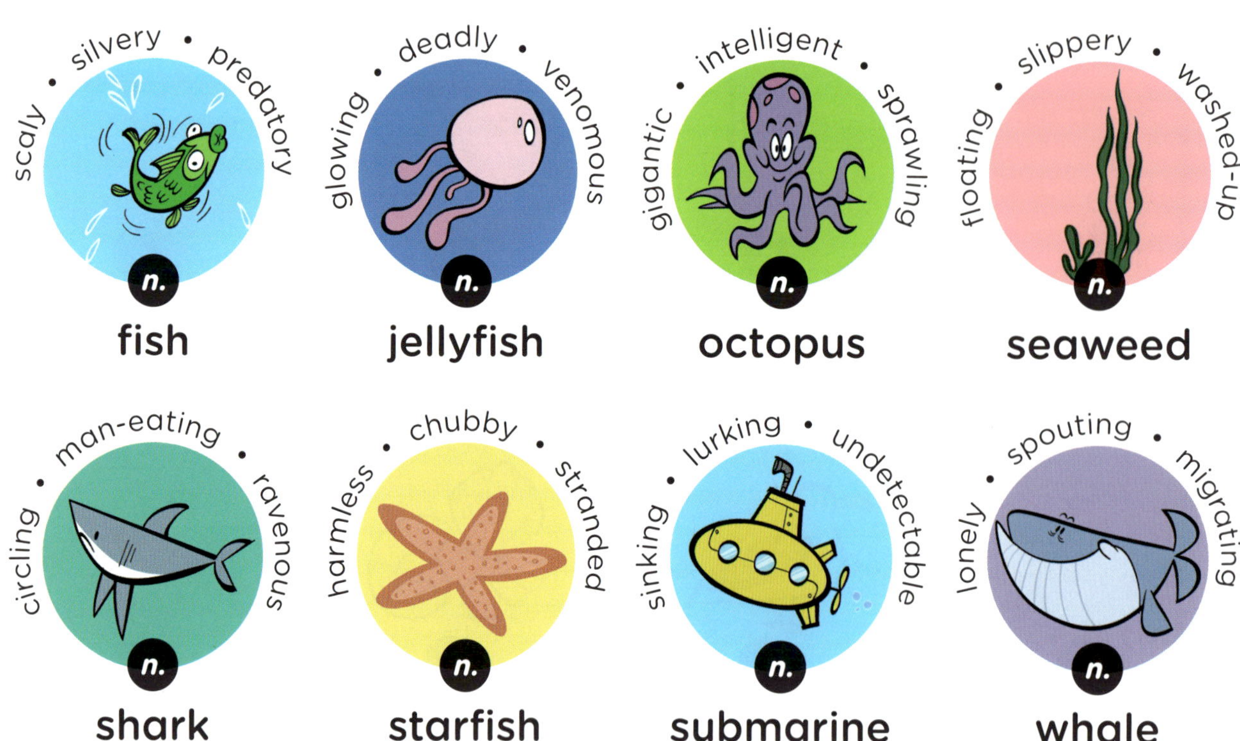

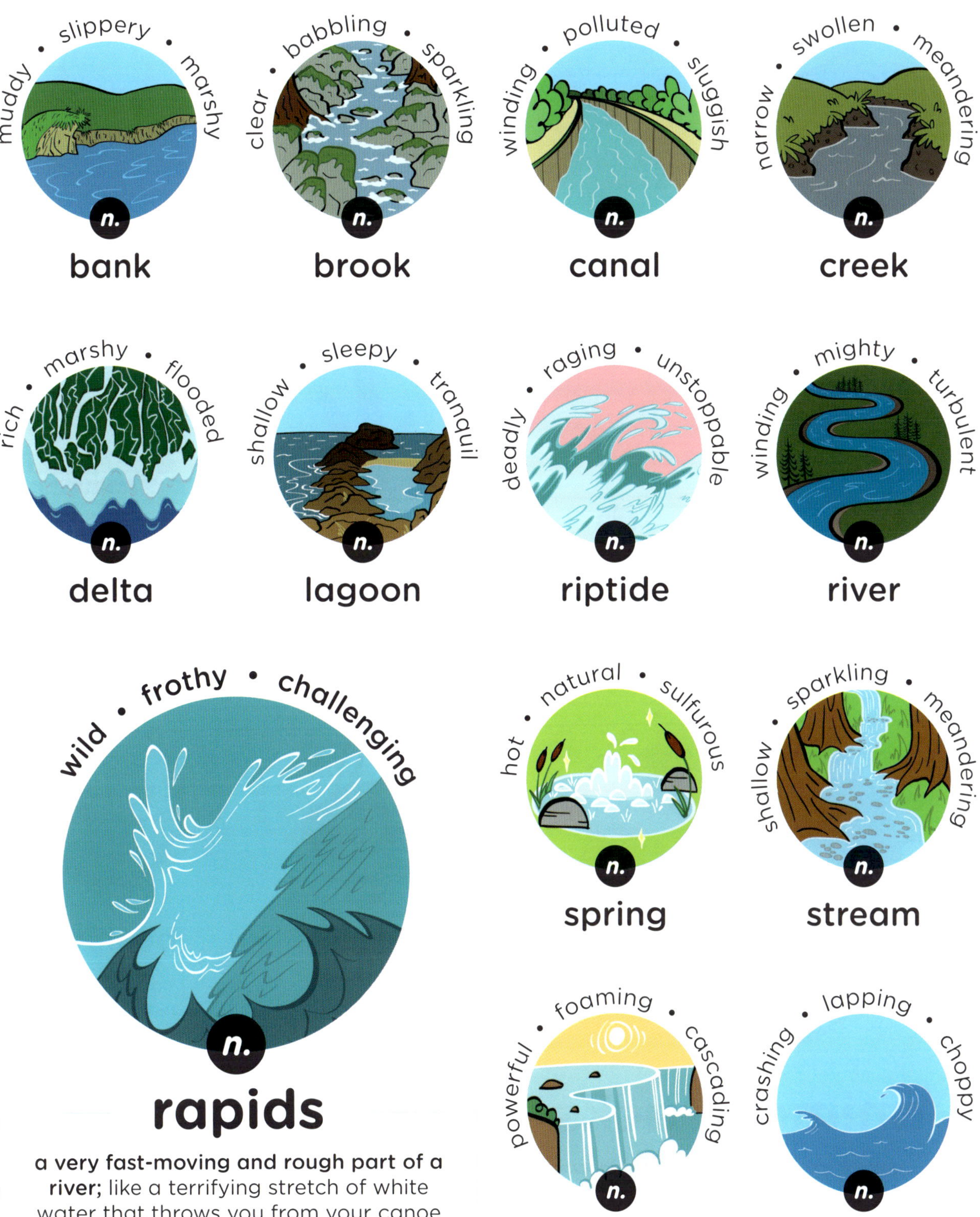

a very fast-moving and rough part of a river; like a terrifying stretch of white water that throws you from your canoe

LANDSCAPESS > WETLAND

LANDSCAPES > WOODLAND

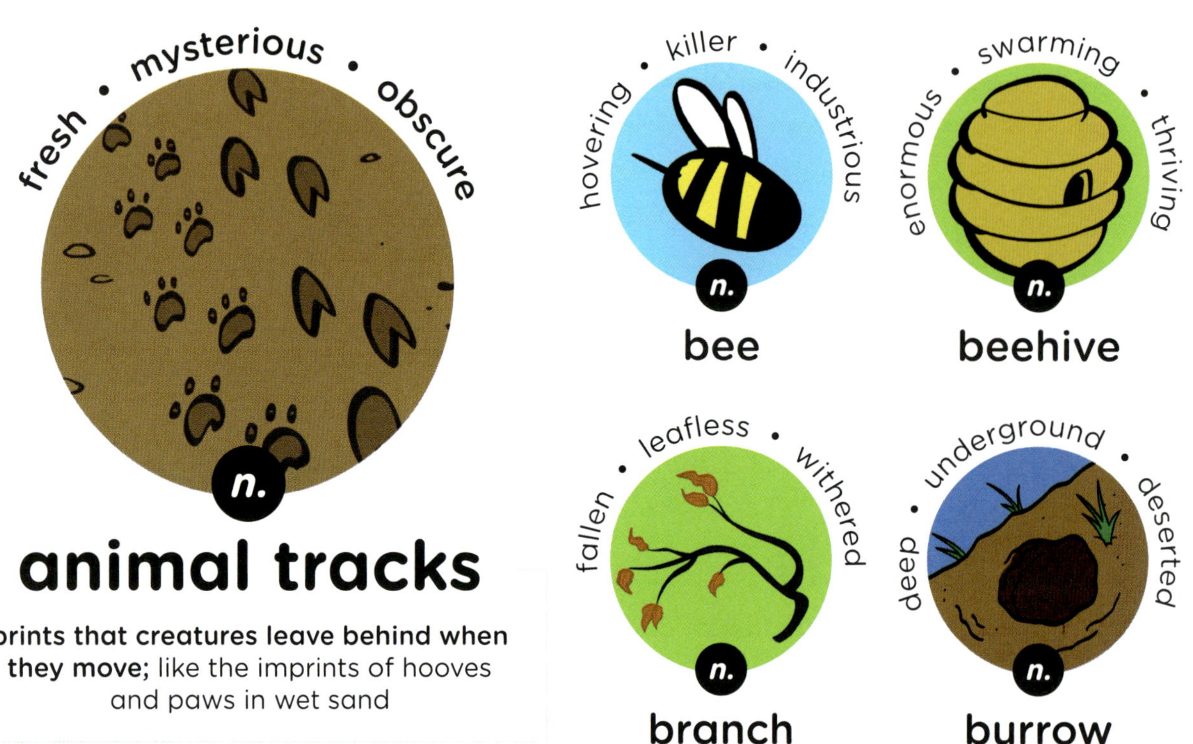

animal tracks

prints that creatures leave behind when they move; like the imprints of hooves and paws in wet sand

LANDSCAPES > WOODLAND

NIGHT AND DAY > DAYTIME

NIGHT AND DAY > NIGHTTIME

SPACE

SPACE

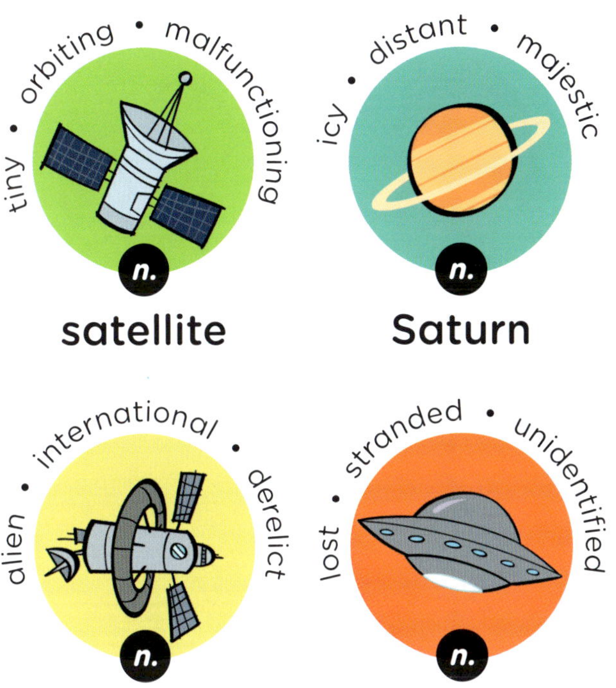

universe

all of space, time, and everything else; all the planets, galaxies, and things you can and can't see

WILDLIFE > ANIMALS

Action | Character | Emotion | Setting | Taste & Smell | Weather

WILDLIFE > ANIMALS

WILDLIFE > BIRDS

WILDLIFE > BIRDS

WILDLIFE > GROUPS OF ANIMALS

Ron had given up completely, and was merely trying to avoid breathing in the **putrid** fumes issuing from his cauldron.

Harry Potter and the Half-Blood Prince
by J.K. Rowling

Taste & Smell

Action | Character | Emotion | Setting | Taste & Smell | Weather

adj.

delicious words

irresistible

DEFINITION

appealing and inviting;
like something so tempting
you can't help reaching for it

SAMPLE SENTENCE

Plato's urge to pop the giant zit on his chin was **irresistible**, he just had to do it.

adj.

delicious words

moist

DEFINITION

damp or not dry;
like a fluffy chocolate cake
that oozes chocolate syrup

SAMPLE SENTENCE

After the rain had fallen,
the worms wriggled happily
in the **moist** earth.

adj.

delicious words

mouthwatering

DEFINITION

looking or smelling delicious; like a giant doughnut that makes you drool when you see it

SAMPLE SENTENCE

Brick drooled into his lap as the **mouthwatering** dish arrived at his table.

delicious words

scrumptious

DEFINITION

tasty or delicious;
like a fancy selection of cakes

SAMPLE SENTENCE

The bakery made the tastiest, most **scrumptious** cakes in town.

adj.

delicious words

succulent

DEFINITION

juicy and fresh;
like perfectly ripe peaches
that are full of delicious juice

SAMPLE SENTENCE

Plato bit into the **succulent** peach and got juice all over his pants.

tantalizing

DEFINITION

tempting and tormenting;
like delicious doughnuts
that you can't reach

SAMPLE SENTENCE

The frying sausages gave
off a **tantalizing** smell that
drew Grit into the kitchen.

or you can try...

Finger-licking, delicious words!

addictive
adj. **irresistible and habit-forming;** like a snack that makes you want more and more of it

comforting
adj. **soothing or satisfying;** like food that makes you feel happy and full

complementing
adj. **combining well with and improving;** like a sauce that makes a particular food taste better

delectable
adj. **tasty or delicious;** like a dessert with wonderful flavors and textures

delicate
adj. **mild or subtle;** like a delicious flavor that you hardly notice

delightful
adj. **delicious or enjoyable;** like food that makes you feel happy when you eat it

distinct
adj. **clear and definite;** like a flavor that you recognize every time you taste it

divine
adj. **delicious or wonderful;** like a dainty pastry that could be served to the gods

exquisite
adj. **fine and beautiful;** like delicate pastries that are fresh from the oven

finger-licking
adj. **tasty or delicious;** like a snack that makes your fingers all sticky

flavorful
adj. **tasty or delicious;** like a stew that brings out the taste of all the different ingredients

full-bodied
adj. **rich and satisfying;** like a thick soup that has lots of flavor

or you can try...

glorious
***adj.* delicious or gorgeous;** like the taste of fresh strawberries on a sunny afternoon

gratifying
***adj.* enjoyable or satisfying;** like a tasty meal at the end of a long day

homemade
***adj.* not bought from a shop;** like jam that you make by boiling your own fruit

juicy
***adj.* tasty and moist;** like a tropical fruit that is soft when you bite into it

lip-smacking
***adj.* delicious and satisfying;** like food that makes you lick your lips with pleasure

luscious
***adj.* delicious and juicy;** like a sweet-tasting melon

lush
***adj.* rich and luxurious;** like ripe fruit that makes your mouth water

oven-fresh
***adj.* warm and delicious;** like a freshly baked pizza

refined
***adj.* elegant or stylish;** like food that is artistically prepared by a five-star chef

sensational
***adj.* gorgeous and impressive;** like a wonderful flavor that you were not expecting

stimulating
***adj.* exciting or interesting;** like a taste that makes you want to eat more

sublime
***adj.* wonderful or magnificent;** like food that tastes better than anything else in the world

tempting
***adj.* delicious and inviting;** like a cake that looks so good that you want to eat it all

toothsome
***adj.* tasty or delicious;** like the taste of freshly baked cupcakes

turn over for disgusting words >

Action | Character | Emotion | Setting | Taste & Smell | Weather

adj.

disgusting words

inedible

DEFINITION

not fit for eating; like a pizza covered in nuts and bolts

SAMPLE SENTENCE

The first pancake Oz made was an **inedible** mess so she threw it out.

adj.

disgusting words

nauseating

DEFINITION

sickening or disgusting; like a rotten sandwich

SAMPLE SENTENCE

Everyone threw up from the **nauseating** stench of Plato's socks.

adj.

disgusting words

rancid

DEFINITION

foul or rotten;
like milk that has been left out for days and gone sour

SAMPLE SENTENCE

The **rancid** smell of rotten eggs wafted from Bogart's bedroom.

adj.

disgusting words

repulsive

DEFINITION

disgusting or gross;
like a horrible, ugly gargoyle that makes you feel sick

SAMPLE SENTENCE

Brick ran away from the **repulsive** odor of the dirty toilet.

disgusting words

adj.

stale

DEFINITION

old, hard, and crusty;
like bread that has gone
rock-solid because you left it out

SAMPLE SENTENCE

The **stale** bread was so hard
that Plato could use it to
hammer a nail into the wall.

adj.

disgusting words

unpalatable

DEFINITION

unappealing or off-putting;
like a can of gross brown dog food

SAMPLE SENTENCE

No one wanted to eat Oz's disgusting, **unpalatable** food.

Gross, disgusting words!

acerbic
adj. **sharp and bitter;** like the taste of vinegar

boring
adj. **plain or unexciting;** like a sandwich with a tasteless filling

burned
adj. **cooked for much too long;** like toast that has turned black and crispy

diluted
adj. **weak or watered down;** like fruit juice that has water added to it

disappointing
adj. **unenjoyable or not satisfying;** like a meal that does not taste as nice as you thought it would

distasteful
adj. **unpleasant or disgusting;** like sour-tasting food that makes you feel a bit sick

doughy
adj. **soft and chewy;** like bread rolls that have been taken out of the oven too soon

dried-out
adj. **stale or no longer fresh;** like a piece of meat that has been left out for a long time

flat
adj. **no longer fizzy;** like soda that has been left in a glass until all the bubbles have gone

greasy
adj. **fatty or oily;** like bacon and eggs cooked in a frying pan

gritty
adj. **grainy or powdery;** like a cake that has little hard pieces that get stuck in your teeth

mediocre
adj. **ordinary or dull;** like food that has been cooked without much thought or care

or you can try...

offensive

***adj.* unpleasant or disgusting;** like food that is so gross that you can't eat it

stomach-churning

***adj.* sickening or revolting;** like a strong taste that makes you feel sick

overcooked

***adj.* cooked for too long;** like vegetables that have become soft and tasteless

underwhelming

***adj.* dull and disappointing;** like a meal that was not as nice as it looked on the menu

rank

***adj.* disgusting or revolting;** like food that has started to go bad

unpleasant

***adj.* uninviting or unpalatable;** like a taste in your mouth that you want to get rid of

raw

***adj.* not cooked;** like crunchy carrots that you eat fresh instead of boiling them

unsavory

***adj.* unpleasant or uninviting;** like food that looks as though it will taste horrible

repellent

***adj.* repulsive or revolting;** like food that is so gross you want to get away from it

unseasoned

***adj.* tasteless or dull;** like a soup that has not had salt or herbs added to it

revolting

***adj.* disgusting or sickening;** like something that makes you feel sick when you think of eating it

vinegary

***adj.* sour and sharp;** like the taste of vinegar

sickening

***adj.* revolting or disgusting;** like food that makes you feel ill when you smell or eat it

weak

***adj.* thin and tasteless;** like a drink that does not have much flavor because it has too much water

turn over for eating words >

v.

eating words

demolish

demolishes • demolishing • demolished

DEFINITION

to destroy or eat up;
when you gobble something up until there's nothing left

SAMPLE SENTENCE

Brick was so hungry that he **demolished** his lunch in ten seconds.

eating words

v.

devour

devours • devouring • devoured

DEFINITION

to eat hungrily or gobble up; when you swallow your dinner quickly in hungry mouthfuls

SAMPLE SENTENCE

Brick could **devour** a pizza whole, swallowing it in one mouthful.

eating words

v.

gorge

gorges • gorging • gorged

DEFINITION

to stuff yourself or overeat; when you eat a giant mountain of food and feel a bit sick

SAMPLE SENTENCE

Grit **gorged** greedily on his chocolate bar without offering a piece to anyone else.

eating words

v.

guzzle

guzzles • guzzling • guzzled

DEFINITION

to gobble or devour;
like gulping down a huge carton of milk all at once

SAMPLE SENTENCE

Shang High nearly choked because he **guzzled** his food so quickly.

v.

eating words

inhale

inhales • inhaling • inhaled

DEFINITION

to breathe in or eat quickly; like sucking up your food in one breath

SAMPLE SENTENCE

Bearnice **inhaled** her food like a vacuum cleaner sucking up dirt.

v.

eating words

savor

savors • savoring • savored

DEFINITION

to enjoy or appreciate;
when you eat something very slowly so you can enjoy every bite

SAMPLE SENTENCE

Oz **savored** the taste of the expensive chocolate by letting it melt in her mouth.

or you can try...

Tasty eating words!

binge
v. **to eat too much all at once;** like eating two tubs of ice cream one after the other

bite
v. **to tear with your teeth;** what you do when you put an apple into your mouth

chew
v. **to eat or munch;** what you do when you slowly break food down with your back teeth

chomp
v. **to chew or munch;** like sheep steadily devouring grass

consume
v. **to eat or swallow;** what you do when you eat a pizza

digest
v. **to absorb or break down;** what your body does to food when it reaches your stomach

dine
v. **to eat or have dinner;** like a family eating together at a restaurant

enjoy
v. **to have a good time doing something;** what you do when you eat your favorite things

feast
v. **to eat a lot of food;** like having a long and luxurious banquet

feed
v. **to eat or dine;** what you do when you put food in your mouth

gnaw
v. **to bite or nibble persistently;** like someone taking regular, small bites of a stick of carrot or celery

gobble
v. **to eat quickly;** when someone is very hungry and eats a lot of food without stopping

or you can try...

graze
***v.* to eat slowly or nibble;** what cattle do when they chew grass in a leisurely way

gulp
***v.* to swallow a lot all at once;** when someone drinks a whole bottle of water all at once

indulge
***v.* to enjoy or take pleasure;** when someone eats a lot of unhealthy food

ingest
***v.* to eat or swallow;** what you do when you take food into your body

lick
***v.* to taste with your tongue;** what you do when you use your tongue to eat a lollipop

munch
***v.* to chew or eat noisily;** like someone steadily devouring a sandwich

nibble
***v.* to bite or gnaw at;** like someone eating nuts by taking regular, small bites

nosh
***v.* to eat or gobble;** like greedily munching on a snack

nourish
***v.* to feed and strengthen;** what healthy food does to your body

peck
***v.* to bite or nibble;** like a bird picking seeds up off the ground

relish
***v.* to enjoy or savor;** the way you take your time over tasty food to make sure you enjoy it

sample
***v.* to taste or try;** like taking a small bite of food to see what it is like

swallow
***v.* to gulp or devour;** what you do when your food goes down your throat and into your stomach

taste
***v.* to feel the flavor of something on your tongue;** like sticking your tongue out to try a new snack

turn over for flavor words >

adj.

flavor words

bland

DEFINITION

plain or flavorless;
like food that is tasteless and boring

SAMPLE SENTENCE

The **bland** taste of the salad had barely any flavor at all.

flavor words

adj.

peppery

DEFINITION

spicy or fiery;
like food that makes your face turn red and your eyes run

SAMPLE SENTENCE

Bearnice's tongue tingled from the **peppery** flavor of the soup.

adj.

flavor words

savory

DEFINITION

salty or spicy;
like pizza sauce or a peppery steak

SAMPLE SENTENCE

Brick couldn't decide whether he wanted a sweet or **savory** snack.

adj.

flavor words

sugary

DEFINITION

very sticky and sweet;
how your bath would taste
if it were full of doughnuts

SAMPLE SENTENCE

Armie got a toothache when he ate too much sweet, **sugary** food.

flavor words

adj.

tangy

DEFINITION

flavorful and sharp;
like the sour taste of a grapefruit

SAMPLE SENTENCE

Plato drizzled a **tangy**, sharp-tasting dressing over his salad.

flavor words

adj.

tart

DEFINITION

sharp and sour;
like the taste of freshly squeezed lemonade

SAMPLE SENTENCE

The small, green apple was too **tart** to eat.

or you can try...

Yummy flavor words!

astringent
adj. **sharp or bitter;** like the flavor of sour cranberries that dry out your mouth

bitter
adj. **sharp or not sweet;** like the taste of a nasty medicine

buttery
adj. **thick and creamy;** like the taste and texture of butter

caramelized
adj. **sweet and sugary;** like fruit that has been cooked in sugar

cheesy
adj. **strong, creamy, and tangy;** like the taste of cheese

complex
adj. **mixed or varied;** like the flavors in a sauce that has many different ingredients

concentrated
adj. **strong or dense;** like fruit juice that has had water removed to make it stronger

creamy
adj. **thick and smooth;** like a rich sauce made with milk and butter

crisp
adj. **hard and crunchy;** like a thin, dry cookie

distinctive
adj. **different or special;** like a flavor that you only find in one particular food

garlicky
adj. **tasting like garlic;** like food that is flavored with, or marinated in, garlic cloves

gamy
adj. **tasting like hunted animals;** like the flavor of deer or wild rabbit

or you can try...

infused

adj. **brewed or saturated;** like tea that has been left in the pot to get its full flavor

marinated

adj. **soaked in a flavorful liquid;** like chicken that has been soaked in lemon juice to make it taste good

mild

adj. **gentle or weak;** like a taste that you only just notice

pickled

adj. **preserved in liquid;** like onions or carrots that you keep in a jar of vinegar

piquant

adj. **sharp or spicy;** like a sauce that makes your mouth feel hot and tingly

rich

adj. **strong and tasty;** like nice food that you can't eat very much of

seasoned

adj. **given added flavor;** like a soup that has salt and herbs added to make it taste good

spiced

adj. **given a strong flavor;** like a meat dish with curry powder or exotic spices

spicy

adj. **peppery or hot;** like a strong chili that makes your tongue tingle

subtle

adj. **mild and delicate;** like a nice flavor that you hardly notice

umami

n. **a pleasant savory taste;** like the flavor of cheese or soy sauce

velvety

adj. **smooth and rich;** like a thick sauce that feels soft against your tongue

vibrant

adj. **intense and exciting;** like an unusual taste that you find surprisingly enjoyable

zesty

adj. **tangy or spicy;** like a refreshing drink made with oranges and lemons

turn over for hungry or thirsty words >

v.

hungry or thirsty words

crave

craves • craving • craved

DEFINITION

to long for or desire;
when you want something so much it's all you can think about

SAMPLE SENTENCE

After eating only salad for weeks, Brick **craved** sugar and junk food.

hungry or thirsty words

adj.

famished

DEFINITION

hungry or starving;
when you feel like you could eat an entire roast turkey in one bite

SAMPLE SENTENCE

The **famished** traveler collapsed from hunger before he made it home.

adj.

hungry or thirsty words

insatiable

DEFINITION

greedy or impossible to satisfy;
so hungry you never fill up

SAMPLE SENTENCE

Bearnice had an **insatiable** appetite so she snacked all day long.

hungry or thirsty words

adj.

parched

DEFINITION

dry or thirsty;
how your throat feels if you run out of water in the desert

SAMPLE SENTENCE

Plato's tongue felt like sandpaper in his dry, **parched** mouth.

hungry or thirsty words

ravenous

DEFINITION

hungry or starving;
when you feel like you could eat an entire Thanksgiving dinner in one bite

SAMPLE SENTENCE

The **ravenous** sharks couldn't wait to get a bite of tasty tuna.

voracious

DEFINITION

greedy or very hungry; like having a never-ending hunger for hamburgers

SAMPLE SENTENCE

The **voracious** predator was always on the lookout for the next animal to hunt.

or you can try...

Desperately hungry and thirsty words!

ache
v. **to really want or hunger for;** when you want something so much that it hurts

barren
adj. **dry and empty;** like land where no trees or crops grow

bone-dry
adj. **completely dry;** like your throat when you haven't had water in a long time

burning
adj. **dry and stinging;** when you're so thirsty your throat feels like it's on fire

covetous
adj. **greedy and envious;** like someone who wants to have other people's possessions

dehydrated
adj. **thirsty and weak;** like the way you feel if you don't drink enough water on a hot day

desirous
adj. **enthusiastic or eager;** like someone who wants a certain thing to happen

desperate
adj. **craving or yearning;** like someone who is so hungry that they start to panic

eager
adj. **excited or impatient;** like someone who can hardly wait to start their dinner

empty
adj. **containing nothing;** like someone whose stomach has nothing in it

faint
adj. **weak or dizzy;** the way you sometimes feel if you have not had enough to eat

gasping
adj. **breathless or extremely thirsty;** like someone who feels they will die if they don't get a drink soon

or you can try...

gluttonous

adj. **very greedy or voracious;** someone who is so greedy that they just can't stop eating

greedy

adj. **very hungry or ravenous;** like someone who always wants more food

hankering

adj. **longing or wishing for;** like someone who is sad because they still don't have what they want

hollow

adj. **empty or unfilled;** like your stomach when you haven't eaten all day

itching

adj. **wanting or needing;** like when you want to eat a specific thing so much that it's annoying

longing

adj. **eager and wishing for;** like someone who has a powerful desire to do something

malnourished

adj. **weak and unhealthy;** like someone who has not had enough healthy food and vitamins for a long time

peckish

adj. **a little bit hungry;** like someone who feels like having a snack

pine

v. **to want badly or crave;** like when you can't stop thinking about food

starved

adj. **dangerously hungry;** like someone who has not been given enough to eat

underfed

adj. **hungry or starving;** like someone who has not eaten enough food for a long time

undernourished

adj. **weak and unhealthy;** like someone who has not had enough to eat for many months

unsatisfied

adj. **disappointed and wanting more;** like someone who is still hungry at the end of a meal

unquenchable

adj. **endlessly thirsty or insatiable;** so thirsty that you always want more water

turn over for meal words >

meal words

adj.

hearty

DEFINITION

filling and wholesome;
like a healthy bowl of stew
on a winter's day

SAMPLE SENTENCE

The cook set down such a
hearty meal that he wasn't
sure he would finish it.

meal words

adj.

humble

DEFINITION

modest, plain, and simple; like a bowl of simple soup for dinner

SAMPLE SENTENCE

The poor farmer could only give the king a **humble** offering.

adj.

meal words

lavish

DEFINITION

sumptuous and luxurious; like a huge banquet for just one person

SAMPLE SENTENCE

Yin laid out a **lavish** banquet to impress her friends with her cooking.

meal words

adj.

meager

DEFINITION

small, limited, or not enough; like a meal made up of a single bean

SAMPLE SENTENCE

The **meager** portion of food wasn't nearly enough to satisfy Bearnice.

meal words

adj.

sumptuous

DEFINITION

lavish and luxurious;
like a banquet made up of
the finest food and drink

SAMPLE SENTENCE

The millionaire ordered
a **sumptuous** dinner to be
laid out for his wedding.

meal words

adj.

wholesome

DEFINITION

healthy or good for you; like a bag of fresh fruit and vegetables

SAMPLE SENTENCE

Oz prepared a **wholesome** meal with vegetables that she had grown herself.

or you can try...

Stuffed meal words!

authentic
adj. **real or genuine;** like food that is made the traditional way

balanced
adj. **complete and healthy;** like a meal that includes all the different foods your body needs

barbecued
adj. **grilled over a fire;** like sausages that have been cooked at an outdoor party

bite-size
adj. **small and easy to swallow;** like a snack that you don't have to cut up before you eat it

casual
adj. **relaxed or informal;** like a meal with friends where nobody dresses formally

chewy
adj. **tough and rubbery;** like meat that you find difficult to swallow

classic
adj. **traditional and popular;** like a meal that people always enjoy even though they eat it often

decadent
adj. **luxurious and not good for you;** like expensive chocolates that you only have as a special treat

filling
adj. **big, heavy, and satisfying;** like a meal that leaves you happy and full

garnished
adj. **decorated or finished off;** like potatoes that have an herb sprinkled over them just before eating

gourmet
adj. **very high-quality;** like food that is made with the best ingredients and prepared by the best chefs

harmonious
adj. **balanced or well-matched;** like different flavors that work well together

or you can try...

healthy
adj. **good for you or wholesome;** like food that helps you to stay fit and energetic

high-end
adj. **expensive and luxurious;** like a restaurant where they serve only the finest food

home-style
adj. **simple or traditional;** like restaurant food that seems like it is homemade

indulgent
adj. **luxurious and too much;** like a large meal that you have as a special treat

innovative
adj. **creative or original;** like a meal that combines ingredients in a way that nobody has done before

layered
adj. **arranged in layers;** like a salad where the different ingredients are placed on top of each other

lean
adj. **with hardly any fat;** like healthy food made with simple ingredients

nutritious
adj. **healthy or wholesome;** like food that helps to keep you fit and strong

opulent
adj. **rich or luxurious;** like the food at a royal feast

palatable
adj. **enjoyable or tasty;** like food that people are happy to eat

satisfying
adj. **pleasant and enough;** like a meal that leaves you feeling nicely full

sophisticated
adj. **elegant and stylish;** like food that is prepared with a lot of thought and fine ingredients

substantial
adj. **large or generous;** like a meal where everyone has a lot of food on their plate

traditional
adj. **typical or handed down;** like a recipe that has been made for many years

turn over for smell words >

smell words

adj.

faint

DEFINITION

barely noticeable or slight; like the trace of a delicious smell carried on the breeze

SAMPLE SENTENCE

"Has someone been baking?" asked Bogart when he noticed the **faint** smell of fresh bread.

fragrance

DEFINITION

a sweet smell or perfume; like the odor of delicious herbs or exotic flowers

SAMPLE SENTENCE

The delicate **fragrance** of the roses was hard to smell next to the stinking garbage cans.

smell words

adj.

musty

DEFINITION

stuffy and stale;
like the smell of an old, stinky sweater that has never been washed

SAMPLE SENTENCE

Brick's old gym bag smelled like damp, **musty** clothes.

n.

smell words

odor

DEFINITION

a smell or stink;
like the fumes from
someone's armpits

SAMPLE SENTENCE

The unpleasant **odor** of Bearnice's feet was so bad that her neighbors moved.

smell words

adj.

overpowering

DEFINITION

overwhelming or unbearable; like a smell so strong that it knocks you over

SAMPLE SENTENCE

The **overpowering** stench of Bogart's breath made his dentist quit his job.

adj.

smell words

pungent

DEFINITION

very strong and smelly; like the stench of stinky, sweaty sneakers after a long day of playing sports

SAMPLE SENTENCE

The cheese was so **pungent** that you could smell it five miles away.

smell words

adj.

putrid

DEFINITION

rotten and decayed;
like an old, moldy sandwich

SAMPLE SENTENCE

The old meat smelled so **putrid** that not even the starving rats wanted to eat it.

smell words

v.

reek

reeks • reeking • reeked

DEFINITION

to stink or to smell;
like the worst breath

SAMPLE SENTENCE

The whole place **reeked** after Yin threw a powerful stink bomb.

n.

smell words

scent

DEFINITION

a smell or aroma;
like the particular smell
that someone leaves behind

SAMPLE SENTENCE

Everyone knew that Bogart
was nearby thanks to his
unmistakable **scent**.

smell words

n.

stench

DEFINITION

an odor or stink;
like the smell of someone who hasn't showered for days

SAMPLE SENTENCE

The fridge was full of the unbearable **stench** of rotting fish.

smell words

adj.

toxic

DEFINITION

poisonous or harmful;
like dangerous radioactive waste

SAMPLE SENTENCE

The **toxic** waste glowed bright green as it slowly burned through the floor.

n.

smell words

whiff

DEFINITION

a sniff or trace;
like the smell of your favorite pie wafting through the air

SAMPLE SENTENCE

Just one delicious **whiff** of fresh-baked bread was enough to make Oz's mouth water.

or you can try...

Funky smell words!

acidic
***adj.* sharp and sour;** like the smell of vinegar

acrid
***adj.* sharp or sour;** like the smell of burning plastic

ambrosial
***adj.* heavenly or extremely lovely;** like the gorgeous smell of a bowl of fresh and exotic fruit

appealing
***adj.* pleasant and inviting;** like the smell of frying food that makes you feel hungry

aroma
***n.* a fragrance or scent;** like the pleasant smell of freshly baked bread

bouquet
***n.* a smell or scent;** like the pleasant scent of a bunch of flowers

cloying
***adj.* overwhelming or sickly sweet;** like the smell of powdered sugar floating in the air

comforting
***adj.* soothing or cheering;** like a pleasant smell that reminds you of home

disagreeable
***adj.* unpleasant or unenjoyable;** like a bad smell that makes you want to open the window

earthy
***adj.* soil-like or muddy;** like how your hands smell after you fall in the mud

enticing
***adj.* tempting or attractive;** like the smell of barbecued food that makes you want to eat it

essence
***n.* a scent or perfume;** like a strong perfume made from flower petals

or you can try...

evocative

adj. **reminding you of something;** like the smell of fresh bread that reminds you of a bakery

exotic

adj. **unfamiliar or tropical;** like the smell of spices from faraway lands

fetid

adj. **nasty or disgusting;** like the smell of dirty socks

flowery

adj. **sweet and perfumed;** like the smell of rose petals

foul

adj. **nasty or disgusting;** like the smell of rotting food

heady

adj. **strong or intoxicating;** like a smell that makes you feel giddy

herbal

adj. **plant-based or fresh;** like the smell of newly cut herbs

incense

n. **something you burn for its smell;** like a substance that people burn in religious ceremonies

intense

adj. **strong or powerful;** like the smell in a room full of scented candles

lingering

adj. **lasting or remaining;** like a smell that stays for a long time after the thing that caused it has gone

metallic

adj. **smelling like metal;** like old coins or rusty scissors

mingled

adj. **mixed or blended;** like smelling two things at the same time

musky

adj. **strong and sweet;** like an old man's cologne

nose

n. **a smell or scent;** like a smell that is particular to a certain food

nostalgic

adj. **reminding you of the past;** like the smell of your grandma's cooking that reminds you of being little

noxious

adj. **harmful, toxic, or unpleasant;** like the smell of poisonous gas fumes

Action | Character | Emotion | Setting | Taste & Smell | Weather

or you can try...

odorless
***adj.* not scented or perfumed;** like a gas that does not smell like anything

peculiar
***adj.* strange or odd;** like a funny smell that you don't recognize

perfume
***n.* a scent or fragrance;** like the sweet smell that flowers give off

potent
***adj.* strong or powerful;** like the smell of a chemical that you can't breathe in for very long

rank
***adj.* foul or disgusting;** like the smell of rotting garbage

redolent
***adj.* smelling strongly of something;** like a place where the air smells like flowers

refreshing
***adj.* pleasant and fresh;** like the smell of a crisp sea breeze

scented
***adj.* sweet-smelling or fragrant;** like a candle that has perfume added to it

sharp
***adj.* strong or noticeable;** like the smell of paint or chemicals

smoky
***adj.* smelling of smoke;** like the smell of burning wood

sniff
***v.* to smell;** what you do when you deliberately draw air up your nose

soothing
***adj.* gentle or comforting;** like a pleasant smell that makes you feel comfortable and relaxed

sour
***adj.* sharp and unpleasant;** like the smell of rotten milk

spicy
***adj.* flavorful or peppery;** like the smell of a kitchen where someone is cooking a curry

stink
***n.* an unpleasant odor or stench;** like the smell of rotten fish

stinky
***adj.* nasty or disgusting;** like a place that smells like sewage and drains

or you can try...

stuffy

adj. **stale or airless;** like a small room with no windows

sweaty

adj. **smelling of sweat;** like an old gym bag full of dirty socks

sweet

adj. **fragrant or nice to smell;** like the scent of flowers

telltale

adj. **revealing or telling;** like a cooking smell that makes it obvious what is in the oven

unfamiliar

adj. **strange or new;** like the smells of food cooking in a country you have never visited before

unmistakable

adj. **recognizable or familiar;** like a smell that reminds you of only one thing

unscented

adj. **not scented or perfumed;** like a plain soap that has no added fragrances

woody

adj. **smelling like wood;** like the smell of a carpenter's workshop

turn over for taste & smell nouns >

decadent taste & smell nouns

Hungry for more? Devour these red-hot nouns and their sizzling word pairs.

BAKING

handheld • buzzing • electric
n.
blender
gooey • dense • decadent
n.
brownie
moist • frosted • scrumptious
n.
cake
towering • tiered • toppling
n.
cake stand
melted • rich • bittersweet
n.
chocolate
warm • freshly baked • fortune
n.
cookie
whipped • clotted • curdled
n.
cream
frosted • gluten-free • decorated
n.
cupcakes
glazed • deep-fried • stale
n.
doughnut
piped • whipped • slathered
n.
frosting
spiced • decorated • fragrant
n.
gingerbread
rich • melted • homemade
n.
ice cream
sugary • crushed • tempting
n.
macarons
blueberry • half-eaten • mini
n.
muffin
floured • heavy • wooden
n.
rolling pin
broken • accurate • precise
n.
scales

BAKING

sweet tooth

a taste for sugary food;
like a person who is always ready for dessert

BREAKFAST

BREAKFAST

COOKING

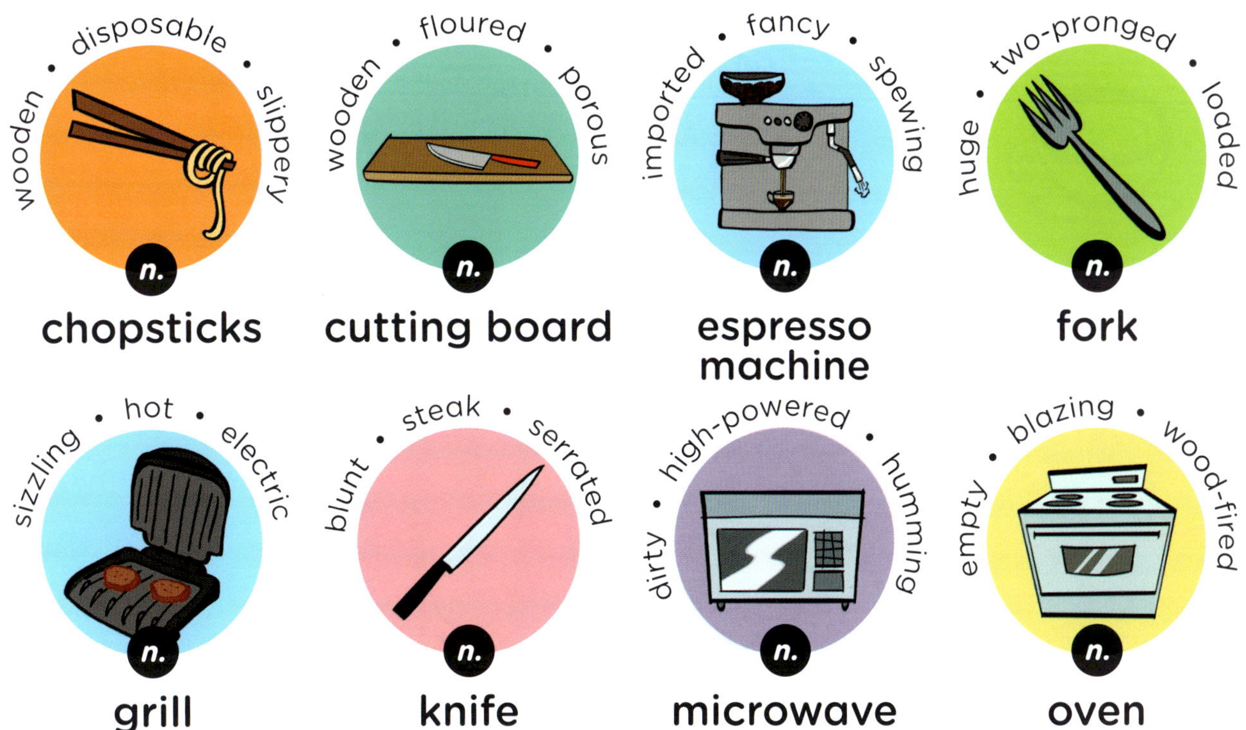

COOKING

DRINKS

DRINKS

FRUIT AND VEGETABLES

FRUIT AND VEGETABLES

FRUIT AND VEGETABLES

vegan

a person who doesn't eat anything from animals; someone who never eats meat, cheese, or eggs

INGREDIENTS

INGREDIENTS

MEAT AND FISH

MEAT AND FISH

RESTAURANTS > EATING OUT

steamed • deep-fried • glutinous
n.
dumplings
salty • greasy • soggy
n.
fries
juicy • towering • succulent
n.
hamburger
grilled • half-eaten • foot-long
n.
hotdog
spicy • authentic • magnificent
n.
kebab
fried • instant • spicy
n.
noodles
frozen • wood-fired • leftover
n.
pizza
soft • spicy • crunchy
n.
taco

STAPLES

fresh • sourdough • moldy
n.
bread
rolled • organic • crunchy
n.
oats
handmade • cheesy • spelt
n.
pasta
roasted • deep-fried • parboiled
n.
potatoes
puffed • expensive • trendy
n.
quinoa
sticky • fried • curried
n.
rice
golden • wild • stone-ground
n.
wheat
mashed • baked • leftover
n.
yams

STORAGE

bottle (n.) — empty • recycled • translucent

bowl (n.) — mixing • ceramic • overturned

can (n.) — rusty • unopened • discarded

carton (n.) — plastic • flattened • corrugated

coffee cup (n.) — steaming • piping-hot • reusable

freezer (n.) — walk-in • locked • unplugged

fridge (n.) — oversized • fully stocked • faulty

jar (n.) — cookie • airtight • ancient

food waste (n.) — rotting • composting • avoidable

scraps or uneaten leftovers;
like fishbones and apple cores that are thrown away after a meal

mug (n.) — dirty • chipped • steaming

plate (n.) — cracked • paper • heaped

teapot (n.) — steaming • scalding • talking

thermos (n.) — sealed • big-bellied • replenished

The wind grew so **tempestuous** during the night, and blew in such gusts against the walls, that the hut trembled and the old beams groaned and creaked.

Heidi **by Johanna Spyri**

Weather

calm and pleasant words

adj.

balmy

DEFINITION

mild or warm;
like weather that makes you want to lie down and daydream

SAMPLE SENTENCE

Grit enjoyed a **balmy** evening relaxing on the river bank.

dewy

DEFINITION

moist or damp;
like grass that is covered in little droplets of water first thing in the morning

SAMPLE SENTENCE

The spider's **dewy** cobweb twinkled in the moonlight.

rustling

DEFINITION

crackling or swishing; the sound of fall leaves being shaken from a tree

SAMPLE SENTENCE

Bogart's silky underwear hung on the line, making a **rustling** noise in the breeze.

serene

DEFINITION

peaceful or calm;
like how you feel when you've done a long, relaxing session of yoga

SAMPLE SENTENCE

The **serene** lake was so still that its surface was like a mirror.

temperate

DEFINITION

mild or pleasant;
like a place where the weather is never too hot and never too cold

SAMPLE SENTENCE

Shang High was a **temperate** person who usually stayed calm.

tranquil

DEFINITION

peaceful or blissfully quiet;
how you feel when you take a little nap in the shade

SAMPLE SENTENCE

Oz enjoyed the **tranquil** atmosphere of her yoga class because it was so peaceful.

or you can try...

Lovely, calm and pleasant words!

benign
adj. **pleasant and gentle;** like warm, dry weather that is good for your health

blissful
adj. **lovely or delightful;** like a perfect summer's day without a cloud in the sky

breezy
adj. **a little windy or gusty;** like wind with gentle gusts that push some leaves around

bright
adj. **sunny or cloudless;** like a beautiful spring morning when the sky is blue

chirping
adj. **singing or tweeting;** like when birds are making a pretty, cheerful sound at dawn

clement
adj. **mild and calm;** like the kind of day that's perfect for a picnic

cloudless
adj. **bright and sunny;** like a perfectly blue summer sky

delightful
adj. **pleasant or enjoyable;** like warm and sunny weather that makes you feel happy all over

favorable
adj. **good or suitable;** like weather that is perfect for plants to grow well

fine
adj. **bright or clear;** like sunny weather that makes you want to spend all day outdoors

fresh
adj. **nice and cool;** like the kind of weather that makes you feel refreshed

gentle
adj. **calm and mild;** like weather that isn't too hot, too cold, or too windy

or you can try...

halcyon

adj. **peaceful and happy;** like a long summer when you don't have a care in the world

rejuvenating

adj. **making you feel healthy again;** like weather that makes you feel relaxed and ready to do anything

heavenly

adj. **beautiful or perfect;** like a warm day spent beside a glistening lake

splendid

adj. **beautiful or wonderful;** like a brilliant dawn making the sky pink and gold

mellow

adj. **calm or relaxing;** like a warm, quiet evening without any rain or strong winds

still

adj. **calm or peaceful;** like a day when there is no wind at all

mild

adj. **calm and warm;** like an unexpected spell of good weather during the winter

sunny

adj. **bright with sunlight;** like a day with a perfectly blue sky

moderate

adj. **calm or mild;** like a winter's day that is not too windy or too cold

tepid

adj. **not too hot and not too cold;** like a hot drink that has cooled down a bit

peaceful

adj. **calm and quiet;** like a small village where everyone is friendly to each other

undisturbed

adj. **quiet and peaceful;** like a place that no tourists ever visit

placid

adj. **very still and calm;** like a lake so still that it looks like a mirror

warm

adj. **not too hot and not cold;** like comfortable weather that makes it easy to relax

turn over for cloudy words >

cloudy words

adj.

billowing

DEFINITION

swelling or expanding;
like a cloud that has grown so big you can bounce on it

SAMPLE SENTENCE

Grit pulled at the rope to control the **billowing** sails that were flapping in the wind.

Action | Character | Emotion | Setting | Taste & Smell | Weather

adj.

cloudy words

dense

DEFINITION

thick, solid, or heavy;
like a cloud so thick you need a knife to cut through it

SAMPLE SENTENCE

The **dense** undergrowth of the forest made a great hiding place for animals.

cloudy words

adj.

hazy

DEFINITION

cloudy or misty;
like a fog that makes
it hard to see clearly

SAMPLE SENTENCE

The old man only had **hazy** recollections of his childhood because it was so long ago.

overcast

DEFINITION

cloudy or gray;
how the sky looks when dark clouds block out all the sunshine

SAMPLE SENTENCE

The sky had been **overcast** for so long that Yin couldn't remember what the sun looked like.

cloudy words

adj.

swirling

DEFINITION

spiraling or twirling;
like clouds spinning around after a plane whizzes past

SAMPLE SENTENCE

The **swirling** mist hung around the tree branches like ghostly scarves.

cloudy words

adj.

wispy

DEFINITION

thin or fine;
like clouds that are feathery and light

SAMPLE SENTENCE

The wise old man had a thin, **wispy** beard that he stroked when he was deep in thought.

or you can try...

Fluffy cloud words!

ash
n. **the fine dust left behind after a fire;** like the dark dust that comes from a volcano in thick clouds

fleecy
adj. **soft and fluffy;** like a sheep's wool

fleeting
adj. **fast-moving or passing;** like clouds that are blown quickly across the sky

fluffy
adj. **soft and furry;** like a rabbit's fur

foggy
adj. **misty or hazy;** like a day when there is a thick mist and you cannot see far in front of you

heavy
adj. **dark or gloomy;** like the sky when it is just about to start raining

insubstantial
adj. **light or thin;** like something that is not very solid and so does not last for long

leaden
adj. **dark and gray;** like the sky when it seems dark even in the middle of the day

looming
adj. **slowly growing and threatening;** like dark clouds building up in the distance

luminous
adj. **bright or shining;** like clouds that have an orange glow when the sun shines through them

murky
adj. **dark and dim;** like a period of twilight when you can't make out shapes very well

nebulous
adj. **cloudy or unclear;** like a mysterious ball of gas that keeps changing its shape

or you can try...

pillow-like

adj. **soft and round;** like an inviting pillow that you sink your head into

puffy

adj. **light and full of air;** like a round, white cloud in a blue sky

purple

adj. **reddish-blue or bruised;** the color of a dark grape

rippling

adj. **flowing and curving;** like clouds that move gently up and down

scattered

adj. **few and far apart;** like two or three small clouds spread across a clear, blue sky

silvery

adj. **light and gray;** like the color of clouds in the light of the sun

stormy

adj. **wild or threatening;** like dark clouds that bring heavy rain with them

swelling

adj. **getting larger and rounder;** like clouds before they start to rain

thin

adj. **light or faint;** like a cloud that is not strong enough to block out the sun

threatening

adj. **dark and menacing;** like dark clouds that warn you that it is going to rain

undulating

adj. **rolling up and down;** the way the tops of the clouds look when you are flying above them

vapor

n. **haze or mist;** like tiny water droplets hanging in the air

weightless

adj. **light and airy;** like a material that is so light that it floats in the air

wooly

adj. **soft and fluffy;** like a sheep's fleece

turn over for cold words >

cold words

adj.

biting

DEFINITION

bitter cold or harsh;
so cold it feels like a monster is nipping your frozen bottom

SAMPLE SENTENCE

The **biting** weather sent a cold shiver down Plato's spine.

cold words

adj.

brisk

DEFINITION

sharp or crisp;
like the cold air on your face when you go for a walk in the winter

SAMPLE SENTENCE

Grit turned up the collar on his leather jacket to keep out the **brisk** wind.

adj.

cold words

excruciating

DEFINITION

extremely painful;
how it would feel to be pricked all over your body by sharp icicles

SAMPLE SENTENCE

Dropping the heavy book on his foot left Armie in **excruciating** pain.

cold words

adj.

frosty

DEFINITION

freezing or icy;
the kind of cold that feels like you have a layer of ice over your skin

SAMPLE SENTENCE

Thanks to the **frosty** weather, Shang High had icicles of snot hanging from his nostrils.

cold words

numbing

DEFINITION

ice-cold or freezing;
like a popsicle that makes your tongue so cold you can't feel it

SAMPLE SENTENCE

The **numbing** effect of the cold weather meant that Oz couldn't feel her toes.

cold words

adj.

penetrating

DEFINITION

piercing or sharp;
like freezing air that goes straight to your bones

SAMPLE SENTENCE

The **penetrating** cold cut through Shang High's extra-warm scarf and made him shiver.

or you can try...

Freezing cold words!

adverse
***adj.* harmful and unfavorable;** like bad weather that forces you to cancel your plans

arctic
***adj.* extremely cold;** like the freezing weather at the North Pole

bitter
***adj.* freezing or harsh;** like cold air that chills you to your bones

blizzard
***n.* a windy and heavy snowstorm;** when it snows so hard that you can't see where you are going

bracing
***adj.* cold and refreshing;** like a windy day at the beach

chilly
***adj.* cold and unpleasant;** like winter air that sucks all the heat from your body

crisp
***adj.* cold and fresh;** like a clear and frosty day in fall

freezing
***adj.* cold and icy;** so cold that icicles form on your window frame

frigid
***adj.* cold or freezing;** like a day when the temperature is so cold that ponds turn to ice

glacial
***adj.* cold and icy;** like a place that is covered in ice all year round

hibernate
***v.* to sleep through the winter;** what animals do when they hide away and sleep from fall until spring

hostile
***adj.* harsh or unfavorable;** like a place where the weather is so bad that it's difficult to survive

or you can try...

iciness
n. **cold or frostiness;** like the slippery conditions when all the sidewalks get frozen

inclement
adj. **harsh and unpleasant;** like a stormy day that wrecks your plans for a picnic

inhospitable
adj. **bleak or unwelcoming;** like a place where the weather is so bad that people cannot live there

nippy
adj. **cold and breezy;** like a day when it is too cold to stay outside for long

powdery
adj. **fine and dusty;** like soft snow that does not hurt you if you fall on it

raw
adj. **cold and unpleasant;** like a day when the wind is so cold that you feel unwell

rigid
adj. **hard or stiff;** like your fingers when it is so cold that you can't move them

severe
adj. **intense or extreme;** like weather that is much colder than what you would normally expect

shivery
adj. **cold and trembling;** the way you feel when it is so cold that you can't stop your body from shaking

slushy
adj. **soft and wet;** like snow that has partly melted

stinging
adj. **burning and tingling;** like weather that is so cold that your skin hurts

subzero
adj. **icy or freezing;** when the temperature is so cold that water turns to ice

tingly
adj. **prickly-feeling or refreshing;** like a winter breeze that sends shivers up your spine

unforgiving
adj. **harsh or cruel;** like the extremely cold weather at the top of a high mountain

turn over for dark and rainy words >

adj.

dark and rainy words

bleak

DEFINITION

gloomy or depressing;
like a miserable day when all your doughnuts have been eaten

SAMPLE SENTENCE

The sad stories on the morning news painted a **bleak** picture of the world.

dark and rainy words

n.

downpour

DEFINITION

a heavy rainstorm;
a big burst of rain that soaks you to the skin

SAMPLE SENTENCE

The tropical **downpour** cooled the sticky island heat.

adj.

dark and rainy words

drab

DEFINITION

dull or gray;
like a dark, gloomy day

SAMPLE SENTENCE

Oz hated her **drab** existence in a boring office.

adj.

dark and rainy words

dreary

DEFINITION

boring or miserable;
like a dull job doing the same thing over and over again

SAMPLE SENTENCE

The prisoner sighed in the **dreary** dungeon, wishing there were something to do.

adj.

dark and rainy words

ominous

DEFINITION

scary, threatening, or menacing; like a huge, dark tornado spinning toward you

SAMPLE SENTENCE

There was panic in the streets as the spaceship cast an **ominous** shadow over the city.

splattered

DEFINITION

splashed or sprinkled; like heavy raindrops that ruin your painting

SAMPLE SENTENCE

Armie was covered in **splattered** ink at the end of a long day scribbling stories.

or you can try...

Dark, rainy words!

cascading
***adj.* pouring or gushing;** like a stream of water flowing down a steep slope

cheerless
***adj.* dull or gloomy;** like a cold day when the sun does not shine

cloudburst
***n.* a storm or downpour;** a sudden, very heavy fall of rain

damp
***adj.* slightly wet or moist;** like a rainy day when everything feels wet

dismal
***adj.* dull or gloomy;** like a spell of wet weather that makes everybody miserable

dribbling
***adj.* dripping or trickling;** like rain that falls in gentle drops

drizzling
***adj.* showery or spitting;** like the weather when you can only feel a few drops of rain in the air

gloomy
***adj.* dark and dim;** like a cold and cloudy day that makes you feel miserable

grim
***adj.* dark and gloomy;** like weather that makes everything look sad and moody

intermittent
***adj.* occasional or irregular;** like showers of rain that keep stopping and then starting again

leaden
***adj.* dark or dull gray;** like the sky when it is the color of lead

miserable
***adj.* gloomy or depressing;** like bad weather that makes you feel unhappy

or you can try...

moody
***adj.* dark and miserable;** like clouds that look like they might become stormy

patchy
***adj.* in small amounts and irregular;** like rain clouds that come and go in patches across the sky

pelting
***adj.* falling quickly and heavily;** like big raindrops that hit you hard

persistent
***adj.* constant or nonstop;** like rain that keeps on falling for the whole day

pouring
***adj.* flowing or streaming;** like rain that comes down hard and completely soaks you

precipitation
***n.* rain or snow;** a substance that falls out of the clouds

sleet
***n.* rain and snow;** soft, wet flakes that are a mixture of rain and snow

smog
***n.* smoky fog;** like a thick fog that happens because the air is full of pollution

sodden
***adj.* wet or soaked;** like clothes that have got so wet that they stick to your skin

soggy
***adj.* wet and heavy;** like the ground after it has been raining for many days

somber
***adj.* dull or gloomy;** like a cloudy day when there is no sun at all

sopping
***adj.* wet and dripping;** like clothes that have been soaked by a rainstorm

sunless
***adj.* dark and cold;** like an underground cave where the sun never shines

waterlogged
***adj.* soaked or flooded;** like a field where it has rained so much that there are puddles of water

turn over for hot words >

hot words

adj.

blistering

DEFINITION

harsh or scorching;
like sun so strong it makes your skin hurt

SAMPLE SENTENCE

The **blistering** heat of the summer sun made Bearnice sweat and pant.

hot words

adj.

clammy

DEFINITION

soggy or moist;
like your skin when you
are sweaty or feverish

SAMPLE SENTENCE

Yin broke out in a nervous sweat
and gave her favorite singer
a **clammy** handshake.

hot words

gleaming

DEFINITION

shining or bright;
like teeth that have been
scrubbed clean by the dentist

SAMPLE SENTENCE

"Yarr..." whispered the pirate,
amazed by the **gleaming** gold.

hot words

adj.

oppressive

DEFINITION

heavy, harsh, or overpowering; like heat so strong you feel like it is crushing you

SAMPLE SENTENCE

The **oppressive** laws meant that you could be sent to prison just for sneezing.

perspire

perspires • perspiring • perspired

DEFINITION

to drip with sweat; what you do when you sit in a very hot sauna

SAMPLE SENTENCE

Plato was so nervous about his speech that he **perspired** visibly and sweat pooled on the floor.

hot words

adj.

radiant

DEFINITION

bright, brilliant, or glowing; like a very large and powerful light bulb

SAMPLE SENTENCE

Oz's **radiant** beauty shone out of her like bright sunbeams.

hot words

adj.

relentless

DEFINITION

constant or nonstop;
like the sun when it beats down on you until you almost melt

SAMPLE SENTENCE

When Yang got lost in the supermarket, Yin led a **relentless** search until she was found.

hot words

adj.

scorching

DEFINITION

red-hot or blazing;
the kind of heat that will toast a marshmallow

SAMPLE SENTENCE

Armie gasped for water as he crawled through the **scorching** desert.

hot words

adj.

searing

DEFINITION

burning or scorching;
like a day so hot you can fry bacon and eggs on the sidewalk

SAMPLE SENTENCE

The **searing** heat of the sun made it too unpleasant to go outside.

Action | Character | Emotion | Setting | Taste & Smell | Weather

hot words

adj.

stifling

DEFINITION

smothering or suffocating; like a day so hot it makes your skin pour with sweat

SAMPLE SENTENCE

The silence in the room was so **stifling** that nobody dared to speak.

Action | Character | Emotion | Setting | Taste & Smell | **Weather**

hot words

adj.

suffocating

DEFINITION

stuffy or smothering;
like clothes so tight around your neck you can't breathe

SAMPLE SENTENCE

Bogart took off his shirt to cool down in the **suffocating** heat.

hot words

adj.

sweltering

DEFINITION

very hot or baking;
like weather that makes you desperate for some shade

SAMPLE SENTENCE

As he watched his ice sculpture melt, Armie regretted making it on such a **sweltering** day.

Hot hot hot words!

airless
***adj.* warm and stuffy;** like weather that is hot and uncomfortable because there is no breeze

baking
***adj.* very hot and dry;** like a day when it is too hot to be out in the sun

blazing
***adj.* hot or fiery;** like a log fire with flames shooting upwards

boiling
***adj.* very hot and scorching;** like water bubbling in a kettle

flaming
***adj.* hot or fiery;** like a log that has been set on fire

glorious
***adj.* lovely or sunny;** like a perfect, bright summer day

heatwave
***n.* a very hot and sunny period;** like a time when it is so hot that you can't sleep at night

humid
***adj.* warm, damp, and muggy;** like hot weather that makes you sweaty

midsummer
***n.* the middle of the summer;** the time of year when the days are longest

muggy
***adj.* warm and damp;** like a hot day when it is likely to rain and the air is heavy

oven-like
***adj.* very hot and dry;** like when it's so hot that the air feels like the inside of an oven

piping
***adj.* hot and steaming;** like food that has come straight out of the oven

or you can try...

red-hot
***adj.* very hot or glowing with heat;** like the extremely high temperature in the middle of a fire

roasting
***adj.* very hot or baking;** like a day when everything is hot to the touch

singed
***adj.* burned or scorched;** like a jacket that is left too close to a fire and gets a black mark on it

sizzling
***adj.* hot and hissing;** like sausages cooking in a frying pan

steamy
***adj.* warm and filled with steam;** like the air in a bathroom after someone takes a hot shower

sticky
***adj.* hot and humid;** like a day when you sweat so much that your clothes cling to you

stuffy
***adj.* airless or muggy;** like a hot room where there is not enough fresh air

sultry
***adj.* hot and airless;** like weather that makes you tired and sleepy

sun-drenched
***adj.* sunny and warm;** like a Caribbean island where the sun shines all the time

sun-kissed
***adj.* sunny and warm;** like an island where the sun shines almost every day

toasty
***adj.* warm and comfortable;** like a room where a large open fire has been burning

torrid
***adj.* hot and dry;** like very hot weather that dries out the soil and kills plants

tropical
***adj.* hot and sunny;** like the weather in a country near the equator

windless
***adj.* still or calm;** like a hot day when there is no breeze at all

turn over for stormy words >

stormy words

n.

deluge

DEFINITION

a flood or overflowing water; like gushing water from a blocked toilet

SAMPLE SENTENCE

After an overnight **deluge**, Shang High woke to find his house totally flooded.

electrifying

DEFINITION

thrilling or stunning;
like something so exciting it makes you feel like there's electricity running up your spine

SAMPLE SENTENCE

Oz's **electrifying** performance had the audience standing on their seats.

stormy words

adj.

incessant

DEFINITION

endless or nonstop;
like a loud phone conversation that goes on and on and on

SAMPLE SENTENCE

Mrs Wordsmith was pleased to finally get away from the **incessant** rain in England.

stormy words

adj.

lashing

DEFINITION

thrashing or beating;
like heavy rain smacking you in the face

SAMPLE SENTENCE

The **lashing** downpour battered the roof of the hut until water started to drip through.

tempestuous

DEFINITION

stormy, wild, or violent;
when the wind and the sea
are out of control

SAMPLE SENTENCE

A **tempestuous** wind blew the
roof off Bogart's beach hut.

stormy words

adj.

torrential

DEFINITION

falling heavily or forcefully; like the rain in a violent storm

SAMPLE SENTENCE

The **torrential** thunderstorm caused flooding across the country.

or you can try...

Rough and stormy words!

apocalyptic
adj. **wild and stormy;** when the conditions are so bad that you think the world is ending

avalanche
n. **a landslide or deluge;** a sudden heavy fall of snow down a mountain

billowing
adj. **rising and swelling;** like huge waves during a storm at sea

brutal
adj. **vicious or cruel;** like a violent hurricane crashing through a city

catastrophic
adj. **harmful or terrible;** like a hurricane that destroys people's houses

destructive
adj. **harmful or damaging;** like a storm that is so strong that it causes buildings to fall down

electrical
adj. **producing electricity;** like a storm when there is thunder and lightning

furious
adj. **angry or violent;** like a wind that seems to want to blow away everything in its path

hailstorm
n. **a storm of heavy hail;** when icy snow falls from the sky

hurricane
n. **a whirlwind or cyclone;** a very powerful wind that flattens trees and buildings

impending
adj. **coming or approaching;** like a storm that is threatening to begin

menacing
adj. **threatening or scary-looking;** like black stormclouds gathering overhead

or you can try...

monsoon
***n.* a storm or downpour;** like a long spell of wet weather in India

overflowing
***adj.* flooding or spilling over;** like a river that has too much water in it after a heavy storm

powerful
***adj.* strong or forceful;** like a storm that can blow things over and damage them

rampant
***adj.* uncontrolled and destructive;** like an unstoppable storm destroying everything in its path

rattling
***adj.* shaking and knocking;** like the sound of a loose part inside a machine

reverberating
***adj.* booming or echoing;** like the sound of thunder when it shakes the walls

rumbling
***adj.* low-pitched and deep;** like the sound of thunder in the distance

savage
***adj.* wild and violent;** like a wind that seems to want to attack and hurt you

shockwave
***n.* a wave of strong force;** like the expanding, noisy blast in the air when lightning strikes

surge
***v.* to swell or rush;** what a wave does when it gets bigger and bigger during a storm

tempest
***n.* a storm or gale;** a very strong storm at sea that sinks ships

thundering
***adj.* loud and booming;** like the deafening noise that a waterfall makes

tornado
***n.* a whirlwind or cyclone;** a powerful storm when the air spins around in a circle very quickly

tumultuous
***adj.* wild and changeable;** like dramatic weather that changes all the time

turn over for wind words >

blustery

DEFINITION

windy or gusty;
like gusts of wind that turn your umbrella inside out

SAMPLE SENTENCE

One **blustery** afternoon, all of Bearnice's underwear was blown off the clothes line.

flurry

DEFINITION

a short, swirling gust;
like a burst of whirling snow that makes you snuggle into your scarf

SAMPLE SENTENCE

The brief **flurry** of snow only fell for five minutes.

gust

DEFINITION

a blast of air or strong breeze; like a puff of wind so strong it blows your doughnuts into the air

SAMPLE SENTENCE

A sudden **gust** came from nowhere and blew a wasp up Bearnice's nose.

wind words

v.

howl

howls • howling • howled

DEFINITION

to cry or wail;
what a strong wind does
when it makes a sound

SAMPLE SENTENCE

Brick **howled** angrily when he found out that his gym shoes had been filled with cheese.

wind words

n.

whirlwind

DEFINITION

a hurricane or tornado;
a violent wind that spins and sweeps everything up from the streets

SAMPLE SENTENCE

The destructive **whirlwind** uprooted trees and knocked over street lamps.

windswept

DEFINITION

windblown and untidy;
how you would look if you were blown around by the wind

SAMPLE SENTENCE

Coconuts blew off the trees in all directions on the **windswept** island.

or you can try...

Wild and windy words!

arctic
adj. **cold and snowy;** like the weather at the North Pole

bitter
adj. **cold or harsh;** like an icy wind that stings your skin

blowy
adj. **windy or gusty;** like a day when the wind blows litter all over the streets

boisterous
adj. **wild or stormy;** like a wind that creates sudden huge waves in the sea

breezy
adj. **gently windy;** like a warm day when you can still feel the wind

chilling
adj. **cold or icy;** like a wind that brings cold air with it

drafty
adj. **full of cold blasts of air;** like an old house whose windows don't keep out the wind

fierce
adj. **strong and violent;** like a wind that blows the tiles off your roof

fresh
adj. **cold and refreshing;** like a wind from the sea that makes you feel full of energy

gale
n. **a wild storm or wind;** like the weather that blows trees and garbage cans over

gentle
adj. **mild and pleasant;** like a light breeze that helps you stay cool in summer

harsh
adj. **wild and rough;** like a cold wind that causes everything to become frozen

or you can try...

icy
***adj.* cold or freezing;** like a wind that makes your fingers frozen and numb

offshore
***adj.* coming from the sea;** like a cool breeze that you feel when you are on the beach

prevailing
***adj.* usual or normal;** like the type of wind that blows on most days of the year

raging
***adj.* angry or violent;** like a wind that makes your window frames rattle during a thunderstorm

rising
***adj.* starting up and getting stronger;** like a wind that starts off gentle but ends up blowing really hard

roaring
***adj.* thunderous or booming;** like wind that sounds like an angry lion

squally
***adj.* windy and violent;** like the weather when you get sudden unexpected bursts of wind

stiff
***adj.* fairly strong or forceful;** like a wind that makes you turn up the collar of your coat

turbulent
***adj.* violent and unstable;** like a powerful wind that can make a little boat capsize

unsettled
***adj.* changing and uncertain;** like the wind when it stops and starts

violent
***adj.* strong and destructive;** like a wind that can tear up trees and damage buildings

whistling
***adj.* sounding high and sharp;** like the noise you make when you blow air through your teeth

wild
***adj.* violent or stormy;** like a wind that creates a sandstorm in a desert

wintry
***adj.* cold or icy;** like a chilly day when you need to wear a scarf and gloves

turn over for weather nouns >

97 whistling weather nouns

Deafening thunder or perfect blue skies? Discover the nouns and word pairs that will transform your story from a gentle breeze into an unstoppable whirlwind.

FORECAST

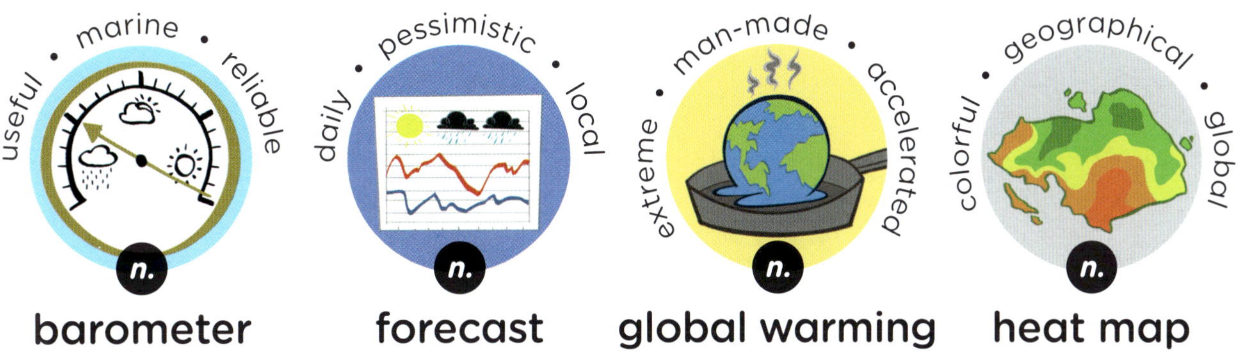

useful • marine • reliable
n.
barometer

daily • pessimistic • local
n.
forecast

extreme • man-made • accelerated
n.
global warming

colorful • geographical • global
n.
heat map

old • global • interactive
n.
map

respected • renowned • incompetent
n.
meteorologist

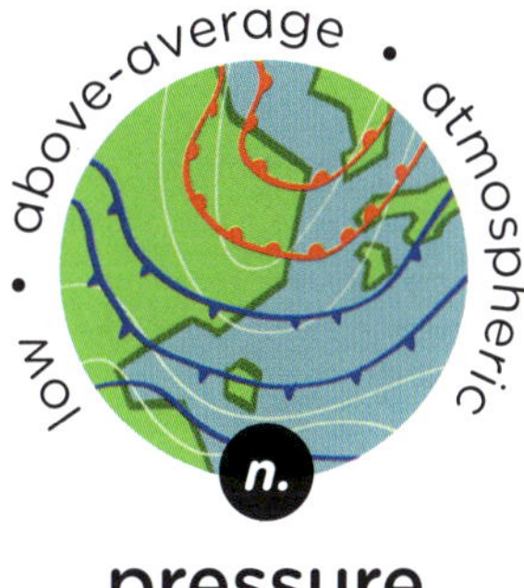

low • above-average • atmospheric
n.
pressure

powerful • early-warning
n.
radar

environmental • electronic • network
n.
sensor

poor • limited • reduced
n.
visibility

rising • freezing • boiling
n.
temperature

how hot or cold something is; like the difference in how the air feels between winter and summer

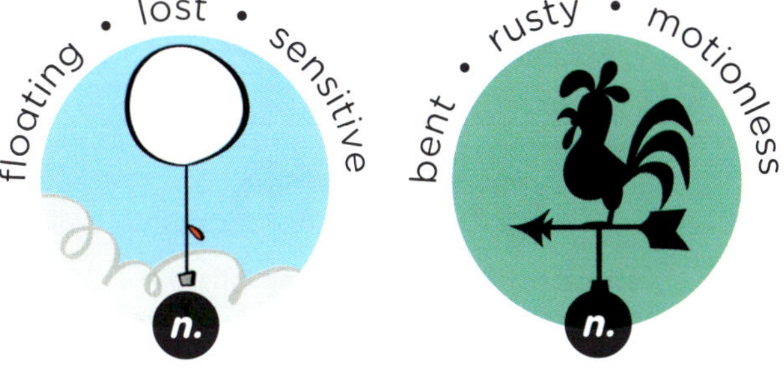

floating • lost • sensitive
n.
weather balloon

bent • rusty • motionless
n.
weathervane

SEASONS > FALL

SEASONS > SPRING

growth

the process of getting bigger or better; like a plant bursting from the ground in spring

SEASONS > SPRING

SEASONS > SUMMER

the energy that makes things hotter; like the warmth coming from the sun on a summer's day

SEASONS > SUMMER

SEASONS > WINTER

WEATHER CONDITIONS > CLOUDY

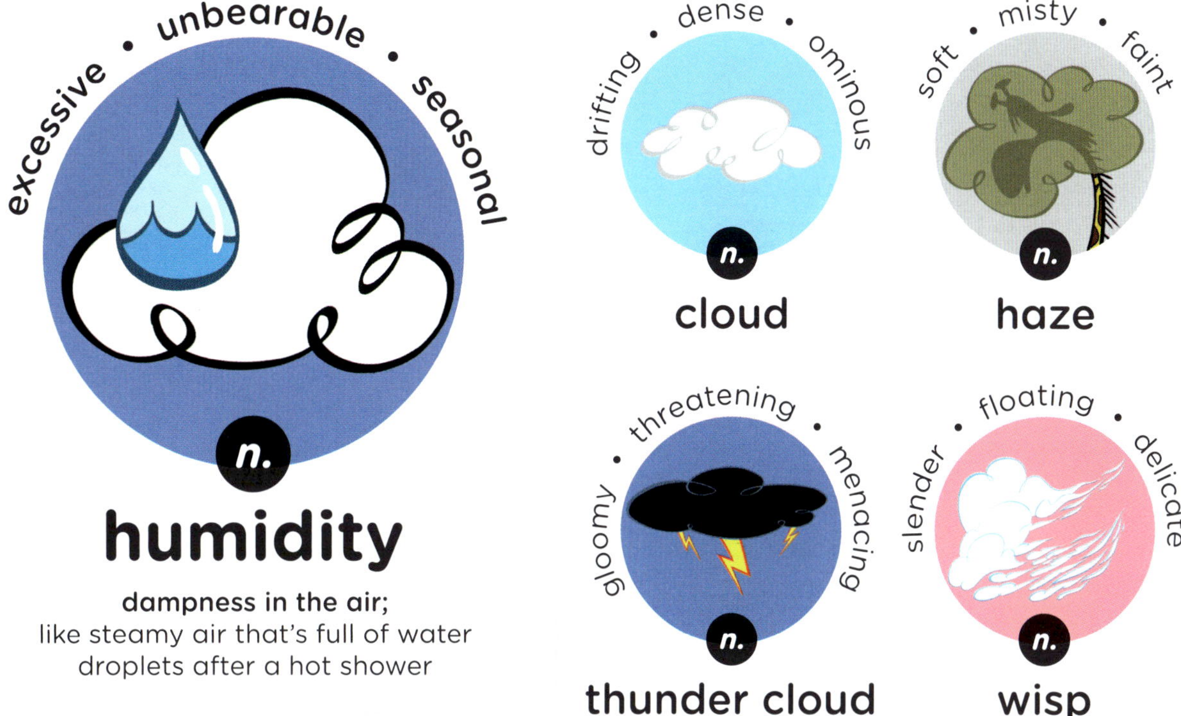

dampness in the air;
like steamy air that's full of water droplets after a hot shower

WEATHER CONDITIONS > EXTREME

WEATHER CONDITIONS > FOGGY

pollution

harmful fumes or dirty waste; like the smoke from a factory that's bad for the environment

WEATHER CONDITIONS > RAINY

WEATHER CONDITIONS > SUNNY

WEATHER CONDITIONS > WINDY

A

abandoned
adj. left or deserted

abnormal
adj. unusual or uncommon

above-average
adj. more than the normal amount

absolute
adj. total or complete

abstract
adj. showing ideas, not real things

abundant
adj. having a large amount or plenty

accelerated
adj. quicker or happening faster

accidental
adj. happening by chance

accomplished
adj. highly trained or skilled

accumulated
adj. piled up over time

accurate
adj. showing correct information

accusing
adj. saying someone is guilty

aching
adj. in constant dull pain

activated
adj. made to start working

addictive
adj. something you really want more of

adjustable
adj. able to be resized or adjusted

adorable
adj. cute, charming, or lovable

advanced
adj. using the latest technology

advancing
adj. moving forward

afternoon
n. time between noon and evening

aged
adj. allowed to mature

agile
adj. able to move quickly and easily

airborne
adj. in the air or flying

airtight
adj. sealed so that no air gets in

airy
adj. open and full of fresh air

alien
n. a creature from outer space

all-you-can-eat
adj. with unlimited portions

alleged
adj. reported or said without proof

alluring
adj. tempting or drawing you in

alpine
adj. relating to high mountains

amazing
adj. stunning or astonishing

amphibious
adj. suited for both land and water

ancient
adj. very old or from long ago

angelic
adj. like an angel

angry
adj. wild, raging, or out of control

ankle-deep
adj. deep enough to cover your feet

annoying
adj. irritating or maddening

annual
adj. every year or in one year

anonymous
adj. unnamed or unknown

antigravity
adj. acting against gravity

antique
adj. old and precious

approaching
adj. coming closer

April
n. the fourth month of the year

arch
adj. main or chief

arched
adj. curved or bent

architectural
adj. to design buildings with

arid
adj. very dry or barren

aristocratic
adj. belonging to a grand family

armed
adj. carrying a weapon

armored
adj. protected or covered by metal

aromatic
adj. having a strong, pleasant smell

artisan
adj. run by a skilled worker

artistic
adj. creative or imaginative

aspiring
adj. ambitious, hopeful, or budding

asthmatic
adj. suffering from asthma

athletic
adj. fit and strong

atmospheric
adj. in the air or atmosphere

A - B

atomic
adj. used for looking at atoms

attentive
adj. helpful and paying attention

austere
adj. harsh and bare

authentic
adj. real or made in the proper way

automated
adj. done using machines

automatic
adj. working by itself

available
adj. free to use

average
adj. ordinary or typical

avid
adj. very keen or enthusiastic

avocado
n. a pear-shaped, green fruit

avoidable
adj. unnecessary or needless

award-winning
adj. having won awards or prizes

babbling
adj. making a continuous noise

back-up
adj. used if the original doesn't work

bad
adj. not good or low quality

baggy
adj. too big or hanging loosely

baked
[1] *adj.* cooked in an oven
[2] *adj.* dried in an oven

bald
adj. without hair

balmy
adj. pleasantly warm or mild

balsamic
adj. dark, sweet, and strong-tasting

bamboo
Go ask a panda!

bandaged
adj. wrapped in protective cloth

barbed-wire
adj. covered in sharp and spiky wire

bare
adj. naked or not covered

barren
adj. with nothing growing in it

basic
adj. only with the important parts

battered
adj. beaten and damaged

beached
adj. lying stranded on a beach

beachfront
adj. looking out over a beach

beachside
adj. next to a beach

beaded
adj. in small, round drops

beady-eyed
adj. with small, shiny, round eyes

bearskin
adj. made from the skin of a bear

beastly
adj. unkind, savage, or cruel

beaten
adj. whisked into a smooth liquid

beating
adj. pounding or drumming

beautiful
You!

bedraggled
adj. messed up and untidy

bejeweled
adj. decorated with jewels

belching
adj. sending out smoke or flames

beloved
adj. deeply loved or precious

bent
adj. twisted, curved, or crooked

big-bellied
adj. having a large belly

big-city
adj. found in a large city

billionaire
n. a person with billions of dollars

billowing
adj. swelling or bulging in the wind

biodegradable
adj. rotting away naturally in soil

bitter
[1] *adj.* angry or grudging [2] *adj.* cold or harsh [3] *adj.* sharp or not sweet

bittersweet
[1] *adj.* making you feel sad and happy
[2] *adj.* tasting both bitter and sweet

black
adj. the darkest color

blackened
adj. turned black

blank
adj. empty or plain

blaring
adj. loud or booming

blazing
adj. very hot or burning

bleak
adj. gloomy or depressing

bleating
adj. making a crying sound

blind
adj. without thinking or judging

B

blinding
[1] *adj.* so bright that you can't see
[2] *adj.* so thick you can't see through

blinking
adj. quickly turning on and off again

blistered
adj. having sore, swollen bubbles

blistering
adj. so hot that your skin blisters

bloated
adj. full and swollen

blocked
adj. not letting things go through

bloodshot
adj. red, sore, and tired

bloodsucking
adj. blood-drinking

bloody
adj. stained or smeared with blood

blooming
adj. producing a flower

blotchy
adj. uneven or patchy

blueberry
n. a small and sweet berry

Bluetooth
n. wireless, short-range connection

blunt
adj. not having a sharp edge

boiled
adj. cooked in very hot water

boiling
[1] *adj.* very hot and bubbling
[2] *adj.* very hot or scorching

bold
adj. brave or daring

bony
[1] *adj.* made of bone or bone-like
[2] *adj.* skinny or scrawny

booming
adj. loud or thundering

borrowed
adj. taken to be used for a short time

botched
adj. done badly or messed up

bottomless
adj. very deep or endless

bouncing
adj. springing off the ground

bouncy
like all the best castles

boundless
adj. never-ending or limitless

bountiful
adj. generous or abundant

bowed
adj. lowered or looking down

branded
adj. stamped or marked with a logo

brave
adj. bold and daring

breathtaking
adj. beautiful or stunning

brief
adj. lasting for a short time

bright
adj. shining, radiant, or colorful

brilliant
adj. bright or shiny

brisk
adj. cold and fresh

bristly
adj. short, stiff, and spiky

brittle
adj. fragile or breakable

broad
adj. wide or long from side to side

broken
[1] *adj.* hurt or despairing [2] *adj.* not working or injured [3] *adj.* smashed or shattered

bronzed
adj. tanned or bronze-colored

brooding
adj. looking intense and sad

broody
adj. ready to lay eggs and sit on them

brown
the same color as chocolate - yum!

bruised
adj. bashed and discolored

brutal
adj. violent, cruel, or savage

bubbling
adj. frothing, foaming, or gurgling

bug-eyed
adj. with bulging, sticking-out eyes

built-in
[1] *adj.* fixed or fitted in [2] *adj.* fixed or fitted into the roof [3] *adj.* fixed or fitted into the walls

bulging
adj. swollen or sticking out

bulky
adj. big or taking up a lot of space

bulletproof
adj. able to block bullets

bumbling
adj. awkward, clumsy, or useless

buoyant
adj. light and able to float

burned
adj. spoiled by heat or overcooked

burned-out
adj. charred and destroyed by fire

burst
adj. broken, torn, or split open

bursting
adj. breaking or splitting open

bushy
adj. thick and full

B - C

bustling
adj. crowded or lively

busy
[1] *adj.* full of people
[2] *adj.* with lots of jobs to do

buttered
adj. covered in butter

buttery
adj. rich and creamy, like butter

buzzing
adj. making a continuous, low noise

caged
adj. kept in a cage

calloused
adj. hardened or roughened

calm
adj. still and peaceful

camouflaged
adj. blending into the background

candied
adj. preserved in sugar syrup

canned
adj. kept in a sealed can

capsized
adj. upside down or flipped

captive
adj. kept prisoner or caged in

captured
adj. caught or taken by force

caramelized
adj. cooked slowly and sweet

carpeted
adj. covered with a carpet

cascading
adj. gushing or falling down quickly

cast-iron
n. easily molded black metal

catastrophic
adj. disastrous or destructive

celebrity
No, you can't have my autograph.

ceramic
adj. made of baked clay

challenging
adj. difficult or dangerous

chaotic
adj. wild and confusing

charming
[1] *adj.* attractive and likable [2] *adj.* attractive or adorable [3] *adj.* attractive or delightful

charred
adj. burned or blackened by heat

cheap
adj. not expensive or low-priced

cheesy
adj. with cheese on top or inside

chemical
adj. made of chemicals or man-made

chewy
adj. tough or hard to chew

chic
adj. stylish or fashionable

chicken
n. a bird used in cooking

chilled
adj. cooled in a fridge

chipped
adj. with a small piece broken off

chiseled
adj. perfectly carved or sculpted

choking
adj. making it hard to breathe

chopped
adj. cut or sliced into pieces

choppy
adj. with lots of little waves

chronic
adj. continuous or long-lasting

chubby
adj. a little fat or round

chunky
adj. thick or with big pieces

cinematic
adj. like something from a movie

circling
adj. moving around in circles

citric
adj. acidic, lemony, and sharp

clammy
adj. soggy, moist, and sticky

clandestine
adj. undercover or secret

clanking
adj. rattling, jangling, or clattering

classic
adj. popular since a long time ago

clattering
adj. noisy and rattling

clean
adj. washed or without any dirt

clear
[1] *adj.* easy to hear or understand [2] *adj.* easy to see through [3] *adj.* easy to spot or notice

clenched
adj. grasped or closed tightly

clever
[1] *adj.* skillful and cunning [2] *adj.* smart or cunning [3] *adj.* well-designed or high-tech

clipped
adj. cut short or trimmed

clogged
adj. blocked or stuffed

close
[1] *adj.* knowing each other very well
[2] *adj.* only won by a few points

clotted
[1] *adj.* dried or thickened into chunks
[2] *adj.* thickened or mixed until it's stiff

cloudless
adj. clear or without clouds

C

cluttered
adj. messy or littered

coarse
adj. rough or scratchy

coastal
adj. on the coast or beside the sea

cobbled
adj. surface made of round stones

cold
Brrrrrrrr.

collapsed
adj. fallen down or crumpled

collected
adj. picked or brought together

colonized
adj. taken as a new place to live

colorful
adj. brightly colored or not dull

colossal
adj. massive or gigantic

comfortable
[1] *adj.* cozy or snug
[2] *adj.* easy to wear and the right size

comfy
adj. soft or nice to wear

comical
adj. funny or amusing

common
adj. ordinary or usual

communal
adj. used by everyone or shared

compact
adj. small and neat

competitive
[1] *adj.* to do with winning and losing
[2] *adj.* wanting to be the best

complete
adj. has all the parts

composting
adj. rotting to be used as fertilizer

concealed
adj. hidden or secret

concealing
adj. hiding something

confusing
Huh?

congested
adj. blocked or too crowded

considerable
adj. big and noticeable

contaminated
[1] *adj.* spoiled by dirt or pollution
[2] *adj.* spoiled or ruined

contemporary
adj. in a modern style

cookie
heavenly circles of deliciousness

cool
adj. popular or fashionable

correct
adj. right or in order

corroded
adj. worn down or burned away

corrosive
adj. harmful or burning

corrugated
adj. ridged or wavy

corrupt
[1] *adj.* dishonest or misusing power
[2] *adj.* ruined or full of mistakes

countless
adj. too many to be counted

covert
adj. secret or undercover

coveted
adj. wanted by lots of people

cowardly
adj. afraid or not confident

cowboy
Yee-haw!!!

cozy
adj. warm and comfortable

cracked
adj. split or with broken lines

crackling
adj. making small, sharp noises

crackly
adj. making short, harsh noises

cramped
adj. small or without enough room

crashed
[1] *adj.* fallen to the ground or smashed
[2] *adj.* smashed into something

crashing
adj. smashing loudly against things

creaky
adj. noisy when stepped on

creamed
adj. blended, smooth, and soft

creamy
adj. as smooth and soft as cream

credible
adj. easy to believe or reliable

creeping
adj. moving slowly over a surface

creepy
adj. scary or spooky

crescent
adj. curved or in a semicircle shape

crisp
adj. cold and fresh

crispy
adj. thin, dry, and crunchy

crooked
adj. bent or wonky

crowded
adj. full of people or things

crude
adj. made very simply or badly

C - D

cruel
adj. mean or unkind

cruising
adj. sailing or traveling

crumbling
adj. falling down little by little

crumpled
adj. crushed out of shape

crunchy
[1] *adj.* making a crushing noise
[2] *adj.* making a noise when you bite

crushed
adj. broken by squeezing or pressing

crushing
adj. squashing or smashing

cuddly
adj. soft and huggable

cunning
adj. clever or crafty

curdled
adj. separated into lumpy bits

cured
adj. dried or smoked to last longer

curious
adj. wanting to find out more

curly
adj. curved or spiraled

curried
adj. flavored with spices

curved
adj. rounded or bent

custom-made
adj. made specially for you

cute
adj. sweet or lovable

cutting-edge
adj. using advanced technology

cynical
adj. negative or full of doubt

daily
adj. for each new day

dairy-free
adj. free from animal milk products

damaging
adj. harmful or destructive

damp
adj. slightly wet or soggy

dangerous
adj. unsafe or likely to cause harm

dapper
adj. neat and stylish

dappled
adj. marked with spots or patches

daring
adj. brave or bold

dark
[1] *adj.* any color close to black
[2] *adj.* with little or no light

dated
adj. old-fashioned or from the past

daunting
adj. seems scary or intimidating

daytime
adj. while the sun is up

dazzling
adj. very bright or amazing

dead
[1] *adj.* no longer alive
[2] *adj.* out of energy

dead-end
adj. with no way out the other side

deadly
adj. dangerous or life-threatening

deafening
adj. very loud or noisy

debilitating
adj. weakening or holding you back

decadent
adj. very luxurious or indulgent

decisive
adj. answering or settling a problem

decorated
adj. made prettier by adding things

dedicated
adj. committed or devoted

deep
adj. goes far down below the top

deep-fried
adj. cooked by being dipped in hot oil

deep-set
adj. fixed or firmly in something

deep-water
adj. growing in very deep water

defective
adj. broken or not working properly

defined
adj. obvious, clear, or outlined

deflated
adj. flat or with the air let out

delayed
adj. later than expected

delectable
adj. very tasty or delicious

delicate
[1] *adj.* fine, elegant, and detailed [2] *adj.* fragile and breakable [3] *adj.* with a mild or subtle flavor

delicious
adj. tasty or enjoyable to eat or drink

dense
adj. thick, solid, or heavy

dented
adj. pushed in from being hit

dependable
adj. reliable or always works well

derailed
adj. driven off the tracks

derelict
adj. run-down or left to fall apart

D - E

deserted
adj. empty or abandoned

desiccated
adj. completely dried out

desolate
adj. bleak, bare, and empty

desperate
adj. anxious, frantic, or without hope

destructive
adj. damaging or devastating

detached
adj. not joined onto another building

detailed
adj. packed with info and facts

devastating
adj. very damaging and destructive

devious
adj. cheating, sneaky, or sly

dewy
adj. covered in little water droplets

diced
adj. chopped into small cubes

die-hard
adj. unchanging or never giving up

digital
adj. using electronics or computers

dilapidated
adj. ruined, run-down, or shabby

dim
adj. faint or not shining brightly

dim-witted
adj. silly or not clever

dimmed
adj. turned down

dingy
adj. dark or gloomy

direct
adj. straight or uninterrupted

dirty
adj. unclean or mucky

discarded
adj. thrown away or rejected

disgusting
adj. gross or revolting

dismal
adj. dark and depressing

disorganized
adj. messy or cluttered

dispersed
adj. spread out over a big area

disposable
adj. thrown away after it's used

distant
adj. far away or faint

distinctive
adj. easy to identify or recognize

distorted
adj. twisted or bent out of shape

disused
adj. not used any more

doomed
adj. unlucky or heading for disaster

double-breasted
adj. overlapping flaps at the front

double-decker
adj. with two floors or decks

downward
adj. toward the ground

downy
adj. filled with soft feathers

drafty
adj. breezy and cold inside

drained
adj. run-down or empty

drawn
adj. closed or pulled shut

dreary
adj. dull and miserable

dried
[1] *adj.* dehydrated or sun-baked
[2] *adj.* dehydrated to make it last

drifting
adj. floating gently away

dripping
adj. wet and with droplets falling off

driverless
adj. automatic and without a driver

drizzled
adj. sprinkled or poured carefully

droning
adj. constantly humming or buzzing

drooling
adj. dribbling or slobbering

drooping
adj. hanging down or sagging

dry
adj. not wet or damp

dull
adj. blunt or not sharp

durable
adj. strong and lasting a long time

dusty
adj. full of dust, dried mud, or soot

dwindling
adj. getting smaller and weaker

eager
adj. excited and enthusiastic

ear-splitting
adj. so loud that it hurt your ears

early
adj. sooner than expected

early-warning
adj. giving a warning ahead of time

eclipsed
adj. blocked out by another thing

E – F

edible
adj. safe to eat

eerie
adj. weird, ghostly, or creepy

effective
adj. working well

ejectable
adj. can be sent flying

elaborate
adj. complex, detailed, or fancy

elbow-length
adj. reaching up to your elbows

electric
adj. powered by electricity

electrified
adj. charged with electricity

electronic
adj. powered by electricity

elegant
adj. graceful and grand

elongated
adj. made longer or stretched

elusive
adj. difficult to find or catch

embroidered
adj. with a stitched design

empty
adj. with nothing inside

enchanted
adj. under a magic spell

encrypted
adj. hidden or protected by a code

endangered
adj. likely to go extinct soon

endless
adj. unlimited or with no end

engraved
adj. with a design carved in

enormous
adj. really big or huge

enraged
adj. very angry or furious

enviable
adj. making other people jealous

environmental
adj. to do with the natural world

erratic
adj. unpredictable or unreliable

escaped
adj. running free

essential
adj. very important or necessary

ethical
adj. moral, honest, and fair

evil
adj. bad or wicked

excess
adj. more than you need

excessive
adj. too much or over the top

excited
adj. lively or enthusiastic

exclusive
adj. only letting a few people in

exotic
adj. unusual and from far away

expensive
adj. costing a lot of money

experimental
adj. testing or based on new ideas

exploding
adj. bursting, popping, or blowing up

exposed
adj. bare or not covered

expressive
adj. showing a lot of emotion

exquisite
adj. excellent or magnificent

external
adj. outside or separate

extortionate
adj. too much or overly expensive

extra
adj. more than the usual

extreme
adj. strong, intense, or severe

fabulous
adj. amazing or wonderful

faded
adj. faint or worn-out

fading
adj. slowly losing its color

failing
adj. not working properly

faint
adj. slight or barely noticeable

faithful
adj. loyal and devoted

fake
adj. not real or not natural

fallen
adj. having dropped to the ground

falling
adj. dropping to the ground

family-owned
adj. owned by one family

famous
adj. known by lots of people

fancy
adj. decorative or expensive

faraway
adj. distant or not nearby

farmed
adj. produced on a farm or fishery

F

fast
Blink and you might miss it.

fast-growing
adj. getting bigger quickly

fast-moving
adj. moving or spreading quickly

fat
adj. round or with a lot of flesh

fatty
adj. with a lot of fat

faulty
adj. not working properly

favorite
adj. liked more than all the others

fearsome
adj. frightening or menacing

feathered
adj. soft and cut at different lengths

feathery
adj. light and soft, like feathers

fenced-in
adj. surrounded by a fence

fermented
adj. gone sour

ferocious
adj. fierce or violent

fertile
adj. fruitful or able to grow things

fierce
adj. violent or savage

fiery
[1] *adj.* burning or producing fire
[2] *adj.* very spicy or hot-tasting

filthy
adj. disgustingly dirty or mucky

fine
[1] *adj.* excellent or top-quality
[2] *adj.* light, thin, or wispy

finest
adj. best or nicest

fireproof
adj. protected against fire

firm
adj. hard or solid

first
adj. at the beginning or before others

first-degree
adj. mild or not very harmful

fishy
adj. tasting or smelling like fish

fitted
adj. made to be the right shape

five-star
adj. of the highest standard

flaky
adj. breaking easily into flakes

flaming
adj. on fire or burning

flamingo
n. a bright pink bird with a long neck

flapping
adj. moving quickly up and down

flared
adj. opened or made wider

flashing
adj. quickly switching on and off

flat
adj. smooth and even

flat-screen
adj. thin and not curved

flattened
adj. squashed or made flat

flattering
adj. making you look better

fleeing
adj. running away or escaping

flesh-eating
adj. eating the meat of humans

flexible
adj. able to bend without breaking

flickering
adj. burning or shining unsteadily

flightless
adj. not able to fly

flimsy
adj. weak, thin, or easy to break

floating
[1] *adj.* sitting on top of the water
[2] *adj.* staying up in the air

flooded
adj. covered with too much water

floppy
adj. limp or hanging loosely

floral
adj. with a flowery pattern

floured
adj. dusted with a layer of flour

flowering
adj. producing flowers

flowing
adj. hanging loosely and smoothly

fluffy
[1] *adj.* light and full of air
[2] *adj.* wooly, fleecy, and soft

fluorescent
[1] *adj.* producing a bright light
[2] *adj.* vividly colorful and bright

fluttering
adj. with wings flapping up and down

flying
adj. moving through the air

foaming
adj. frothing or making tiny bubbles

folded
adj. with one part turned over

folding
adj. able to be made smaller or neater

fond
adj. loving or affectionate

F - G

foot-long
the length of a grown-up's smelly foot

forensic
adj. using science to find the truth

formal
adj. right for important occasions

formidable
adj. impressive and intimidating

fortune
n. luck or chance in life

fossilized
adj. preserved in a rock

foul
adj. disgusting or revolting

fragile
adj. easy to break or ruin

fragrant
adj. sweet-smelling or perfumed

frayed
adj. with worn-out edges

free
adj. without any cost or payment

free-flying
adj. able to move easily in the air

free-range
adj. not raised in small cages

freezing
adj. below zero or very cold

frenzied
adj. wildly excited or frantic

fresh
adj. made or created recently

freshly baked
adj. just out of the oven

freshly squeezed
adj. recently pressed from fruit

fried
adj. cooked in a pan with oil

friendly
adj. kind, sociable, and welcoming

frightened
adj. scared or fearful

front
adj. on the side that faces forward

frosted
adj. covered with frosting

frosty
adj. freezing or icy

frothy
adj. foamy and bubbly

frozen
adj. iced-over or kept in a freezer

fruit
n. a sweet, healthy food from plants

fruity
adj. tasting or smelling like fruit

full
adj. complete or without empty space

full-length
adj. as long as your body

fully stocked
adj. with everything you might need

fur-lined
adj. with a layer of fur inside

furious
adj. wild, angry, and violent

furry
adj. soft, fluffy, and hairy

futuristic
[1] *adj.* using the latest technology
[2] *adj.* with a very modern design

fuzzy
adj. wooly, fluffy, or frizzy

galloping
adj. racing or sprinting

gaping
adj. open very wide

gargantuan
adj. huge or enormous

garish
adj. much too bright and flashy

gaudy
adj. bright, glaring, or flashy

gaunt
adj. far too thin and scrawny

general
adj. common or from all around

genetic
adj. involving DNA or genes

gentle
adj. calm, soft, or mild

geographical
adj. to do with a certain area

ghostly
[1] *adj.* creepy or like a ghost
[2] *adj.* creepy or scary

giant
fee, fi, fo, fum

gifted
adj. talented or skilled

gigantic
adj. huge or enormous

gladiator
n. an armed Roman warrior

glass
adj. made of a clear, hard material

glazed
adj. with a thin layer of frosting

gleaming
adj. shining or bright

glimmering
adj. glowing faintly or twinkling

glistening
adj. shining or sparkling

glitching
adj. not working properly

G - H

glitchy
adj. often working incorrectly

glittering
adj. shiny or sparkling

global
adj. of the whole world

gloomy
adj. dark and depressing

glorious
adj. beautiful and magnificent

glossy
adj. shiny and smooth

glowing
[1] *adj.* bright and healthy-looking
[2] *adj.* bright or shining

gluten-free
adj. without gluten

glutinous
adj. sticky, gooey, or glue-like

golden
adj. of the color of gold

gooey
adj. with a soft and sticky texture

goopy
adj. thick and sticky

gossipy
adj. talking about other people

graceful
adj. elegant and beautiful

gracious
adj. polite, kind, and pleasant

gradual
adj. happening slowly

grand
adj. big and impressive

grassy
adj. like grass or covered in grass

grated
adj. cut into thin slices by a grater

grazed
adj. lightly scraped and bleeding

grazing
adj. slowly eating grass

greasy
adj. oily or waxy

greedy
adj. wanting too much

green
You don't need help with this one!

greenish
adj. slightly green

grilled
adj. cooked on a hot grill

grim
adj. serious, gloomy, or unpleasant

grimy
adj. dirty or covered with grime

gristly
adj. with hard-to-chew tough bits

grizzly
adj. with patches of gray

groaning
adj. creaking under heavy weight

groomed
adj. looked after or styled

growling
adj. making noise due to hunger

grubby
adj. a little dirty or grimy

gruesome
adj. horrible or disgusting to look at

grunting
adj. making a short, low sound

gushing
adj. coming out quickly

hacked
adj. broken into with a computer

hairy
adj. covered with hairs

half-eaten
adj. only partly eaten

half-finished
adj. only partly finished

halved
adj. cut into two equal pieces

hand-painted
adj. painted by a person

hand-picked
adj. picked by a person

handheld
adj. small enough to hold

handmade
adj. made by a person

handwritten
adj. written with a pen or pencil

handy
adj. helpful or convenient

hanging
adj. drooping or dangling

hard
adj. solid or firm

hard-fought
adj. played with lots of effort

hardened
adj. harder than before or not soft

harmful
adj. dangerous or unhealthy

harmless
adj. not causing harm or damage

harnessed
adj. wearing straps for guiding

harsh
adj. sharp or unpleasantly intense

haunted
adj. lived in by ghosts

H - I

hazardous
adj. dangerous or unsafe

headless
adj. without a head

healthy
adj. fit and well or good for you

heaped
adj. in a big pile or completely full

heart-shaped
adj. in the shape of a heart

hearty
adj. filling and wholesome

heated
adj. made hot or warm

heavy
[1] *adj.* sad or miserable [2] *adj.* weighty, thick, or hard to lift [3] *adj.* forceful or in big amounts

heavy-duty
adj. not easily worn out

heavyweight
adj. above the normal weight

helpless
adj. weak, powerless, or unprotected

herbal
adj. made using herbs

hidden
adj. secret or kept out of sight

high
adj. tall or near the top

high-end
adj. expensive or luxury

high-powered
adj. with a lot of power or energy

high-rise
adj. in a tall, multi-story building

high-security
adj. strictly guarded or protected

high-tech
adj. using the latest science

hilarious
adj. very funny or hysterical

hilly
adj. with lots of hills

hissing
adj. making a 'sssss' sound

holey
adj. full of holes

hollow
adj. empty or with nothing inside

homemade
adj. made at home

homing
adj. able to find and hit a target

honking
adj. beeping or hooting

hooked
adj. curved or bent

hopping
adj. jumping or leaping

horned
adj. with a horn on its head

horrific
adj. terrible and shocking

horse-drawn
adj. pulled by horses

hostile
adj. unfriendly and aggressive

hot
the flavor of Word Sauce

hovering
adj. floating or fluttering in the air

howling
adj. crying or wailing

huge
adj. very big or enormous

hulking
adj. big and heavy

human
Look in a mirror!

humble
adj. modest, plain, and simple

humid
adj. muggy or with damp air

humming
adj. making a continuous sound

hunched
adj. bent over or arched

hungry
Warning: This dictionary is not edible.

hurtling
adj. moving very fast or rushing

hydroelectric
adj. using water to make electricity

hypnotic
adj. mesmerizing or captivating

ice-cold
adj. as cold as ice

iced
adj. served cold and with ice

iconic
adj. famous and recognizable

icy
adj. with ice or covered in ice

idyllic
adj. ideal or perfect

illegal
adj. against the law

immaculate
adj. perfect or spotless

immense
adj. very large or huge

immersive
adj. making you completely involved

immortal
adj. living forever or never dying

I - K

immune
adj. not affected by certain illnesses

impenetrable
adj. dense or inaccessible

important
adj. valuable or significant

imported
adj. brought from another country

imposing
adj. grand or impressive

impractical
adj. not useful or sensible

impregnable
adj. impossible to enter or defeat

impressive
adj. admirably good or big

incessant
adj. constant or never stopping

incoming
adj. approaching or arriving

incompetent
adj. lacking skill or useless

incorrect
adj. wrong or not accurate

incurable
adj. unable to be made better

indestructible
adj. impossible to break or destroy

indulgent
adj. luxurious or pampering

industrial
adj. relating to factories or industry

industrious
adj. hard-working

infected
adj. affected by virus or disease

infinite
adj. going on forever

inflatable
adj. able to be filled with air

inflated
adj. filled with air

infrared
adj. using invisible light rays

ingenious
adj. clever and inventive

ingrown
adj. growing backwards or sideways

injured
adj. hurt or wounded

innocent
adj. harmless, pure, or not guilty

innovative
adj. new, advanced, and original

inquisitive
adj. wanting to discover things

inspiring
adj. exciting and motivating

instant
adj. immediate or very quick to make

intelligent
adj. clever or able to work things out

intense
adj. strong, powerful, or extreme

interactive
adj. responding to what you do

international
adj. involving different countries

interplanetary
adj. going between planets

interstellar
adj. going between stars

intoxicating
adj. making you feel drunk

intruding
adj. going where not wanted

intrusive
adj. unwelcome and annoying

intuitive
adj. easily understood without training

invasive
adj. growing aggressively

invigorating
adj. making you feel lively and alert

invisible
adj. impossible to see

inviting
adj. attractive or tempting

iridescent
adj. colored like a rainbow

isolated
adj. alone or far from others

itchy
adj. making you want to scratch

ivy-covered
adj. covered with a climbing plant

jagged
adj. with sharp or pointy edges

jealous
adj. wanting what someone else has

jittery
adj. nervous, scared, and jumpy

jolly
adj. happy and joyful

jolting
adj. moving suddenly and roughly

juicy
adj. full of juice or moisture

jumbo
adj. especially big or large

key
adj. important or essential

khaki
adj. grayish-green

K – L

killer
adj. deadly or dangerous

kind
adj. friendly, generous, and caring

knee-high
adj. reaching up to your knees

knitted
adj. made by knitting wool

knobby
adj. with lumps and bumps

lakeside
adj. next to a lake

lanky
adj. tall, thin, and ungraceful

lapping
adj. gently flowing or splashing

large
adj. big or great in size

late-night
adj. staying open late at night

latest
adj. newest or most recent

lazy
adj. not working hard

leafless
adj. bare and without leaves

leafy
adj. with lots of leaves

leaky
adj. letting water in through holes

leather
adj. made of animal skin

leather-clad
adj. covered in leather

leering
adj. gazing, ogling, or gawking

leftover
adj. uneaten by the end of a meal

legendary
adj. famous or told of in stories

lethal
adj. deadly or very harmful

life-saving
adj. able to cure people

life-size
adj. full-size or the actual size

lifelike
adj. very like a living thing

lifelong
adj. for your whole life

light
adj. not thick or heavy

lightweight
[1] *adj.* thin or not heavy
[2] *adj.* thin or not weighing much

limited
adj. not very good or poor

lingering
adj. lasting or not ending

lit
adj. on fire or burning

littered
adj. covered in trash or messy

little
adj. small or tiny

live
adj. not dead

livid
adj. raging or furious

loaded
adj. full or carrying a lot

loathsome
adj. making you feel hatred

local
adj. in or from a nearby area

locked
adj. sealed shut with a lock and key

lofty
adj. very tall or high up

lone
adj. on its own or solitary

lonely
adj. alone or isolated

long
[1] *adj.* far from beginning to end
[2] *adj.* lasting a while or not fast

long-lasting
adj. not ending quickly

longtime
adj. for many years

loose
adj. baggy or not tight

loose-leaf
adj. made using loose tea leaves

lopsided
adj. drooping or leaning to one side

lost
W-w-where am I? HELP!

loud
adj. noisy or easy to hear

lovable
adj. adorable or sweet

low
adj. less than the normal amount

low-fat
adj. not containing much fat

low-flying
adj. flying low in the sky

low-sodium
adj. not containing much sodium

loyal
adj. faithful and reliable

lucky
adj. bringing good luck

lukewarm
adj. a little warm

L - M

luminous
adj. bright, shining, or glowing

lumpy
adj. uneven or with lots of bumps

lurking
adj. hiding and waiting to attack

luscious
adj. rich, sweet, and delicious

lush
adj. rich and growing healthily

luxurious
adj. very comfortable and expensive

luxury
n. richness or comfort

magic
n. mysterious or unexplained power

magical
[1] *adj.* with mysterious power
[2] *adj.* wonderful or special

magnificent
adj. very beautiful or impressive

majestic
adj. beautiful or powerful

makeshift
adj. temporary and not very good

malfunctioning
adj. not working properly

malicious
adj. spiteful or meaning harm

mammoth
adj. very large or giant

man-eating
adj. likes feeding on human flesh

man-made
adj. created by humans

manicured
adj. tidy and well looked after

marauding
adj. looking for things to kill or steal

marbled
adj. streaky like marble

marinated
adj. soaked in spices or flavors

marine
adj. used at sea

marshy
adj. wet and boggy

mashed
adj. crushed or blended into a pulp

masked
adj. disguised or covered

massive
adj. very large or giant

matted
adj. tangled or knotted

meandering
adj. wandering or taking a long path

meaty
adj. large, weighty, or fleshy

mechanical
adj. controlled by a machine

meddling
adj. getting involved or interfering

medieval
adj. from the Middle Ages

mellow
adj. soft and soothing

melted
adj. turned from solid to liquid

melting
adj. turning from solid to liquid

menacing
adj. threatening to do harm

mesmerizing
adj. very attractive or bewitching

messy
adj. untidy or dirty

metal
n. a hard, shiny material

metallic
adj. looking like metal

mighty
adj. big, strong, and powerful

migrating
adj. moving from one place to another

mild
adj. not very strong or not spicy

military
adj. to do with the army or soldiers

mindless
adj. foolish or senseless

mini
adj. smaller than usual

mint
n. a plant used in cooking

minted
adj. flavored with mint

miraculous
adj. wonderful or magical

mirrored
[1] *adj.* reflective or with a mirror
[2] *adj.* shiny or mirror-like

mischievous
adj. naughty and playful

mismatched
adj. not the same color or pattern

misplaced
adj. in the wrong place

missing
adj. lost or gone

mistreated
adj. treated badly or cruelly

misty
adj. like a thin fog

misunderstood
adj. not understood or appreciated

M – O

mixing
adj. combining things together

mobile
adj. able to be carried around

modern
adj. in the latest or current style

moist
adj. damp or not dry

moldy
adj. rotten or covered with mold

monstrous
adj. horrible or like a monster

moonlit
adj. lit up by the moon

moored
adj. tied up with a rope or anchor

moth-eaten
adj. full of holes made by insects

motionless
adj. still or not moving

motorized
adj. powered by a motor

mournful
adj. very sad or full of regret

much-needed
adj. very important and necessary

mud
n. a mixture of water and soil

muddled
adj. confused or mixed-up

muddy
adj. covered in mud

muffled
adj. quiet and not heard properly

murky
adj. dark, muddy, or cloudy

muscular
adj. strong and powerful

mushy
adj. mashed or pulpy

musty
adj. stuffy, moldy, or stale

mutated
adj. changed into something else

mysterious
adj. strange, eerie, or unexplained

mythical
adj. existing only in stories

narrow
adj. small or not far from side to side

nasty
adj. very bad or unpleasant

natural
adj. made by nature

neglected
adj. not well looked after

nesting
adj. building a home or nest

network
n. a system of connected things

new
adj. just made or just bought

nimble
adj. moving quickly and skillfully

nocturnal
adj. active at night

noise-canceling
adj. blocking out other sounds

noisy
WHAT? I CAN'T HEAR YOU.

non-stick
adj. not letting food stick

nondescript
adj. not unusual or not memorable

number-one
adj. the best or highest-rated

nutty
adj. tasting of or containing nuts

oaty
adj. made with oats

obscure
adj. hidden or unclear

obsessive
adj. too interested or addicted

obvious
adj. easy to see or notice

odd-looking
adj. looking unusual or strange

offshore
adj. out at sea

old
adj. having existed for a long time

ominous
adj. scary, threatening, or menacing

oncoming
adj. moving toward you

oozing
adj. slowly trickling or leaking

open
[1] *adj.* not shut or not closed
[2] *adj.* wide and exposed

open-air
adj. outside or not walled in

open-plan
adj. with no dividing walls

oppressive
adj. cruel, harsh, and overpowering

optical
adj. relating to eyes and sight

opulent
adj. rich and luxurious

orbiting
adj. circling or moving around

organic
adj. made without using chemicals

O - P

ornamental
adj. fancy or decorative

ornate
adj. detailed and decorated

orphaned
adj. without a mother or father

outdoor
adj. not inside

outer
adj. on the outside

outspread
adj. spread open or wide apart

overcast
adj. cloudy or gray

overcrowded
adj. full of too many people

overflowing
adj. too full and spilling over

overgrown
adj. grown too big or thick

overhanging
adj. above or hanging over

overhead
adj. above your head or in the sky

overloaded
adj. carrying too much stuff

overnight
adj. during the night

overripe
adj. too ripe or past its best

oversized
adj. bigger than normal

overstocked
adj. filled with too many things

overstuffed
adj. stuffed with too many things

overturned
adj. tipped upside down

packed
adj. full or overcrowded

padded
adj. stuffed with a soft material

painful
adj. causing pain or distress

painted
adj. covered with paint

palatial
adj. vast or splendid

paper
n. thin sheets made from trees

parboiled
adj. boiled until partly cooked

parked
adj. left somewhere without moving

passing
[1] *adj.* moving or going past
[2] *adj.* not lasting long

patchy
adj. uneven or not everywhere

patterned
adj. with a repeated design

peaceful
adj. calm and tranquil

pebbly
adj. with a lot of pebbles

peeled
adj. with the outer peel removed

peeling
adj. coming off or shedding

peep
adj. showing or poking out

pelting
adj. bombarding or battering

perennial
adj. living for many years

perfect
adj. ideal or flawless

perilous
adj. dangerous and full of risk

personal
adj. belonging to you or for you

pesky
adj. causing trouble or annoying

pessimistic
adj. gloomy or negative

phenomenal
adj. fantastic or extraordinary

photographic
adj. using photos or in photos

pickled
adj. preserved in a vinegary liquid

picturesque
adj. attractive or scenic

pink
adj. the color of red and white mixed

pinstripe
adj. with very thin stripes

pioneering
adj. new and innovative

piped
adj. applied in thin stripes

piping-hot
adj. extremely hot

pirate
Ahoy, matey!

pitted
adj. with the pits removed

pivotal
adj. very important or critical

plastic
n. an easily molded material

platform
n. a raised level or surface

playful
adj. fun-loving and lively

P

pleasant
adj. enjoyable or nice

plentiful
adj. in large amounts

plowed
adj. with the soil turned over

plucked
adj. with feathers or hairs pulled off

plump
adj. round and fat

plush
adj. rich, soft, and luxurious

poached
adj. cooked in a hot liquid

pointed
adj. ending in a sharp point

pointy
adj. with a pointed tip

poisonous
adj. deadly or toxic

poky
adj. tiny or cramped

polar
adj. near the North or South Pole

polished
adj. made shiny by being rubbed

polluted
adj. dirty or full of waste

poor
adj. low-quality or not very good

pop-up
adj. spring-loaded

popular
adj. liked by many people

porous
adj. with lots of tiny holes

portable
adj. easy to carry or move

possible
adj. likely or able to happen

potted
adj. grown in a pot

powdery
adj. fine and powder-like

powerful
adj. strong, mighty, or effective

precious
adj. loved, valued, or expensive

precipitous
adj. steep or dangerously high

precise
adj. exact or accurate

predatory
adj. hunting other creatures

preening
adj. grooming itself with its beak

pregnant
adj. going to have a baby soon

preserved
adj. protected from going bad

pressed
adj. flattened to get rid of creases

prestigious
adj. important and respected

prickly
adj. covered in sharp spikes

primitive
adj. basic, rough, or crude

princely
adj. good enough for a prince

pristine
adj. brand-new or spotless

private
adj. for one person or not for everyone

prize-winning
adj. good enough to get an award

prized
adj. valued very highly

professional
adj. trained or expert

profitable
adj. making money

profuse
adj. a lot of or abundant

projectile
adj. pushed forward forcefully

prolific
adj. producing a lot

prominent
adj. easy to see or noticeable

promising
adj. hopeful or having potential

prosthetic
adj. made to replace the real thing

protected
adj. kept safe from harm

protective
adj. keeping you safe from harm

protruding
adj. sticking out or bulging

proud
adj. feeling important and confident

prowling
adj. roaming and looking for prey

pruned
adj. with the branches cut back

public
adj. for everyone to use

puffed
adj. swollen or bigger than before

puffed-up
adj. sticking out proudly

punctured
adj. damaged by making a hole

P - R

pungent
adj. strongly smelling or tasting

pure
adj. not mixed with anything else

purple
color you turn if you hold your breath

purring
adj. making a low, and happy hum

quaint
adj. charming and picturesque

quaking
adj. shaking or trembling

queasy
adj. feeling sick or nauseous

quick
adj. able to learn in a short time

quiet
Shhhh!

quilted
adj. with a layer of soft padding

quirky
adj. in an unusual or eccentric style

rabid
adj. wild and violent

radiant
adj. bright, brilliant, or glowing

radioactive
adj. sending out toxic waves

ragged
adj. old and torn

raging
adj. furious or uncontrollable

rainbow-billed
adj. with a beak full of colors

ramshackle
adj. falling to pieces

random
[1] *adj.* chosen without a reason
[2] *adj.* odd or irregular

ransacked
adj. damaged and robbed

rapid
adj. very fast or quick

rapid-fire
adj. firing quickly one after another

rare
[1] *adj.* very few or not often seen
[2] *adj.* very lightly cooked

raucous
adj. making a harsh, loud noise

ravenous
adj. hungry or starving

raw
adj. uncooked or unprocessed

razor-sharp
adj. able to cut things very easily

reborn
adj. made new again

rechargeable
adj. able to be refilled with energy

reclining
adj. able to be tilted backwards

record-breaking
adj. more than ever before

recycled
adj. reused again for something new

red-brick
adj. made with red-colored bricks

red-hot
adj. so hot that it glows red

reduced
adj. lowered or lessened

reedy
adj. with tall grass everywhere

refreshing
adj. making you feel energized

refurbished
adj. repaired, fixed, or revamped

regular
adj. always at the same time

reinforced
adj. made stronger or tougher

rejuvenating
adj. making you feel better or younger

relentless
adj. constant or nonstop

reliable
adj. trusted and dependable

remote
adj. far away or distant

renowned
adj. well-known and respected

rented
adj. paid to be used for a short time

replenished
adj. refilled or topped up

reputable
adj. well-respected and reliable

rescued
adj. saved from danger

respected
adj. admired or thought highly of

responsible
adj. sensible and trusted

restless
adj. unsettled or constantly moving

restored
adj. repaired or fixed

retired
adj. not working anymore

retractable
adj. able to be drawn back in

retro
adj. old-fashioned and cool

reusable
adj. can be used again and again

R - S

revolutionary
adj. bringing about a big change

revolving
adj. moving in a circle

rich
[1] *adj.* creamy, heavy, and delicious
[2] *adj.* lush, fertile, and full of life

rickety
adj. wobbly, shaky, or poorly made

ridiculous
adj. funny, silly, or absurd

ripe
adj. soft and ready to eat

ripped
adj. torn or pulled apart

rippling
adj. flowing in small waves

rising
adj. getting higher or moving up

roaring
[1] *adj.* full of loud and powerful flames
[2] *adj.* making a loud and deep noise

roasted
adj. cooked for a long time

roasting
adj. used to roast

robotic
adj. mechanical or like a robot

robust
adj. strong and tough

rocket-boosted
adj. made faster using rockets

rocky
adj. made of rock or stone

rogue
adj. rebellious and different

rolled
adj. turned over and flattened

rolling
[1] *adj.* rippling, wavy, or tumbling
[2] *adj.* turning around and around

romantic
adj. showing love and passion

roof-mounted
adj. fixed to the top of a roof

rotating
adj. spinning or turning

rotten
adj. decayed, old, and stinking

rotting
adj. going bad or decaying

rough
adj. carelessly made or badly made

rounded
adj. smooth and curved

royal
adj. for the family of a king or queen

rubber
n. a soft, bendy material

rubbery
adj. flexible and tough

rude
You smell.

ruffled
adj. scrunched up in a design

rugged
adj. rough, uneven, or craggy

rumbling
adj. deep, muffled, and continuous

rumpled
adj. wrinkled or creased

run-down
adj. old and needing repairs

runaway
adj. escaped or out of control

running
adj. moving quickly on foot

runny
adj. liquid or flowing easily

ruptured
adj. broken open or burst

rustic
adj. typical of the countryside

rusty
adj. covered in rust or red flakes

sabotaged
adj. broken or ruined on purpose

sacred
adj. holy, religious, or spiritual

sad
Turn that frown upside down!

safari
n. a trip to look at or hunt animals

sagging
adj. drooping or hanging loosely

salted
adj. containing or covered in salt

saltwater
adj. containing salty water

salty
adj. tasting like salt

salvaged
adj. saved or rescued

sandy
adj. covered with sand

satin
n. a smooth, glossy fabric

savage
adj. cruel, violent, and uncontrolled

scalding
adj. extremely hot or burning

scaly
adj. covered in scales

scampering
adj. scurrying or dashing

scarlet
adj. vivid red in color

S

scattered
adj. spread randomly

scenic
adj. with beautiful views

scented
adj. with a nice smell

scheming
adj. plotting devious tricks

scientific
adj. to do with science

scorching
adj. red-hot or blazing

scraped
adj. grazed or scratched

scrappy
adj. determined and feisty

scrawny
adj. thin and bony

screeching
adj. squawking or squealing

scruffy
adj. shabby or untidy

scrumptious
adj. tasty or delicious

scuffed
adj. lightly damaged from scraping

sculpted
adj. beautifully shaped or carved

scuttling
adj. running with short steps

sea
Why is the sea friendly? It waves.

sealed
adj. shut tightly

seared
adj. quickly cooked on the surface

seaside
adj. by the sea

seasonal
adj. happening in certain seasons

seasoned
adj. with salt, pepper, or spices

secluded
adj. quiet or kept hidden

secret
My lips are sealed.

secure
adj. safe against danger or attacks

seedless
adj. without seeds

self-service
adj. letting people serve themselves

sensible
adj. wise and responsible

sensitive
adj. able to notice small changes

sentient
adj. able to feel things

serene
adj. peaceful or calm

serious
adj. important or not to be ignored

serrated
adj. sharp, rough, and jagged

serving
adj. used for giving out portions

severe
adj. very serious or harsh

shabby
adj. scruffy and worn

shaded
adj. sheltered from the sun

shady
adj. giving shelter from the sun

shaggy
adj. long, thick, and messy

shallow
adj. not deep

sharp
[1] *adj.* able to cut or pierce things easily
[2] *adj.* quick, clear, and noticeable

sharp-eyed
adj. quick to spot things

sharpened
adj. made more pointy

shattered
adj. smashed into small pieces

shaved
adj. shredded into thin flakes

sheltering
adj. protecting or covering

shifting
adj. moving in different directions

shimmering
adj. glinting and flickering

shocking
adj. surprising and distressing

shooting
adj. moving very fast

shorn
adj. with its fleece cut off

short
adj. not very long

shredded
adj. cut or torn into thin pieces

shrill
adj. sharp or very high-pitched

shriveled
adj. wrinkled or shrunken

shuttered
adj. closed with shutters

shy
adj. nervous, timid, or hiding

sifted
adj. put through a sieve

S

silk
n. a strong, soft and thin fabric

silver
adj. pale gray and shiny

silvery
adj. light gray and reflective

simple
adj. basic and plain

single
adj. only one or with no others

sinking
adj. moving slowly downwards

sizzling
adj. very hot or hissing with heat

sizzling-hot
adj. hot or extremely spicy

skilled
adj. trained or experienced

skillful
adj. talented or expert

skimpy
adj. small and revealing

skinny
[1] *adj.* made with less fat [2] *adj.* slim and tight-fitting [3] adj. thin or scrawny

sky-high
adj. very tall or very high

sky-piercing
adj. taller than the sky

slanting
adj. sloping at an angle

slathered
adj. spread on thickly or heavily

sleek
adj. smooth and shiny

sleeping
adj. asleep or not awake

sleepy
adj. quiet and peaceful

slender
adj. slim and graceful

sliced
adj. cut into thin pieces

slimy
adj. slippery, wet, and gooey

slippery
adj. smooth, wet, or difficult to grip

slithering
adj. slips, slides, or moves smoothly

slivered
adj. cut into very thin pieces

slobbering
adj. drooling or dripping saliva

slow
adj. taking a long time or not fast

slow-moving
adj. moving slowly or barely moving

sluggish
adj. slow, lazy, or lifeless

sly
adj. clever and dishonest

small
adj. little in size or not big

smart
adj. looking good or neat

smashed
adj. very broken or shattered

smelly
You smelt it, you dealt it.

smoked
adj. preserved using smoke

smoky
adj. sending out smoke

smudged
adj. blurred, rubbed, or smeared

snarling
adj. making a growling noise

sneaky
adj. good at lying and hiding

snooty
adj. rudely looking down on others

snow-capped
adj. covered with snow at the top

snowy
adj. covered with snow

snug
adj. cozy and comfortable

soaked
adj. extremely wet

soaring
adj. high, flying, or gliding

sodden
adj. soaking or completely wet

soft
[1] *adj.* faint or dim [2] *adj.* mild and mellow [3] *adj.* mushy or not hard

soggy
adj. wet and soft

solar
adj. powered by sunlight

solemn
adj. serious and formal

solid
[1] *adj.* firm and reliable
[2] *adj.* hard and thick

solitary
adj. living or spending time alone

somber
adj. sad, gloomy, or dark

soothing
adj. comforting and calming

sore
[1] *adj.* angry or annoyed
[2] *adj.* painful or aching

soundproofed
adj. not letting sound in or out

sour
adj. bitter, sharp, and acidic

S

sourdough
n. a sour or bitter type of dough

spacious
adj. big or with a lot of room inside

spare
adj. extra or backup

sparkling
adj. shining or glimmering

sparkly
adj. shiny or glittery

spattered
adj. splashed, stained, or speckled

special
adj. important or unique

speckled
adj. marked with small dots

speeding
adj. moving too fast

speedy
adj. fast or quick

spelt
n. a healthy type of flour

spewing
adj. gushing, spitting, or oozing

spiced
adj. with added flavor from spice

spicy
adj. tasting hot and fiery

spiked
adj. with sharp points or spikes

spilled
adj. falling out or overflowing

spiral
adj. coiled, twisted, or curved

spiraling
adj. winding around and around

spirited
adj. lively and determined

spiritual
adj. religious and emotional

splendid
adj. bright, glorious, or impressive

splintered
adj. broken into thin, sharp pieces

spooked
adj. scared, frightened, and jumpy

spoon-bending
adj. so stiff it can bend metal

spotless
adj. completely clean

spouting
adj. sending out a jet of water

sprawling
adj. stretching over a large area

spray-painted
adj. painted using a spray

springy
adj. bouncy, or moving like elastic

square
like a circle, but with corners

squashed
adj. crushed or squeezed

squat
adj. short and stubby

squawking
adj. a harsh screeching or shrieking

squeaky
adj. making a high-pitched noise

squealing
adj. making a loud, high noise

squeezed
adj. with the juice pressed out

squirming
adj. wriggling uncomfortably

stacked
adj. piled up, one on top of the other

stagnant
adj. still and stale

stained
adj. marked or discolored

stale
adj. old, hard, and crusty

stampeding
adj. rushing wildly in a group

startled
adj. surprised or frightened

steady
adj. constant and unchanging

steak
n. a thick slice of meat

stealthy
adj. sneaky or secretive

steamed
adj. cooked with heat from steam

steaming
adj. giving off misty fumes

steamy
adj. clouded by misty fumes

steep
adj. going sharply up or down

sterile
adj. completely free from germs

stewed
adj. cooked slowly in liquid

sticky
adj. gluey or fixing to things

stiff
[1] *adj.* straight and severe
[2] *adj.* unbending or hard to move

stifling
adj. so hot you can barely breathe

stinging
adj. painful to touch

stinking
adj. smelling nasty

S - T

stolen
adj. taken illegally or without asking

stone-ground
adj. crushed up finely using stones

stony
[1] *adj.* covered in small rocks
[2] *adj.* unfriendly or unfeeling

stormy
adj. rainy, thundery, and windy

strained
adj. tense, tired, or painful

stranded
adj. left, stuck, or abandoned

strange
adj. odd or unusual

strapless
adj. without straps

strappy
adj. held together with straps

stray
adj. escaped or without an owner

streaky
adj. marked with stripes

streamlined
adj. made simple and easy to use

stretched
adj. pulled tight and not loose

strict
adj. sticking to the rules

striped
adj. patterned with lines

strong
[1] *adj.* firm and muscular [2] *adj.* intense and full of flavor [3] *adj.* powerful, tough, and mighty

strutting
adj. walking upright and confidently

stubborn
adj. difficult to get rid of or move

stubby
adj. short and thick

studded
adj. decorated with pieces of metal

stuffed
adj. filled or packed with something

stumpy
adj. short, thick, and squat

stunning
adj. beautiful and impressive

stunted
adj. stopped from growing fully

sturdy
adj. strong and solidly built

stylish
adj. fashionable or elegant

submerged
adj. completely underwater

subtle
adj. faint and delicate

succulent
adj. juicy, fresh, and tasty

sudden
adj. unexpected or without warning

sufficient
adj. enough or plenty

suffocating
adj. making it hard to breathe

sugar-loaded
adj. full of sugar

sugary
adj. very sticky and sweet

sulfurous
adj. smelling like rotten eggs

sun-kissed
adj. warmed or browned by the sun

sunken
[1] *adj.* lower or beneath a surface
[2] *adj.* under water or submerged

sunny
adj. lit up by the sun

super-strong
adj. very powerful

supercharged
adj. very powerful or lasting longer

superfast
adj. extremely speedy

surfacing
adj. coming up above the water

surgical
adj. used in surgery

suspected
adj. thought to be guilty

sustainable
adj. caught safely and responsibly

swarming
adj. moving together in a big group

swaying
adj. moving gently from side to side

sweet
adj. pleasant and sugary

sweetened
adj. made to taste sugary

swelling
adj. growing bigger or expanding

sweltering
adj. very hot or baking

swimming
adj. moving through water

swirling
adj. spiraling or twirling

swollen
adj. bulging, expanded, or inflamed

swooping
adj. flying downwards quickly

sympathetic
adj. understanding and comforting

table
n. a surface for eating or working

T

tailored
adj. specially made to fit you

tainted
adj. spoiled or contaminated

talented
adj. skilled and gifted

talkative
adj. chatty or talks a lot

talking
adj. saying words out loud

tall
adj. high off the ground

tame
adj. well-trained and obedient

tangled
adj. twisted, knotted, or messy

tart
adj. sharp and sour

tasty
adj. delicious or yummy

tattered
adj. old, torn, and worn-out

teeming
adj. full or crowded

teen
n. a person aged 13 to 19

telepathic
adj. reading thoughts

televised
adj. shown on the television

temperamental
adj. emotional, moody, or fiery

tempestuous
adj. wild, stormy, and unpredictable

temporary
adj. lasting for a short time

tempting
adj. attractive or hard to say no to

terrible
adj. very bad or awful

tethered
adj. tied up or chained

thatched
adj. made with straw or hay

thawing
adj. melting into water

therapeutic
adj. healing or making you feel better

thick
[1] *adj.* chunky, wide, and heavy [2] *adj.* closely packed in or dense [3] *adj.* not very runny

thieving
adj. robbing or stealing

thirsty
adj. in need of water

thorny
adj. having lots of thorns

threadbare
adj. old and worn thin

threatening
adj. ominous or scary

three-legged
adj. with three legs

thriving
adj. growing and doing very well

throbbing
adj. pulsing in pain

thundering
adj. making a sound like thunder

thunderous
adj. very loud or like thunder

ticking
adj. a short and repetitive sound

ticklish
adj. making you wriggle and giggle

tie-dyed
adj. with round color patterns

tiered
adj. with one row on top of another

tight
[1] *adj.* close-fitting or figure-hugging
[2] *adj.* dense or pressed firmly together

tiled
adj. covered in flat stone slabs

timid
adj. shy or fearful

tinted
adj. with a faint color

tiny
adj. very small

tired
adj. worn out and sleepy

toasted
adj. heated until crispy and brown

toasty
adj. keeping you warm

top
adj. best or of the highest standard

toppling
adj. tumbling or about to fall over

torn
adj. cut or split

torrential
adj. falling heavily and forcefully

total
adj. complete or absolute

touchscreen
adj. controlled by pressing a screen

tough
[1] *adj.* difficult to cut or chew
[2] *adj.* strong and resilient

towering
adj. extremely tall

toxic
adj. poisonous or deadly

trained
adj. prepared and practiced

T - U

trampled
adj. walked over and crushed

trampling
adj. stomping and crushing

tranquil
adj. peaceful or blissfully quiet

tranquilized
adj. made sleepy or calm with a drug

translucent
adj. letting light through

transplanted
adj. moved from another body

trapped
adj. stuck or caught

treacherous
[1] *adj.* dangerous or unsafe
[2] *adj.* lying and not to be trusted

treasured
adj. loved and valued

trembling
adj. shaking with nerves or fear

trendy
adj. fashionable or in style

trophy
n. a prize given to winners

tropical
adj. in or from a hot country

trusted
adj. loyal, reliable, and honest

trusty
adj. tried and tested, or reliable

turbocharged
adj. made extra fast or strong

turbulent
adj. violent and unpredictable

twinkling
adj. sparkling and flickering

twirling
adj. spinning or swirling

twisting
adj. bending or curling around

twitching
adj. fluttering or jerking

two-headed
adj. with two heads

two-person
adj. with space for two people

two-pronged
adj. with just two sharp points

two-time
adj. having happened twice before

ugly
adj. unattractive or hideous

unattended
adj. left alone or not watched

unbearable
adj. impossible to take or put up with

unbeatable
adj. impossible to trick or beat

unbreakable
adj. very strong or not easily broken

unbuttoned
adj. with the buttons undone

uncharted
adj. unexplored or not mapped

uncomfortable
adj. unpleasant or not comfortable

unconvincing
adj. not very believable

undeciphered
adj. impossible to read or understand

undefeated
adj. never beaten before

undercover
adj. working secretly or in disguise

underground
adj. under the surface of the ground

undetectable
adj. impossible for others to see

undrinkable
adj. too disgusting to drink

uneven
adj. bumpy or not level

unexpected
adj. surprising or without warning

unfeeling
adj. without emotions

unflushed
adj. left full of gross waste

unforgiving
adj. showing no mercy

unicorn
n. a magical horse with a single horn

unidentified
adj. unknown or unrecognized

uninflated
adj. not filled with air

uninhabitable
adj. not possible to live in

unique
adj. the only one of its kind

unkempt
adj. messy or untidy

unknowable
adj. impossible to know about

unlikely
adj. unexpected or not probable

unlit
adj. dark and without lights

unlocked
adj. not shut with a lock

unlucky
adj. unfortunate or out of luck

unmade
adj. not arranged neatly

U - W

unmanned
adj. without people on board

unopened
adj. closed or not opened

unpaid
adj. still needing to be paid

unpatrolled
adj. not checked by inspectors

unplugged
adj. not plugged into electricity

unripe
adj. not ready to be eaten

unscooped
adj. left or not picked up

unseen
adj. hidden or out of sight

unsightly
adj. ugly or not pleasant to look at

unsinkable
adj. will never stop floating

unstoppable
adj. impossible to stop

unsuccessful
adj. failed or giving bad results

unsung
adj. uncelebrated or not praised

unsuspecting
adj. not realizing what is going on

unswept
adj. unchecked or uncleared

unswerving
adj. steady or constant

untidy
adj. messy or cluttered

untuned
adj. sounding wrong

unwanted
adj. rejected or not wanted

unwieldy
adj. large and difficult to use

unwitting
adj. not aware of the facts

upcoming
adj. happening soon

upright
adj. standing up straight

upscale
adj. fashionable and expensive

upturned
adj. tipped over or upside down

useful
adj. handy or helpful

useless
adj. pointless or without use

user-friendly
adj. easy for anyone to use

vacant
adj. empty or not lived in

valiant
adj. brave or fearless

varicose
adj. painfully swollen or twisted

vast
adj. very large or enormous

vegan
adj. avoiding all food from animals

vegetable
What grown ups make you eat.

velvety
adj. soft, smooth, and silky

vengeful
adj. wanting revenge

venomous
adj. poisonous or toxic

versatile
adj. able to do lots of different things

vicious
adj. cruel, brutal, and violent

vintage
adj. old, high-quality, and stylish

visceral
adj. deeply felt and uncontrolled

viscous
adj. thick and sticky

vivid
adj. full of bright colors

volcanic
adj. made by volcanoes

voluminous
adj. large and full

waddling
adj. walking in short, wobbly steps

wagging
adj. shaking or waving up and down

wailing
adj. moaning or howling

walk-in
adj. big enough to walk into

warm
[1] *adj.* hot, but not too hot
[2] *adj.* keeps in the heat

wary
adj. careful or cautious

washed-up
adj. dumped on a beach by the tide

watchful
adj. alert or observant

waterproof
[1] *adj.* not letting water through
[2] *adj.* won't stop working in water

weak
adj. watery or not very strong

weekly
adj. happens every week

weightless
adj. not held down by gravity

W - Z

welcome
adj. wanted or pleasing

welcoming
adj. making people want to go in

well-cut
adj. well-made and of high quality

well-done
adj. cooked for longer than normal

well-earned
adj. deserved after hard work

well-lit
adj. covered in light and easy to see

well-run
adj. efficient and organized

well-worn
adj. old and worn-out

wet
adj. covered in water or full of water

wheezy
adj. panting, gasping, and hissing

whipped
adj. thickened using a whisk

whirling
adj. moving around in quick circles

whirring
adj. making a continuous, low sound

whistling
adj. making a high-pitched sound

white
adj. of the color of snow

whitewashed
adj. painted with a thin, white liquid

whole
adj. in one piece or not cut up

whole-grain
adj. made using complete grains

wicked
adj. evil or bad

wide
adj. broad or with the sides far apart

widespread
adj. covering a large area

wild
[1] *adj.* not grown on a farm
[2] *adj.* violent or uncontrolled

willing
adj. eager or happy to agree

wilted
adj. cooked until slightly soft

wilting
adj. dying from lack of water

winding
adj. bending or moving in a curve

windowless
adj. without any windows

windswept
adj. windblown or beaten by winds

winged
adj. with wings attached

winning
You have to be in it to win it.

wintry
adj. looking or feeling like winter

wire-framed
adj. with thin metal frames

wireless
adj. without any wires

wise
adj. clever and sensible

wispy
adj. thin or fine

withered
adj. wilted, dried-up, and drooping

wobbly
adj. shaky or unsteady

wood-burning
adj. using wood as fuel

wood-fired
adj. burning wood for heat

wooden
adj. made of wood

wooly
adj. made of wool

world-class
adj. one of the best in the world

worn-out
adj. damaged from being used a lot

worthy
adj. respectable and deserving

wounded
adj. hurt or injured

wriggling
adj. twisting and turning

wrinkled
adj. with lots of little creases

writhing
adj. wriggling or squirming

yellow
adj. of the color of bananas

young
adj. not having lived for long

zesty
adj. fruity and sharp-tasting

zingy
adj. lively and sharp-tasting

zooming
adj. moving very quickly

A

C

D

E

F

G

H

I

J

K

L

M

N

P

Q

R

S

X

Y

Mrs Wordsmith is on a mission to bring words to life, one hilarious illustration at a time.

Founded in London, and now spread around the world, we won't rest until every child, young storyteller and family, has the words they need to achieve awesomeness. Combining genuine Hollywood creativity from the artist behind *Madagascar's* unforgettable characters, with world-leading data science, this is literacy at near-light speed.

Credits to...

Editor-in-Chief
Sofia Fenichell

Art Director
Craig Kellman

Artists
Agniah Mardiyah
Brett Coulson
Daniel Permutt
Holly Jones
Joan Varitek
Nico Mereu
Phil Mamuyac
Wendell Luebbe

Senior Writers
Graeme Keeton
Mark Holland
Tatiana Barnes

Editors & Lexicographers
Federico Espinosa
Ian Brookes
Nicole Le Vine
Penny Hands

Academic Advisors
Emma Madden
Prof. Susan Neuman

Graphic Designers
Gemma Kindness
James Sales
Lady San Pedro
Sarah Bennion

Machine Learning
Benjamin Pettit
Rob Koeling
Stanislaw Pstrokonski

Producers
Rebecca Man
Leon Welters

DISCLAIMER:

Under no circumstances should you ever attempt to eat Word Sauce!